"Securing the Cloud: Strategies for Protecting Your Digital Horizon"

Table of Content

Chapter 1: The Evolving Threat Landscape

- Define the concept of cyber threats and their significance in the digital age.
- Explore various types of cyber threats, including malware, phishing, and ransomware.
- Explain the concept of zero-day vulnerabilities and their role in cyber-attacks.
- Explore the psychological aspects of social engineering used by cybercriminals.
- Discuss specific threats that are unique to cloud environments.
- Examine how AI is both a tool for cyber attackers and defenders.
- Provide an overview of current global cybersecurity trends.
- Introduce the concept of risk assessment in the context of the evolving threat landscape.
- Highlight the role of human factors in cybersecurity incidents.
- Discuss proactive measures and strategies for staying ahead of future cyber threats.

Chapter 2: Building a Robust Security Infrastructure

- Define the components of a security infrastructure in the context of cloud computing.
- Introduce the concept of security by design and its relevance in building secure cloud architectures.
- Explore best practices for securing cloud networks.
- Discuss physical and virtual security measures for data centers in the cloud.
- Address the challenges and solutions related to securing endpoints in a cloud environment.
- Explore the principles of IAM in cloud security.
- Discuss the role of automation in improving security operations.
- Explain the importance of continuous monitoring for identifying and responding to security threats.
- Address the challenges and strategies associated with third-party security in the cloud.
- Explore how security infrastructure can adapt to the dynamic nature of cloud environments.

Chapter 3: Encryption Essentials: Safeguarding Your Data

- Provide a comprehensive overview of encryption principles.
- Differentiate between symmetric and asymmetric encryption methods.
- Explore the importance of end-to-end encryption in securing communication channels.
- Discuss strategies and best practices for encrypting data stored in the cloud.
- Explain the significance of effective key management in encryption.
- Explore how encryption is applied to secure cloud storage services.
- Address challenges and solutions for implementing encryption in multi-cloud scenarios.
- Introduce the potential impact of quantum computing on traditional encryption methods.
- Explore how encryption aligns with regulatory requirements in various industries.
- Emphasize the role of user awareness in maintaining the effectiveness of encryption.

Chapter 4: Identity Management in the Cloud Era

- Highlight the central role of identity management in cloud security.
- Explain the concept of SSO and its benefits in cloud environments.
- Explore the significance of MFA in enhancing identity verification.
- Discuss the challenges and solutions for identity federation in a multi-cloud environment.
- Explain the principles of RBAC and its application in cloud security.
- Discuss the importance of efficient user provisioning and de-provisioning processes.
- Explore how identity governance ensures compliance with security policies.
- Explore the use of biometric authentication as an additional layer of identity verification.
- Address common challenges and pitfalls in cloud identity management.
- Discuss emerging trends and technologies in cloud identity management.

Chapter 5: Securing Cloud Applications: Best Practices

- Define the unique challenges and considerations in securing cloud-based applications.
- Explore the principles of incorporating security into the development process.
- Explain the importance of securing application programming interfaces (APIs).
- Explore the security challenges associated with containerized applications.
- Discuss the security implications of serverless computing.
- Explain the role of WAF in protecting web applications from common vulnerabilities.
- Discuss strategies for protecting sensitive data within cloud applications.
- Highlight the importance of continuous monitoring for identifying and addressing application vulnerabilities.
- Outline a framework for incident response specific to cloud-based applications.
- Emphasize the role of education in empowering developers to build secure applications.

Chapter 6: Compliance and Governance in Cloud Security

- Define the concept of compliance and its relevance in cloud security.
- Explore established frameworks for cloud security compliance.
- Discuss the impact of data privacy regulations on cloud security.
- Explain the role of risk assessment in achieving and maintaining compliance.
- Discuss the importance of regular auditing for assessing compliance.
- Address legal aspects related to cloud security, including contractual agreements.
- Explore the development and implementation of governance policies in cloud security.
- Emphasize the role of training and awareness programs in maintaining compliance.
- Discuss the importance of metrics in measuring and reporting on cloud security compliance.
- Highlight the iterative nature of compliance efforts.

Chapter 7: Incident Response and Recovery Strategies

- Define incident response and its crucial role in mitigating security threats.

- Explore methods for promptly identifying and classifying security incidents.

- Discuss the development of a tailored incident response plan for cloud environments.

- Highlight the importance of collaboration with cloud service providers during incident response.

- Outline a step-by-step approach to responding to data breaches in the cloud.

- Explore recovery strategies for cloud-based systems after a security incident.

- Discuss the significance of post-incident analysis in improving future incident response.

- Discuss legal and compliance aspects related to incident response activities.

- Address the importance of clear and effective communication during security incidents.

- Emphasize the iterative nature of incident response improvement.

Chapter 8: Future Trends in Cloud Security

- Discuss the rapid evolution of technology and its impact on cloud security.
- Explore the principles of a zero-trust security model.
- Discuss the increasing role of AI and machine learning in cybersecurity.
- Explore the security challenges associated with edge computing.
- Discuss the potential impact of quantum computing on traditional cryptography.
- Explore the concept of continuous authentication for enhanced identity security.
- Discuss advancements in security automation and orchestration.
- Discuss the evolution of biometric authentication technologies.
- Discuss anticipated regulatory developments in cloud security.
- Address the ongoing importance of human factors in cybersecurity.

Introduction

In an era overwhelmingly shaped by the pervasive influence of digital transformation, the cloud has emerged as the linchpin of our interconnected world. This paradigm shift has prompted businesses and individuals alike to migrate their data and operations to cloud environments, ushering in unprecedented convenience and scalability. However, as this migration gains momentum, the concomitant need for robust security strategies has never been more critical. "Securing the Cloud: Strategies for Protecting Your Digital Horizon" stands as a beacon in this evolving landscape, offering a comprehensive guide that empowers readers with the knowledge and tools necessary to navigate the intricacies of cloud security.

At the heart of the digital revolution lies the cloud, a dynamic and flexible infrastructure that has redefined the way we store, process, and access data. This transformative shift has unlocked unparalleled opportunities for innovation, efficiency, and collaboration. Yet, with these advantages come profound challenges, particularly in the realm of cybersecurity. As organizations entrust their most sensitive data to cloud providers, the imperative to safeguard against evolving threats becomes paramount. "Securing the Cloud" addresses this imperative head-on, delving into the multifaceted dimensions of cloud security to equip readers with a nuanced understanding of the risks and the strategies required to mitigate them.

The guide begins by unraveling the intricacies of cloud architecture, elucidating the various service models (Infrastructure as a Service, Platform as a Service, and Software as a Service) and deployment models (public, private, hybrid, and multicloud). Understanding the nuances of these models is foundational to crafting a robust security posture tailored to the specific demands of each organization's digital footprint. As the narrative unfolds, readers are guided through the intricate web of shared responsibilities between cloud service providers and their clients, a pivotal concept that underlines the collaborative nature of securing the cloud.

With a foundation laid, "Securing the Cloud" delves into the arsenal of security measures available to fortify digital landscapes. Encryption emerges as a linchpin, as the guide expounds on the nuances of data encryption in transit and at rest, illustrating its role as a stalwart defender against unauthorized access. Identity and access management (IAM) takes center stage, illuminating the significance of stringent controls over user privileges and authentication mechanisms. The guide navigates the reader through the labyrinth of secure coding practices, shedding light on the pivotal role of application security in fortifying cloud-based services against cyber threats.

As the digital horizon expands, so does the threat landscape. "Securing the Cloud" confronts emerging challenges head-on, exploring the intricacies of threat intelligence, anomaly detection, and incident response within the context of cloud environments. The guide unravels the complexities of compliance and regulatory frameworks, providing insights into how organizations can navigate the intricate web of legal requirements while upholding robust security standards. It further elucidates the role of security audits and continuous monitoring in maintaining a proactive security posture, emphasizing the need for an adaptive and resilient approach to cybersecurity.

In the age of interconnectedness, collaboration is not limited to human actors alone. The guide examines the burgeoning field of cloud-native security solutions, leveraging artificial intelligence and machine learning to autonomously identify and respond to threats in real time. From container security to serverless computing, the evolving landscape of cloud technologies is dissected to reveal the security implications inherent in each innovation.

"Securing the Cloud" also places a magnifying glass on the human element, acknowledging that the weakest link in the security chain often lies in the actions of users. It delves into the realms of security awareness training and cultural shifts necessary to foster a security-centric mindset across organizations. Through case studies and real-world examples, the guide illustrates the tangible impact of security incidents, underscoring the need for a holistic and proactive approach to security that extends beyond technological solutions.

In conclusion, "Securing the Cloud: Strategies for Protecting Your Digital Horizon" is not merely a guide; it is a manifesto for the digital age. As businesses and individuals continue their inexorable march towards cloud adoption, the need for a deep and nuanced understanding of cloud security becomes non-negotiable. This guide, with its comprehensive exploration of the myriad facets of cloud security, serves as an indispensable companion in the journey towards a secure and resilient digital future. It empowers its readers to not only grasp the intricacies of the cloud security landscape but also to actively shape and fortify the digital horizons they inhabit. In a world where the cloud is the backbone of our interconnected existence, this guide stands as a testament to the imperative of securing the very foundation upon which our digital future rests.

Chapter 1: The Evolving Threat Landscape

Define the concept of cyber threats and their significance in the digital age.

In the rapidly evolving landscape of the digital age, cyber threats have emerged as formidable adversaries, posing significant challenges to the integrity, confidentiality, and availability of information systems. At their core, cyber threats encompass a wide array of malicious activities orchestrated by individuals, groups, or even nation-states with the intent to exploit vulnerabilities in computer networks, software, and electronic devices. These threats manifest in various forms, including but not limited to malware, ransomware, phishing attacks, and denial-of-service incidents. Their significance lies not only in the potential financial losses and operational disruptions they can inflict upon individuals, organizations, and governments but also in their capacity to compromise sensitive data, erode privacy, and undermine the very fabric of trust in our interconnected digital world.

One of the most pervasive cyber threats is malware, encompassing a diverse range of malicious software designed to infiltrate, damage, or gain unauthorized access to computer systems. The sophistication of malware has evolved over time, with attackers employing advanced techniques such as polymorphism and encryption to evade traditional security measures. Ransomware, a particularly insidious form of malware, encrypts a victim's files and demands a ransom for their release. The proliferation of ransomware attacks has not only crippled critical infrastructure but has also highlighted the pressing need for robust cybersecurity measures to mitigate these threats.

Phishing attacks represent another significant facet of cyber threats, relying on deceptive tactics to trick individuals into divulging sensitive information, such as login credentials or financial details. As the boundary between personal and professional lives becomes increasingly blurred in the digital realm, cybercriminals exploit this interconnectedness to target both individuals and organizations alike. The consequences of successful phishing attacks extend beyond immediate financial losses, encompassing reputational damage and a pervasive erosion of trust in online interactions.

Denial-of-service (DoS) and distributed denial-of-service (DDoS) attacks underscore the vulnerability of digital infrastructures to disruption. By overwhelming targeted systems with a flood of traffic, these attacks can render websites, services, or entire networks inaccessible. Beyond the immediate impact on business continuity, DoS and DDoS attacks can serve as smokescreens for more insidious activities, diverting attention while attackers exploit vulnerabilities or exfiltrate sensitive data.

In the geopolitical arena, cyber threats have transcended individual criminal enterprises to become a tool of statecraft. Nation-states engage in cyber espionage, cyber warfare, and cyber influence operations, leveraging digital means to achieve political, economic, or military objectives. The blurring of lines between state-sponsored and non-state cyber actors has further complicated the attribution of cyber attacks, posing a formidable challenge to international efforts to establish norms and rules governing cyberspace.

The increasing interconnectivity brought about by the Internet of Things (IoT) has expanded the attack surface, providing cyber adversaries with new vectors to exploit. Insecure IoT devices, ranging from smart home appliances to industrial control systems, can be manipulated to launch large-scale attacks or serve as entry points for more extensive intrusions. The security implications of this pervasive connectivity demand a holistic and proactive approach to safeguarding the digital ecosystem.

The significance of cyber threats is heightened by the critical role that digital technologies play in our daily lives. From financial transactions to healthcare systems, from smart cities to autonomous vehicles, the reliance on interconnected digital infrastructure underscores the urgency of addressing cybersecurity challenges. The potential for cascading and systemic failures necessitates a collective and coordinated response from governments, industry stakeholders, and the cybersecurity community to fortify the resilience of our digital society.

As we confront the ever-evolving landscape of cyber threats, the paradigm of cybersecurity must shift from a reactive stance to a proactive and adaptive approach. This entails continuous investment in research and development to stay ahead of emerging threats, fostering international collaboration to establish norms and frameworks for responsible behavior in cyberspace, and promoting a cybersecurity culture that emphasizes awareness, education, and a shared commitment to collective defense. In the face of escalating cyber threats, the imperative to fortify the foundations of our digital infrastructure has never been more pressing, demanding concerted efforts to secure the digital age for the benefit of individuals, organizations, and societies worldwide.

Explore various types of cyber threats, including malware, phishing, and ransomware.

The realm of cybersecurity is confronted by a diverse array of cyber threats, each posing distinct challenges to the integrity, confidentiality, and availability of digital systems. Among the most pervasive and adaptable threats is malware, a term derived from "malicious software." Malware encompasses a vast spectrum of harmful programs designed with the intent to infiltrate, damage, or gain unauthorized access to computer systems. This category includes viruses, worms, Trojans, spyware, and adware, each exhibiting unique characteristics and methods of propagation. Viruses attach themselves to legitimate programs and spread when the infected program is executed, while worms are standalone entities capable of self-replication and spreading across networks. Trojans disguise themselves as benign software to deceive users, and spyware clandestinely observes and transmits user activities, posing significant privacy concerns. Adware inundates users with unwanted advertisements, often accompanied by tracking functionalities. The evolution of malware tactics, such as polymorphism and obfuscation, challenges traditional security measures, emphasizing the need for advanced detection and mitigation strategies.

Phishing represents another insidious form of cyber threat, leveraging deceptive techniques to manipulate individuals into divulging sensitive information. Typically executed through emails, social engineering, or malicious websites, phishing attacks exploit human psychology and trust. Attackers may impersonate reputable entities, such as banks or government agencies, creating convincing replicas of legitimate communication to induce recipients into providing login credentials, financial information, or other sensitive data. Spear phishing targets specific individuals or organizations, tailoring the attack to exploit personalized information. Whaling is a variant that specifically targets high-profile individuals within an organization. The success of phishing attacks often hinges on the ability to craft convincing and socially engineered messages that bypass traditional email security measures, underscoring the importance of user awareness, education, and robust email filtering systems.

Ransomware has emerged as a particularly menacing cyber threat, combining elements of malware and extortion. This malicious software encrypts a victim's files, rendering them inaccessible, and demands a ransom, usually in cryptocurrency, for the decryption key. Ransomware attacks have inflicted substantial financial losses on individuals, businesses, and even critical infrastructure, disrupting operations and causing data loss. Notable variants include WannaCry, NotPetya, and Ryuk, each exploiting vulnerabilities in software or employing phishing techniques for initial infection. The growing sophistication of ransomware, including the development of ransomware-as-a-service (RaaS) models, has democratized access to these tools, enabling even less technically proficient individuals to engage in extortion activities. Mitigating the impact of ransomware necessitates a multi-faceted approach, combining robust cybersecurity practices, regular backups, and the timely patching of software vulnerabilities.

Denial-of-service (DoS) and distributed denial-of-service (DDoS) attacks underscore the vulnerability of digital infrastructures to disruption. In a DoS attack, a single source overwhelms a targeted system with a flood of traffic, rendering it inaccessible to legitimate users. DDoS attacks, on the other hand, harness a network of compromised devices, forming a botnet to amplify the scale of the assault. These attacks exploit vulnerabilities in network protocols, servers, or applications, often accompanied by extortion attempts or as a diversion for other malicious activities. The consequences of DoS and DDoS attacks extend beyond immediate disruption, encompassing financial losses, reputational damage, and potential exploitation of underlying vulnerabilities. Mitigating the impact of these attacks involves the deployment of robust network defenses, traffic filtering, and, in some cases, collaboration with internet service providers to identify and neutralize malicious traffic.

In the realm of cyber threats, advanced persistent threats (APTs) represent a sophisticated and targeted form of cyber espionage. APTs are typically orchestrated by well-resourced and organized entities, such as nation-states or advanced cybercriminal groups, with the objective of gaining prolonged and unauthorized access to sensitive information. These attacks often involve a combination of social engineering, zero-day exploits, and stealthy malware to maintain persistence within targeted networks. APT actors pursue strategic objectives, such as intellectual property theft, political influence, or the compromise of critical infrastructure. Detecting and mitigating APTs demand a proactive and multi-layered security approach, including continuous monitoring, threat intelligence integration, and incident response capabilities.

As the Internet of Things (IoT) continues to proliferate, cyber threats have expanded to exploit the inherent vulnerabilities in interconnected devices. Insecure IoT devices, ranging from smart home appliances to industrial control systems, are susceptible to manipulation for various malicious purposes. Botnets composed of compromised IoT devices can be leveraged for large-scale DDoS attacks, while vulnerabilities in IoT security may expose critical infrastructure to unauthorized access. The diversity of IoT devices, coupled with lax security practices in their design and deployment, underscores the urgent need for robust security standards, regular updates, and collaboration among manufacturers, regulators, and the cybersecurity community to mitigate the evolving risks associated with IoT.

The significance of these diverse cyber threats lies not only in the immediate financial and operational consequences they impose but also in their potential to erode trust, compromise privacy, and disrupt the very fabric of our interconnected society. As technology advances and the digital landscape evolves, the cat-and-mouse game between cyber defenders and adversaries continues, necessitating a proactive, adaptive, and collaborative approach to cybersecurity. This entails ongoing research and development, international cooperation, user education, and a commitment to cultivating a cybersecurity culture that prioritizes resilience and collective defense in the face of an ever-expanding array of cyber threats.

Explain the concept of zero-day vulnerabilities and their role in cyber-attacks.

In the intricate landscape of cybersecurity, zero-day vulnerabilities emerge as critical elements that underscore the perpetual cat-and-mouse game between attackers and defenders. A zero-day vulnerability refers to a flaw or weakness in software, hardware, or firmware that is unknown to the vendor or the entity responsible for developing and maintaining the technology. The term "zero-day" denotes that the developers have had zero days to address or patch the vulnerability since its discovery. Consequently, these vulnerabilities present an attractive and potent avenue for cyber attackers, as they are unmitigated by available security measures, leaving systems exposed to exploitation.

The life cycle of a zero-day vulnerability typically commences with its discovery, often by independent security researchers, cybercriminals, or intelligence agencies. Once identified, the vulnerability can be exploited for malicious purposes, ranging from unauthorized access to systems, data exfiltration, or the deployment of malware. The crucial element that distinguishes zero-day vulnerabilities from other security flaws lies in the absence of a pre-existing patch or solution. This characteristic renders traditional security measures, such as antivirus software or intrusion detection systems, ineffectual in preventing or mitigating attacks leveraging these vulnerabilities.

The covert nature of zero-day vulnerabilities contributes to their prominence in targeted and sophisticated cyber-attacks. Advanced Persistent Threat (APT) actors, including nation-state-sponsored entities and well-organized cybercriminal groups, often leverage zero-day vulnerabilities as part of their arsenal. APTs operate with strategic objectives, seeking to maintain unauthorized access to target networks over extended periods. By exploiting zero-day vulnerabilities, APTs can infiltrate systems without triggering alarms, remaining undetected and maintaining a persistent presence to achieve their goals, be it espionage, data theft, or the compromise of critical infrastructure.

The discovery and subsequent exploitation of zero-day vulnerabilities require a unique set of skills, often possessed by individuals or groups operating at the cutting edge of cybersecurity research or cybercrime. The motivation behind zero-day discovery may vary; ethical hackers may uncover these vulnerabilities to responsibly disclose them to the affected vendors, contributing to improved cybersecurity, while malicious actors exploit them for financial gain, political objectives, or other nefarious purposes. The existence of a thriving market for zero-day exploits, where these vulnerabilities are bought and sold, further complicates the landscape, providing a lucrative incentive for individuals or groups to keep their findings undisclosed.

A critical aspect of zero-day vulnerabilities is their transient nature. Once a zero-day vulnerability becomes known to the public or the affected vendor, it ceases to be a zero-day, as efforts to patch or mitigate the vulnerability are initiated. The race between attackers seeking to exploit the vulnerability and defenders working to develop and deploy effective countermeasures defines this transient window of vulnerability. As organizations race to apply patches or implement mitigations, the duration of exposure dwindles, highlighting the temporal significance of zero-day vulnerabilities in the cyber threat landscape.

The role of zero-day vulnerabilities is not confined to specific types of software or systems; they can affect operating systems, web browsers, office productivity suites, and even embedded systems in critical infrastructure. This broad applicability amplifies the potential impact of zero-day exploits, as successful attacks can compromise a wide range of systems across various sectors. The Stuxnet worm, which targeted supervisory control and data acquisition (SCADA) systems, exemplifies the potent consequences of leveraging zero-day vulnerabilities in targeted attacks with significant geopolitical implications.

Mitigating the risk posed by zero-day vulnerabilities demands a multifaceted approach. Vendors play a pivotal role by instituting robust secure coding practices, conducting thorough security audits, and establishing effective vulnerability disclosure programs. Timely and transparent communication between security researchers and vendors facilitates the prompt development and dissemination of patches once vulnerabilities are identified. End-users and organizations, in turn, bear the responsibility of promptly applying security updates and patches to minimize exposure to known vulnerabilities.

The evolving nature of zero-day vulnerabilities underscores the importance of threat intelligence and information sharing within the cybersecurity community. By disseminating information about newly discovered vulnerabilities and associated exploits, security professionals can collectively enhance their defenses, proactively identifying and addressing potential threats. Collaborative efforts between government agencies, private-sector organizations, and the broader cybersecurity community contribute to a more resilient and adaptive defense against the exploitation of zero-day vulnerabilities.

In conclusion, zero-day vulnerabilities represent a dynamic and influential facet of the cybersecurity landscape, shaping the tactics of cyber attackers and the strategies of defenders. Their clandestine nature, combined with the potential for significant impact, underscores the critical importance of ongoing research, collaboration, and proactive cybersecurity practices. As the digital ecosystem continues to evolve, the role of zero-day vulnerabilities in cyber-attacks will persist, necessitating a collective and unwavering commitment to innovation and collaboration to stay ahead of emerging threats.

Explore the psychological aspects of social engineering used by cybercriminals.

In the intricate landscape of cybersecurity, the art of social engineering emerges as a psychological battleground where cybercriminals exploit human behavior, trust, and vulnerabilities to achieve their nefarious objectives. Social engineering is a deceptive and manipulative technique employed by cybercriminals to exploit the weakest link in the cybersecurity chain: the human factor. At its core, social engineering involves the psychological manipulation of individuals to divulge confidential information, perform actions against their best interests, or unwittingly assist in cybercriminal activities.

The success of social engineering hinges on the fundamental understanding of human psychology, including cognitive biases, emotions, and the innate desire to trust and help others. One of the foundational principles that cybercriminals leverage is the concept of reciprocity, wherein individuals feel obligated to return favors. By presenting themselves as helpful or trustworthy entities, attackers exploit this innate tendency, fostering a sense of obligation that compels the victim to reciprocate, often by providing sensitive information or performing actions they would otherwise avoid.

In the realm of social engineering, phishing stands out as a prevalent and effective tactic. Phishing attacks often take the form of deceptive emails, messages, or websites that masquerade as legitimate communication from trusted sources. Attackers meticulously craft these communications to trigger emotional responses, such as fear, urgency, or curiosity, prompting victims to act hastily without scrutinizing the legitimacy of the request. By exploiting emotional triggers, cybercriminals manipulate human psychology to override rational thought, increasing the likelihood of successful deception.

The principle of authority is another psychological lever exploited by social engineers. Individuals tend to comply with requests from perceived authority figures or trusted entities. Cybercriminals adeptly impersonate authoritative figures, such as IT support personnel, law enforcement, or company executives, creating a facade that induces victims to comply with requests for sensitive information or actions that compromise security. The psychological impact of this manipulation is profound, as individuals instinctively defer to authority, often bypassing critical skepticism.

The concept of scarcity, deeply ingrained in human psychology, is frequently exploited by cybercriminals to create a sense of urgency. Whether posing as a financial institution warning of an imminent account compromise or a government agency threatening legal consequences, attackers manipulate the fear of loss or punishment to coerce victims into immediate compliance. This urgency diminishes the likelihood that individuals will critically evaluate the legitimacy of the communication, as the perceived consequences of inaction loom large.

Social engineers also capitalize on the human tendency to trust others, particularly in familiar or seemingly benign contexts. Through pretexting, cybercriminals construct elaborate scenarios or personas to establish a sense of legitimacy, often posing as colleagues, service providers, or trusted acquaintances. By weaving a convincing narrative, attackers exploit the inherent human inclination to trust familiar faces or situations, thereby lowering the barriers to manipulation and increasing the likelihood of successful social engineering attacks.

The psychology of conformity plays a pivotal role in social engineering tactics. People have an innate desire to conform to social norms and expectations, often resulting in behavior that aligns with the perceived actions of others. Cybercriminals exploit this inclination by crafting messages or scenarios that suggest widespread compliance or endorsement. By creating a false sense of consensus, attackers manipulate individuals into conforming to actions they might otherwise question, fostering an environment conducive to successful social engineering exploits.

The evolving landscape of social media introduces new dimensions to social engineering, with cybercriminals leveraging personal information shared on these platforms to tailor their attacks. The psychological impact of receiving a personalized message containing accurate details about one's life or connections creates a false sense of familiarity and trust. This familiarity, combined with the illusion of legitimacy, significantly increases the likelihood that individuals will fall victim to social engineering attacks that exploit their personal relationships.

Moreover, the psychology of trust plays a crucial role in social engineering exploits. Humans are naturally inclined to trust others, especially in familiar or seemingly secure contexts. Cybercriminals exploit this trust dynamic by impersonating trusted entities or manipulating social connections. Through the art of impersonation, attackers create deceptive scenarios that bypass individuals' natural skepticism, leading them to disclose sensitive information or take actions that compromise security.

The psychological aspects of social engineering extend beyond individual exploits to more elaborate schemes, such as business email compromise (BEC) attacks. In BEC attacks, cybercriminals often impersonate high-ranking executives or trusted vendors, exploiting the psychological pressure associated with hierarchical structures and financial transactions. The urgency of financial matters and the perceived authority of the impersonated executive create an environment where employees may bypass regular security protocols, transferring funds or disclosing sensitive information under the assumption of fulfilling legitimate requests.

Understanding the psychology of social engineering is paramount for effective defense against these manipulative tactics. Cybersecurity awareness and training programs play a pivotal role in empowering individuals to recognize and resist social engineering attempts. By educating users about common tactics, emotional triggers, and red flags associated with social engineering, organizations can bolster their human firewall, making it more resilient to manipulation.

In conclusion, the psychological aspects of social engineering represent a dynamic interplay between human behavior and the evolving tactics of cybercriminals. The success of social engineering exploits relies on the exploitation of innate human tendencies, including trust, reciprocity, authority, conformity, and the desire to avoid loss. As technology advances and attackers refine their tactics, cultivating a cybersecurity culture that emphasizes awareness, skepticism, and critical thinking becomes increasingly crucial. By acknowledging the psychological dimensions of social engineering and investing in education and training, individuals and organizations can fortify their defenses against these deceptive maneuvers in the ever-evolving landscape of cybersecurity.

Discuss specific threats that are unique to cloud environments.

In the dynamic landscape of cloud computing, unique and evolving threats have emerged, necessitating a nuanced understanding of the security challenges inherent to cloud environments. One prominent threat is data breaches, where unauthorized access to sensitive information stored in the cloud poses significant risks. Cloud service providers (CSPs) store vast amounts of data from numerous clients on shared infrastructure, making them attractive targets for cybercriminals seeking to exploit vulnerabilities in the multi-tenant architecture. The interconnected nature of cloud services also introduces the risk of lateral movement, enabling attackers to navigate between different cloud resources once a breach occurs, potentially compromising entire ecosystems.

Another distinctive threat in cloud environments is misconfigured security settings, a consequence of the shared responsibility model between cloud providers and their clients. Organizations, while benefiting from the convenience and scalability of cloud services, must actively manage their security configurations. Misconfigurations, such as improperly configured access controls or insecure storage settings, can inadvertently expose sensitive data to unauthorized parties. The complexity of cloud configurations and the potential for human error amplify the risk, underscoring the importance of robust security hygiene and continuous monitoring.

Cloud-specific attacks also encompass vulnerabilities associated with application programming interfaces (APIs), which serve as the linchpin for communication between different cloud services. API-related threats include insecure direct object references, where attackers manipulate references to gain unauthorized access to data, and API endpoint vulnerabilities that can be exploited for unauthorized data access or denial-of-service attacks. As organizations increasingly rely on APIs for seamless integration of cloud services, securing these interfaces becomes paramount to prevent potential exploitation.

The shared nature of cloud environments introduces the risk of co-tenancy vulnerabilities, where malicious actors exploit weaknesses in the underlying infrastructure to compromise the security of neighboring tenants. Hypervisor vulnerabilities, for example, could allow an attacker to escape their virtualized environment and access data or resources belonging to other tenants on the same physical server. Co-tenancy threats highlight the importance of robust isolation mechanisms and continuous monitoring to detect and mitigate potential breaches.

Cryptocurrency mining attacks, commonly known as crypto-jacking, have found a fertile ground in cloud environments. Cyber-criminals compromise cloud resources to deploy unauthorized cryptocurrency mining operations, utilizing the computational power of the compromised infrastructure. The elasticity of cloud services makes it an attractive target, allowing attackers to scale their operations dynamically. Organizations face the challenge of detecting and preventing cryptojacking activities, which can lead to increased operational costs, performance degradation, and potential data breaches.

Supply chain attacks present a unique challenge in cloud environments, where dependencies on third-party services and components are prevalent. Adversaries may compromise the security of a cloud service provider's supply chain, introducing malicious code or backdoors into the services offered. This can have cascading effects, impacting multiple clients relying on the compromised services. Vigilant vetting of third-party providers, robust supply chain security practices, and continuous monitoring are essential measures to mitigate the risks associated with supply chain attacks in the cloud.

Man-in-the-middle attacks are also a concern in cloud environments, where data traverses networks, including the internet, to reach cloud services. Attackers may intercept and manipulate this communication, leading to data exfiltration, unauthorized access, or the injection of malicious code. The use of secure communication protocols, encryption, and comprehensive network security measures becomes crucial to mitigate the risk of man-in-the-middle attacks in the cloud.

Advanced Persistent Threats (APTs) have adapted to exploit the characteristics of cloud environments, conducting long-term, targeted campaigns with a focus on stealth and persistence. APTs in the cloud often involve sophisticated tactics, such as leveraging compromised credentials, evading detection through encryption, and utilizing cloud-native tools for lateral movement. Detecting and responding to APTs in the cloud requires a holistic approach, combining threat intelligence, behavioral analytics, and continuous monitoring to identify anomalous activities indicative of persistent threats.

The phenomenon of "shadow IT" poses a unique challenge to cloud security, as employees may use unauthorized cloud services or applications without the knowledge or approval of the IT department. While the intent may be to enhance productivity, the uncontrolled proliferation of shadow IT introduces unknown risks, including data exposure, compliance violations, and unmanaged access points for cyber threats. Organizations must implement robust policies, education programs, and technical controls to address the challenges posed by shadow IT and ensure the security of cloud environments.

In conclusion, the adoption of cloud computing introduces a spectrum of unique security threats that demand vigilant attention and strategic mitigation efforts. From data breaches and misconfigurations to API vulnerabilities, co-tenancy risks, and novel attack vectors like cryptojacking, the dynamic nature of cloud environments requires organizations to adopt a comprehensive and adaptive security posture. As cloud technologies continue to evolve, the collaboration between cloud service providers, organizations, and the broader cybersecurity community becomes imperative to stay ahead of emerging threats and safeguard the integrity, confidentiality, and availability of data in the cloud.

Examine how AI is both a tool for cyber attackers and defenders.

In the complex landscape of cybersecurity, artificial intelligence (AI) has emerged as a double-edged sword, serving both as a potent tool for cyber attackers and a crucial asset for defenders. As attackers continually evolve their tactics to exploit vulnerabilities and bypass traditional security measures, the integration of AI into offensive strategies has become increasingly prevalent. One prominent application is the use of AI in crafting sophisticated and targeted phishing attacks. AI-driven tools can analyze vast datasets to generate highly convincing phishing emails, leveraging natural language processing and contextual understanding to tailor messages that deceive even vigilant users. This AI-enabled evolution of phishing tactics raises the bar for detection, as these attacks can mimic legitimate communication with unprecedented realism.

AI's role extends beyond phishing, encompassing the development of more advanced and evasive malware. Adversarial machine learning, a technique where AI models are manipulated to generate malicious code that can evade traditional detection mechanisms, represents a notable threat. AI-driven malware can adapt its behavior in real-time, making it challenging for signature-based antivirus solutions to keep pace. Moreover, AI facilitates the automation of the entire cyber attack lifecycle, from reconnaissance and weaponization to delivery, exploitation, installation, command and control, and actions on objectives (the so-called APT29 model), enabling cyber-criminals to operate at scale with heightened sophistication.

The realm of AI-powered attacks also includes the manipulation of machine learning models. Attackers can exploit vulnerabilities in AI systems, injecting malicious data or subtly modifying input to deceive models and cause them to make incorrect predictions or classifications. This adversarial machine learning poses a significant challenge for industries deploying AI for critical applications such as finance, healthcare, and autonomous systems, as it introduces the risk of manipulated decision-making with potentially severe consequences.

On the flip side, the defender's arsenal has also been fortified by AI technologies, marking a paradigm shift in cybersecurity strategies. One of the primary contributions of AI to defense lies in its capacity to enhance threat detection and response. Machine learning algorithms can analyze vast datasets, discern patterns, and identify anomalies indicative of potential security incidents. This enables organizations to detect and respond to threats in real-time, reducing the dwell time of attackers within networks and minimizing the potential impact of breaches.

AI-driven threat intelligence is another crucial aspect of the defender's toolkit. Automated analysis of threat feeds, open-source intelligence, and dark web forums allows security teams to stay ahead of emerging threats and vulnerabilities. Predictive analytics powered by AI can assist in forecasting potential attack vectors and preparing proactive defense measures. Additionally, AI enables the automation of routine security tasks, freeing up human resources to focus on more complex and strategic aspects of cybersecurity.

In the realm of vulnerability management, AI plays a pivotal role in identifying and prioritizing potential weaknesses in systems. Automated scanning and analysis of network configurations and software applications can significantly accelerate the identification of vulnerabilities, enabling organizations to patch or mitigate risks promptly. This proactive approach is crucial in an era where the sheer volume and complexity of vulnerabilities make manual assessment processes increasingly impractical.

Behavioral analytics, facilitated by AI, represents a game-changing advancement in the realm of user and entity behavior analytics (UEBA). By establishing baselines of normal behavior for users and systems, AI-driven analytics can identify deviations that may indicate a security incident, such as unauthorized access or lateral movement within a network. This proactive identification of suspicious activities allows defenders to respond swiftly, mitigating the potential impact of breaches.

AI-driven incident response capabilities empower organizations to automate and orchestrate the response to security incidents. Rapid containment and eradication of threats become achievable through automated workflows, reducing the time and resources required to mitigate the consequences of a security breach. This aspect is particularly critical in the face of advanced persistent threats (APTs) and other sophisticated attacks where timely response is paramount.

The application of AI in predictive modeling is instrumental in risk management. By assessing the potential impact and likelihood of security incidents, organizations can allocate resources effectively, prioritizing high-risk areas and fortifying defenses where they matter most. This risk-centric approach enables organizations to navigate the evolving threat landscape with a strategic and informed perspective.

Moreover, AI is instrumental in securing cloud environments. As organizations migrate their infrastructure to the cloud, the complexity of managing security in dynamic, multi-cloud environments necessitates the capabilities that AI brings. Automated threat detection, identity and access management, and anomaly detection in cloud activities are all areas where AI significantly enhances security in the cloud.

While AI serves as a powerful ally for defenders, it is essential to acknowledge the ongoing arms race between attackers and defenders in the realm of artificial intelligence. As AI becomes more prevalent in cybersecurity, attackers are likely to employ increasingly sophisticated AI-driven tactics to circumvent defenses. The dynamic nature of AI-driven attacks requires defenders to continuously innovate and adapt their strategies, emphasizing the importance of a holistic and multi-layered security approach.

In conclusion, the duality of AI in cybersecurity reflects the broader technological landscape's complexities. As both attackers and defenders harness the power of AI, the battleground for cybersecurity becomes a dynamic arena of innovation and adaptation. While AI empowers cybercriminals to craft more sophisticated attacks, it simultaneously equips defenders with the tools needed to detect, respond to, and mitigate these threats. The future of cybersecurity hinges on the ability of organizations to leverage AI strategically, staying ahead of evolving threats and ensuring the resilience of digital ecosystems in the face of an ever-changing threat landscape.

Provide an overview of current global cybersecurity trends.

In the contemporary digital landscape, the ever-evolving field of cybersecurity is shaped by dynamic and multifaceted trends that reflect the complex interplay of technological advancements, threat landscapes, and the expanding attack surface. One prominent trend is the escalation of ransomware attacks to unprecedented levels, posing significant threats to individuals, businesses, and critical infrastructure globally. Cybercriminals have refined their tactics, employing advanced techniques such as double extortion, where stolen data is not only encrypted but also threatened with public exposure, compelling victims to pay ransoms. The impact of ransomware extends beyond financial losses to reputational damage, operational disruptions, and the critical need for organizations to fortify their defenses against this pervasive and evolving threat.

A parallel trend is the surge in supply chain attacks, reflecting the realization among cyber adversaries that compromising trusted third-party services or software providers offers a potent avenue for infiltrating target organizations. High-profile incidents, such as the SolarWinds supply chain compromise, have underscored the sophisticated nature of these attacks and their potential to compromise a vast number of entities indirectly connected to the initial breach. Supply chain attacks emphasize the importance of comprehensive cybersecurity measures, including rigorous vetting of third-party providers, continuous monitoring, and the establishment of resilient security postures.

The rapid adoption of cloud computing has transformed the digital landscape, introducing a new frontier for cybersecurity challenges. Cloud security trends encompass a spectrum of considerations, including misconfigurations, identity and access management, and the evolving nature of threats targeting cloud environments. As organizations migrate critical infrastructure to the cloud, the shared responsibility model emphasizes the need for robust security practices and continuous monitoring to mitigate the unique risks associated with cloud computing. Security tools tailored for cloud environments, along with comprehensive training programs, are pivotal in navigating the complexities of cloud security.

Another significant trend revolves around the role of artificial intelligence (AI) and machine learning in both cyber attacks and defense strategies. Cybercriminals leverage AI to enhance the sophistication of their tactics, ranging from more convincing phishing attacks to the development of adaptive malware that can evade traditional detection mechanisms. Simultaneously, defenders harness the power of AI for threat detection, behavioral analytics, and predictive modeling to bolster their security postures. The AI-driven arms race in cybersecurity underscores the importance of continuous innovation and strategic adaptation to stay ahead of evolving threats.

The expanding attack surface fueled by the Internet of Things (IoT) introduces a plethora of cybersecurity challenges. With the proliferation of connected devices in homes, industries, and critical infrastructure, the potential for exploitation and compromise grows exponentially. IoT security trends include the need for standardized security protocols, device identity management, and comprehensive risk assessments to address the vulnerabilities inherent in the diverse ecosystem of IoT devices. As IoT becomes more integral to daily life and business operations, a proactive approach to securing these interconnected devices becomes imperative.

In the realm of nation-state cyber activities, geopolitical tensions manifest in the form of state-sponsored cyber attacks, espionage, and influence operations. Nation-state actors leverage sophisticated tactics to achieve political, economic, or military objectives in cyberspace. The blurred lines between state-sponsored and non-state cyber actors complicate attribution efforts, emphasizing the need for international cooperation, norms, and regulations to establish a framework for responsible behavior in the digital domain.

Privacy concerns and regulatory developments continue to shape cybersecurity trends globally. The implementation of stringent data protection regulations, such as the General Data Protection Regulation (GDPR) in Europe and similar initiatives worldwide, places an emphasis on the responsible handling of personal information. Organizations face the challenge of aligning their cybersecurity practices with regulatory requirements, mitigating the risk of data breaches, and fostering a privacy-centric culture within their operations.

Cybersecurity workforce shortages represent a persistent and escalating challenge. The increasing complexity of cyber threats, coupled with the expanding attack surface, demands a skilled and diverse cybersecurity workforce. Organizations struggle to recruit and retain qualified professionals, exacerbating the need for strategic investments in cybersecurity education, training, and diversity initiatives to cultivate a robust talent pool capable of addressing the evolving demands of the field.

The intersection of cybersecurity and artificial intelligence extends to the domain of threat hunting and collaborative defense mechanisms. Threat intelligence sharing, both within and across sectors, represents a critical trend in fostering collective resilience against cyber threats. Collaborative efforts, such as Information Sharing and Analysis Centers (ISACs) and public-private partnerships, enable organizations to pool resources, share insights, and respond collectively to emerging threats. As threat landscapes become increasingly interconnected, collaborative defense mechanisms become indispensable in fortifying global cybersecurity postures.

The integration of zero-trust security models is gaining prominence as organizations recognize the limitations of traditional perimeter-based approaches. Zero-trust frameworks assume that no entity, whether inside or outside the network, can be inherently trusted. This approach emphasizes continuous authentication, micro-segmentation, and the principle of least privilege to mitigate the risk of lateral movement and contain potential breaches. The zero-trust paradigm aligns with the evolving nature of cyber threats and the need for adaptive security architectures.

In conclusion, the landscape of global cybersecurity is marked by a dynamic interplay of trends that underscore the multifaceted challenges faced by individuals, organizations, and nations. From the surge in ransomware attacks and supply chain compromises to the transformative impact of cloud computing and the imperative for AI-driven defense strategies, the cybersecurity arena demands continuous adaptation, innovation, and collaboration. Addressing these trends requires a holistic approach that combines advanced technologies, comprehensive training, regulatory compliance, and collaborative efforts to fortify the collective defense against the evolving and sophisticated nature of cyber threats.

Introduce the concept of risk assessment in the context of the evolving threat landscape.

In the ever-evolving landscape of cybersecurity, where threats are dynamic and multifaceted, the concept of risk assessment stands as a pivotal element in the strategic arsenal of organizations seeking to fortify their digital defenses. At its core, risk assessment is a systematic and comprehensive process designed to identify, evaluate, and prioritize potential risks to an organization's assets, operations, and sensitive information. This process is indispensable in navigating the complexities of the contemporary threat landscape, where cyber adversaries continually innovate and adapt their tactics to exploit vulnerabilities, both known and novel.

The foundation of risk assessment lies in understanding that risk is an inherent aspect of any digital ecosystem, stemming from the interconnected nature of technology, the proliferation of data, and the expanding attack surface. As organizations embrace digital transformation, leveraging technologies such as cloud computing, Internet of Things (IoT), and artificial intelligence (AI), they simultane-ously expose themselves to new and diverse risk vectors. Risk assess-ment becomes a proactive and strategic endeavor, equipping organi-zations with the insights needed to make informed decisions, allo-cate resources effectively, and prioritize security measures based on the potential impact and likelihood of various threats.

The risk assessment process typically commences with the iden-tification of assets within the organizational landscape. Assets en-compass not only tangible elements like hardware, software, and net-works but also intangible components such as intellectual property, customer data, and the organization's reputation. This holistic view allows organizations to comprehend the full spectrum of elements that contribute to their operational fabric and are susceptible to po-tential risks.

Following asset identification, the risk assessment delves into the realm of threat identification. In the contemporary threat land-scape, threats manifest in diverse forms, from traditional malware and phishing attacks to advanced persistent threats (APTs), supply chain compromises, and zero-day vulnerabilities. The dynamic na-ture of threats requires organizations to stay abreast of emerging tactics, techniques, and procedures employed by cyber adversaries. Threat intelligence feeds, collaboration with industry peers, and monitoring of global cybersecurity trends become integral compo-nents in identifying the breadth and sophistication of potential threats.

Vulnerability assessment is another critical facet of the risk as-sessment process. This involves identifying weaknesses and suscepti-bilities within the organization's infrastructure, systems, and appli-cations that could be exploited by adversaries. Vulnerabilities may arise from misconfigurations, outdated software, unpatched systems, or lapses in security hygiene. The goal of vulnerability assessment is to create an inventory of potential entry points for attackers and prioritize remediation efforts based on the level of risk posed by each vulnerability.

Once assets, threats, and vulnerabilities are identified, the risk assessment process progresses to the evaluation phase. This involves assessing the potential impact and likelihood of various risk scenarios. Impact assessment considers the consequences of a successful exploitation of a vulnerability or a specific threat event, encompassing financial losses, operational disruptions, reputational damage, and legal ramifications. Likelihood assessment, on the other hand, gauges the probability of these risk scenarios materializing based on historical data, threat intelligence, and the organization's security posture.

Risk assessment employs a risk matrix or a similar framework to categorize and prioritize risks based on their potential impact and likelihood. This enables organizations to distinguish between high-risk scenarios that require immediate attention and lower-priority risks that can be addressed through proactive mitigation measures. The risk matrix serves as a visual aid, providing a clear representation of the risk landscape and guiding decision-makers in allocating resources strategically.

As the risk assessment process advances, organizations delve into the development of risk mitigation strategies. Mitigation involves implementing controls and measures to reduce the likelihood of risk events occurring or to minimize their impact if they do occur. Mitigation strategies encompass a spectrum of activities, from implementing technical safeguards and security policies to conducting employee training and enhancing incident response capabilities. The goal is to create a layered defense mechanism that addresses vulnerabilities, counters specific threats, and fortifies the organization's overall security posture.

An integral component of risk mitigation is the concept of the risk appetite and risk tolerance. Risk appetite defines the level of risk that an organization is willing to accept in pursuit of its objectives. It represents a conscious decision by organizational leadership to balance innovation and growth with the need for security and resilience. Risk tolerance, on the other hand, represents the organization's threshold for accepting variations in performance or deviations from expected outcomes. Establishing clear risk appetite and risk tolerance parameters guides decision-making processes and ensures that risk management aligns with organizational objectives.

The risk assessment process does not conclude with the implementation of mitigation measures. Continuous monitoring and reassessment are imperative in the face of the dynamic threat landscape. Threats evolve, new vulnerabilities emerge, and the organization's assets and operations undergo changes. Periodic reviews of the risk landscape allow organizations to adapt their risk management strategies, fine-tune mitigation measures, and respond to emerging threats in a timely and effective manner.

Risk assessment is not a one-size-fits-all endeavor; it is contextual and should be tailored to the unique characteristics and requirements of each organization. The risk landscape for a financial institution may differ significantly from that of a healthcare provider or a manufacturing company. Therefore, organizations must cultivate a risk-aware culture that permeates every level of the organization, from executive leadership to front-line employees. This culture emphasizes the shared responsibility of managing risk, promotes communication and collaboration, and fosters a proactive approach to cybersecurity.

In conclusion, risk assessment emerges as a cornerstone of effective cybersecurity in the face of an ever-evolving threat landscape. It is a dynamic and iterative process that demands continuous attention, adaptation, and collaboration. By systematically identifying assets, assessing threats and vulnerabilities, and developing strategic mitigation measures, organizations can navigate the complexities of the digital landscape with resilience and foresight. Risk assessment empowers organizations to make informed decisions, align cyberse-curity efforts with business objectives, and foster a cybersecurity pos-ture that is not merely reactive but anticipatory and proactive.

Highlight the role of human factors in cybersecurity inci-dents.

The role of human factors in cybersecurity incidents is a per-vasive and complex dimension that significantly influences the ef-fectiveness of security measures. Despite the technological advance-ments in cybersecurity, humans remain both the weakest link and an essential component in the defense against cyber threats. The human element introduces a dynamic interplay of cognitive, behavioral, and social factors that can either fortify or compromise the security pos-ture of organizations. One prominent human factor is the phenom-enon of social engineering, where cyber attackers exploit psycholog-ical manipulations to deceive individuals into divulging sensitive in-formation or performing actions against their best interests.

Social engineering tactics leverage the inherent human traits of trust, reciprocity, and the inclination to assist others. Phishing, a prevalent form of social engineering, involves deceptive communica-tion, often through emails or messages, masquerading as legitimate entities to trick individuals into providing login credentials, financial information, or sensitive data. The success of phishing attacks under-scores the psychological impact of well-crafted messages that trigger emotional responses, such as fear, urgency, or curiosity, bypassing ra-tional thought and leading individuals to unwittingly assist in com-promising security.

Moreover, the psychological aspect of trust plays a crucial role in social engineering exploits. Humans naturally tend to trust famil-iar entities or those posing as authoritative figures. Cybercriminals adeptly impersonate trusted sources, such as IT support personnel, colleagues, or supervisors, to manipulate individuals into complying with requests for sensitive information or actions that compromise security. The psychology of trust amplifies the effectiveness of social engineering tactics, emphasizing the need for robust cybersecurity awareness and education to instill skepticism and critical thinking among users.

The human factor extends beyond social engineering to encompass the broader realm of employee behavior within organizations. Insider threats, whether unintentional or malicious, exemplify the impact of human behavior on cybersecurity incidents. Employees may inadvertently compromise security through actions such as clicking on malicious links, sharing passwords, or mishandling sensitive information. Malicious insiders, on the other hand, exploit their access and knowledge to intentionally cause harm, exfiltrate data, or sabotage systems. Addressing insider threats requires a multifaceted approach, involving not only technological controls but also organizational culture, training, and employee engagement.

The psychology of decision-making is a crucial aspect of human factors in cybersecurity incidents. Individuals often face cognitive biases and heuristics that influence their judgments and decisions. The optimism bias, for example, leads individuals to underestimate their susceptibility to cyber threats, fostering a false sense of security. Confirmation bias can influence the way individuals interpret information, potentially leading them to overlook warning signs or dismiss security alerts. Understanding these cognitive biases is paramount in designing effective cybersecurity awareness programs that resonate with individuals, promote realistic risk perceptions, and empower users to make informed decisions in the face of cyber threats.

The complexity of human factors is further compounded by the challenges associated with the intersection of personal and professional digital lives. Bring Your Own Device (BYOD) policies and remote work arrangements introduce a blurred boundary between personal and corporate digital environments. This convergence amplifies the risk of individuals using insecure devices, accessing unsecured networks, or engaging in risky online behaviors that can inadvertently expose organizations to cyber threats. Balancing the benefits of flexibility and productivity with the imperative for security requires a nuanced approach that integrates technical controls, policy enforcement, and user education.

The role of human factors in cybersecurity incidents extends to the domain of password security. Despite the emphasis on strong, unique passwords, individuals often succumb to the convenience of using easily guessable passwords or reusing them across multiple accounts. The human tendency to prioritize convenience over security creates vulnerabilities that attackers exploit through credential stuffing attacks or brute-force techniques. Educating users on the importance of password hygiene, implementing multi-factor authentication, and leveraging technical solutions to detect and prevent compromised credentials become integral components of a comprehensive cybersecurity strategy.

Additionally, the concept of cybersecurity fatigue reflects the weariness and desensitization that individuals experience in response to the continuous barrage of security warnings, alerts, and requirements. The overwhelming nature of security-related decisions, coupled with the prevalence of complex password policies and frequent updates, can lead to fatigue-induced lapses in security hygiene. Organizations need to strike a balance between enforcing necessary security measures and alleviating the burden on users through user-friendly interfaces, simplified security procedures, and continuous education efforts that reinforce the importance of individual contributions to overall cybersecurity.

The insider threat landscape further unfolds with unintentional actions driven by lack of awareness or training. Employees may unwittingly introduce risks through activities such as downloading malware-infected files, connecting unauthorized devices to corporate networks, or falling victim to scams. Building a resilient human firewall necessitates ongoing cybersecurity education that not only imparts knowledge about emerging threats and best practices but also instills a sense of responsibility and vigilance among employees. Human-centric cybersecurity approaches recognize that individuals are integral components of the defense strategy, and investing in their cybersecurity literacy is crucial for overall resilience.

The realm of social media introduces yet another layer to the human factors in cybersecurity incidents. Individuals share vast amounts of personal and professional information on social platforms, creating a rich environment for cyber adversaries seeking to conduct reconnaissance or launch targeted attacks. Social engineering tactics often leverage this information to craft convincing spear-phishing campaigns that exploit personal relationships, job roles, or organizational structures. The challenge for organizations lies in promoting responsible social media use, balancing the benefits of professional networking with the imperative for maintaining a vigilant and security-conscious online presence.

The intersection of human factors and cybersecurity is particularly pronounced in the context of incident response and recovery. Human error, whether in the form of delayed detection, miscommunication during incident response, or inadequate coordination among response teams, can exacerbate the impact of cybersecurity incidents. The psychological stress and pressure associated with responding to a breach further underscore the importance of robust incident response planning, regular drills, and clear communication channels that mitigate the risk of human-induced errors during critical moments.

Organizational culture plays a pivotal role in shaping human factors in cybersecurity. A culture that prioritizes security, fosters open communication about potential threats, and encourages a shared responsibility for cybersecurity contributes to a resilient defense posture. Conversely, a culture that downplays the significance of security, places undue emphasis on convenience over robustness, or fosters a blame-centric approach in the face of security incidents creates an environment where human factors become liabilities rather than assets.

In conclusion, the role of human factors in cybersecurity incidents is multifaceted and intrinsic to the overall security posture of organizations. Recognizing the complexities of human behavior, cognitive biases, and the interplay between personal and professional digital lives is essential in crafting effective cybersecurity strategies. Human-centric approaches that integrate education, awareness, and cultural initiatives empower individuals to become proactive contributors to cybersecurity resilience. As organizations navigate the evolving threat landscape, they must acknowledge the pivotal role of human factors and cultivate a cybersecurity culture that values the human element as a critical component of the defense against cyber threats.

Discuss proactive measures and strategies for staying ahead of future cyber threats.

Proactively staying ahead of future cyber threats demands a multifaceted and adaptive approach that integrates technological innovation, strategic planning, collaboration, and continuous education. One pivotal strategy involves the cultivation of a robust cybersecurity culture within organizations. Fostering a culture that prioritizes security awareness, responsible digital behavior, and a shared sense of responsibility among employees is foundational. Cybersecurity education programs, regular training sessions, and awareness campaigns empower individuals to recognize and respond to evolving threats. A culture of openness and reporting ensures that potential threats are identified and addressed swiftly, creating a resilient human firewall as a frontline defense against cyber adversaries.

Embracing the principles of a zero-trust security model is instrumental in proactively mitigating cyber threats. Zero-trust assumes that no entity, whether inside or outside the network, can be inherently trusted. This approach mandates continuous authentication, micro-segmentation, and the principle of least privilege to minimize the attack surface and contain potential breaches. Implementing a zero-trust framework requires a comprehensive understanding of the organization's digital ecosystem, mapping data flows, and deploying adaptive access controls that scrutinize every user and device interaction, thereby enhancing the overall security posture.

The integration of advanced threat intelligence is indispensable for staying ahead of emerging cyber threats. Threat intelligence involves the proactive gathering, analysis, and dissemination of information about potential threats and vulnerabilities. Leveraging threat intelligence feeds, collaborating with industry peers, and monitoring global cybersecurity trends provide organizations with insights into the tactics, techniques, and procedures employed by cyber adversaries. This foresight enables proactive defense measures, allowing organizations to anticipate and prepare for specific threats rather than merely reacting after an incident has occurred.

Continuous vulnerability management is a cornerstone of proactive cybersecurity. Identifying and patching vulnerabilities in a timely manner is essential for preventing exploitation by cybercriminals. Automated vulnerability scanning tools, regular penetration testing, and a well-defined patch management process enable organizations to detect and remediate weaknesses in their systems, applications, and infrastructure. Furthermore, a proactive approach involves engaging in ethical hacking or bug bounty programs to leverage the collective expertise of the cybersecurity community in identifying and addressing vulnerabilities before malicious actors can exploit them.

The proactive use of artificial intelligence (AI) and machine learning (ML) technologies significantly enhances the ability to detect and respond to emerging cyber threats. AI-driven threat detection systems can analyze vast datasets, discern patterns, and identify anomalies indicative of potential security incidents. Machine learning models, when trained on historical data, contribute to predictive analytics that forecast potential attack vectors and vulnerabilities. The dynamic nature of cyber threats demands adaptive defense mechanisms, and AI and ML technologies provide the agility required to stay ahead of evolving tactics employed by cyber adversaries.

Embracing a DevSecOps (Development, Security, Operations) approach is pivotal for integrating security seamlessly into the software development lifecycle. Proactively incorporating security measures into the development process ensures that potential vulnerabilities are identified and addressed early in the lifecycle, reducing the risk of deploying insecure applications. DevSecOps emphasizes collaboration and communication between development, security, and operations teams, fostering a culture of shared responsibility for security throughout the development and deployment processes.

The proactive monitoring and analysis of network traffic and user behavior are critical components of staying ahead of cyber threats. Security information and event management (SIEM) systems, combined with behavioral analytics, enable organizations to detect anomalous activities indicative of potential security incidents. Machine learning algorithms can establish baselines of normal behavior, facilitating the identification of deviations that may signal unauthorized access, lateral movement, or other malicious activities. Proactive threat hunting, conducted by skilled cybersecurity professionals, involves actively searching for signs of potential threats within an organization's network and endpoints, complementing automated detection systems.

Engaging in red teaming exercises provides organizations with a proactive and realistic simulation of cyber threats. Red teams, composed of skilled ethical hackers, mimic the tactics, techniques, and procedures of real-world adversaries to identify vulnerabilities and weaknesses in an organization's defenses. Red teaming goes beyond automated testing, offering a human-centric approach that assesses not only technical controls but also the effectiveness of response processes and the resilience of the overall cybersecurity strategy.

The proactive sharing of threat intelligence and collaborative defense initiatives amplify the collective resilience against cyber threats. Information Sharing and Analysis Centers (ISACs), public-private partnerships, and industry collaboration forums enable organizations to pool resources, share insights, and respond collectively to emerging threats. Collaborative efforts contribute to a more comprehensive understanding of the threat landscape, allowing organizations to benefit from the experiences and insights of their peers.

Staying ahead of future cyber threats requires organizations to embrace a risk-centric approach to cybersecurity. This involves understanding that not all risks can be eliminated but can be managed effectively through informed decision-making and strategic prioritization. Risk assessments, conducted regularly and comprehensively, provide organizations with insights into their unique risk landscape, enabling the prioritization of resources and efforts based on the potential impact and likelihood of specific threats.

As organizations increasingly rely on third-party vendors and services, a proactive approach involves robust supply chain security practices. Assessing the security posture of third-party providers, conducting regular audits, and ensuring contractual agreements include stringent security requirements are essential components of supply chain risk management. Proactively vetting and monitoring third-party relationships mitigate the risk of compromises originating from the supply chain, enhancing the overall resilience of the organization.

Finally, staying ahead of future cyber threats necessitates a commitment to continuous learning and adaptation. The cybersecurity landscape evolves rapidly, and organizations must remain agile in response to emerging threats. Establishing a cybersecurity team that is well-versed in the latest technologies, threat landscapes, and defense strategies is crucial. Investing in professional development, certifications, and industry engagement ensures that the cybersecurity workforce is equipped to navigate the complexities of the evolving threat landscape proactively.

In conclusion, proactively staying ahead of future cyber threats demands a holistic and adaptive approach that integrates technological innovation, strategic planning, collaboration, and continuous education. From cultivating a cybersecurity culture and embracing a zero-trust model to leveraging advanced threat intelligence, AI, and machine learning, organizations must adopt a multifaceted strategy. Continuous vulnerability management, DevSecOps practices, red teaming exercises, collaborative defense initiatives, and a risk-centric approach contribute to a proactive defense posture. Embracing a mindset of continuous learning and adaptation ensures that organizations remain resilient in the face of the dynamic and evolving cyber threat landscape.

Chapter 2: Building a Robust Security Infrastructure

Define the components of a security infrastructure in the context of cloud computing.

In the dynamic landscape of cloud computing, building a robust security infrastructure is paramount to safeguarding sensitive data, ensuring compliance, and mitigating the evolving threats that organizations face in the digital realm. The components of a security infrastructure in the context of cloud computing encompass a comprehensive set of technologies, processes, and policies designed to address the unique challenges and opportunities presented by cloud environments.

At the core of a cloud security infrastructure lies identity and access management (IAM). IAM encompasses the policies, technologies, and processes that govern and control access to cloud resources. This includes user authentication, authorization, and the management of privileges. Implementing strong IAM practices ensures that only authorized individuals or systems can access and manipulate cloud resources, reducing the risk of unauthorized access, data breaches, or malicious activities within the cloud environment.

Encryption plays a pivotal role in securing data both in transit and at rest within cloud environments. Data in transit, as it travels between users and cloud servers or between cloud services, is vulnerable to interception. Transport Layer Security (TLS) or Secure Sockets Layer (SSL) protocols provide encryption for this data, safeguarding it from eavesdropping or tampering. At rest, encryption ensures that stored data remains confidential and secure, particularly in scenarios where cloud service providers manage data storage. A robust cloud security infrastructure integrates encryption mechanisms to protect sensitive information from unauthorized access, even if physical controls of the underlying infrastructure are beyond the user's control.

Network security is another critical component of a cloud security infrastructure. As organizations leverage cloud services, data traverses various networks, both within and outside the cloud provider's infrastructure. Implementing firewalls, intrusion detection and prevention systems, and virtual private networks (VPNs) helps secure network traffic, monitor for malicious activities, and establish secure communication channels between different components of the cloud environment. Network security measures are vital for preventing unauthorized access, detecting anomalies, and maintaining the confidentiality and integrity of data as it traverses the cloud.

Vulnerability management is an ongoing process within a cloud security infrastructure that involves identifying, assessing, and remediating potential weaknesses in cloud systems and applications. Automated scanning tools, regular security assessments, and penetration testing aid in identifying vulnerabilities, ensuring that security patches are promptly applied, and minimizing the risk of exploitation by cyber adversaries. Given the dynamic nature of cloud environments, where resources can scale up or down rapidly, vulnerability management becomes integral to adapting to changes and maintaining a resilient security posture.

Security information and event management (SIEM) systems form a critical part of a cloud security infrastructure, offering real-time monitoring, correlation of security events, and centralized log management. SIEM tools aggregate and analyze logs from various cloud services, applications, and infrastructure components, enabling security teams to detect and respond to security incidents promptly. Advanced SIEM solutions leverage machine learning and artificial intelligence to identify patterns indicative of potential threats, providing a proactive defense mechanism against cyber attacks within the cloud environment.

Cloud security posture management (CSPM) tools are specifically designed to assess and manage the security configuration of cloud resources. These tools automatically evaluate the security settings of cloud services against best practices and compliance standards, highlighting misconfigurations or deviations from security policies. By continuously monitoring and remediating security configuration issues, CSPM tools contribute to maintaining a secure and compliant cloud environment.

Threat intelligence is a valuable component that enhances the proactive capabilities of a cloud security infrastructure. Threat intelligence feeds provide information about emerging threats, vulnerabilities, and the tactics, techniques, and procedures (TTPs) of cyber adversaries. Integrating threat intelligence into the security infrastructure allows organizations to anticipate potential threats, prioritize security measures, and respond effectively to the evolving threat landscape. Threat intelligence is particularly relevant in cloud environments where the rapid deployment of resources necessitates a proactive and adaptive defense strategy.

Container security has become increasingly important as organizations adopt containerization technologies, such as Docker and Kubernetes, within their cloud environments. Containers offer a lightweight and scalable approach to deploying applications, but they also introduce unique security challenges. Container security tools address these challenges by scanning container images for vulnerabilities, monitoring runtime activities, and ensuring secure configuration. As microservices and container orchestration become integral to cloud architectures, container security becomes a vital component of a holistic cloud security infrastructure.

Incident response and management are crucial components of a cloud security infrastructure, ensuring that organizations can effectively contain and mitigate the impact of security incidents. Cloud environments require tailored incident response plans that consider the distributed nature of resources and the unique challenges posed by virtualized infrastructure. Automated incident response workflows, playbooks, and coordination with cloud service providers facilitate a swift and coordinated response to security incidents, minimizing downtime and potential data breaches.

Governance, risk, and compliance (GRC) are overarching components that guide the establishment and maintenance of security controls within a cloud environment. Governance involves defining policies, procedures, and responsibilities, ensuring that security measures align with organizational objectives. Risk management involves identifying, assessing, and mitigating risks associated with cloud services and applications. Compliance ensures adherence to regulatory requirements, industry standards, and internal policies. A robust GRC framework provides the foundation for a resilient cloud security infrastructure, guiding decision-making, resource allocation, and strategic planning.

Cloud security orchestration and automation streamline security processes within a cloud environment. As organizations scale their infrastructure, automating routine security tasks becomes imperative. Security orchestration platforms enable the integration of different security tools, facilitating automated incident response, threat hunting, and remediation. Automation not only enhances operational efficiency but also ensures a rapid and consistent response to security events, reducing the dwell time of potential threats within the cloud environment.

User and entity behavior analytics (UEBA) represent an advanced component that leverages machine learning algorithms to analyze patterns of behavior within a cloud environment. UEBA tools establish baselines of normal behavior for users and entities, enabling the identification of anomalous activities that may indicate security incidents. By detecting deviations from established behavioral patterns, UEBA tools contribute to the early detection of insider threats, compromised accounts, or other malicious activities within the cloud.

Finally, continuous monitoring and auditing form a fundamental aspect of a cloud security infrastructure. Continuous monitoring involves real-time observation of activities, events, and changes within the cloud environment, enabling rapid detection of potential security incidents. Regular auditing of cloud configurations, access logs, and security controls ensures ongoing compliance, identifies security gaps, and provides insights for continuous improvement. Continuous monitoring and auditing contribute to the overall resilience of the cloud security infrastructure by maintaining visibility into the evolving threat landscape and the effectiveness of implemented security measures.

In conclusion, the components of a security infrastructure in the context of cloud computing are diverse and multifaceted, reflecting the dynamic nature of the digital landscape. From identity and access management to encryption, network security, and advanced technologies such as threat intelligence and container security, each component plays a crucial role in establishing a resilient defense against cyber threats within the cloud. A holistic approach that integrates these components, coupled with proactive measures such as vulnerability management, incident response, and continuous monitoring, ensures that organizations can navigate the complexities of cloud security and maintain a secure and compliant digital ecosystem.

Introduce the concept of security by design and its relevance in building secure cloud architectures.

Security by Design (SbD) is a holistic and proactive approach that integrates security considerations into every phase of the software development lifecycle and system architecture. The concept seeks to embed security principles and practices from the initial design stages rather than treating security as an add-on or an afterthought. In the context of building secure cloud architectures, Security by Design becomes particularly relevant due to the unique challenges and opportunities presented by cloud environments. As organizations migrate their infrastructure and applications to the cloud, the need for a robust and resilient security foundation becomes imperative, and SbD emerges as a guiding principle to address these challenges effectively.

The significance of Security by Design in the cloud era lies in its ability to align security measures with the dynamic and distributed nature of cloud architectures. Cloud computing introduces a paradigm shift, transforming the traditional model of on-premises infrastructure into a virtualized, scalable, and often multi-tenant environment. Security by Design recognizes that the principles governing security in traditional environments may not fully apply to the cloud, and hence, a paradigm shift in security thinking is necessary. By embedding security into the design and development processes of cloud architectures, organizations can build a foundation that is adaptive, resilient, and capable of addressing the unique challenges posed by the cloud environment.

One of the key pillars of Security by Design in cloud architectures is identity and access management. Traditional perimeter-based security models are inadequate in the cloud, where resources are dynamic, and users can access data from various locations and devices. Security by Design emphasizes the implementation of robust identity and access controls from the outset. This involves defining and enforcing strong authentication mechanisms, implementing least privilege principles, and ensuring that access permissions are continuously monitored and adjusted. By integrating identity and access management into the core design of cloud architectures, organizations establish a foundation that addresses the challenges of secure resource access in the cloud.

Encryption is another fundamental aspect of Security by Design in the cloud. With data traversing networks and residing in shared storage environments, the risk of unauthorized access is heightened. Security by Design advocates for a default encryption approach, ensuring that data is encrypted both in transit and at rest. This involves implementing strong encryption algorithms, managing encryption keys securely, and integrating encryption into the design of applications and services. By making encryption an integral part of the architectural design, organizations enhance the confidentiality and integrity of data, even in scenarios where the underlying infrastructure is beyond their direct control.

The dynamic nature of cloud environments necessitates a robust approach to network security, and Security by Design addresses this through the proactive consideration of network architecture and controls. Traditional network perimeters are dissolved in the cloud, and Security by Design encourages the implementation of micro-segmentation, network segmentation, and the use of virtual private clouds (VPCs) to isolate and control traffic. Additionally, the adoption of cloud-native security services, such as cloud firewalls and web application firewalls (WAFs), is integral to designing secure network architectures. By incorporating these principles into the initial design stages, organizations create a resilient network security posture that aligns with the flexible and scalable nature of cloud environments.

Vulnerability management is a continuous and integral component of Security by Design. Traditional approaches that focus on periodic scans and reactive patching are insufficient in the cloud, where resources are ephemeral, and the attack surface is dynamic. Security by Design promotes the implementation of automated vulnerability scanning tools, continuous monitoring, and a DevSecOps (Development, Security, Operations) approach. By integrating vulnerability management into the DevOps pipeline, organizations can identify and remediate vulnerabilities in real-time, reducing the window of exposure and enhancing the overall security posture of cloud architectures.

Security by Design places a strong emphasis on the principle of least privilege. In the cloud, where resources are shared among multiple tenants, limiting user and application permissions to the minimum necessary level is crucial. Security by Design advocates for a fine-grained access control model, ensuring that users and applications have only the permissions required to perform their specific functions. This principle extends to cloud service roles, APIs, and serverless computing environments. By adhering to the principle of least privilege, organizations reduce the risk of lateral movement and unauthorized access within the cloud environment.

As organizations adopt microservices architectures and containerization technologies within the cloud, Security by Design becomes particularly relevant in the context of container security. Containers offer a lightweight and scalable approach to application deployment, but they also introduce unique security challenges. Security by Design for containers involves secure image registries, scanning container images for vulnerabilities, implementing secure runtime configurations, and ensuring that container orchestration platforms, such as Kubernetes, are configured securely. By integrating container security measures into the design phase, organizations build a secure foundation for deploying and managing containerized applications in the cloud.

Threat modeling is a proactive practice endorsed by Security by Design to anticipate and mitigate potential security threats. By systematically analyzing the system architecture, identifying potential threats, and assessing the impact of potential vulnerabilities, organizations can make informed decisions about security controls and mitigation measures. Threat modeling encourages a comprehensive understanding of the threat landscape specific to the cloud environment, guiding the selection and implementation of security controls based on identified risks. Through threat modeling, organizations align their security measures with the specific nuances of the cloud, addressing potential threats before they can be exploited.

Automation is a key enabler of Security by Design in the cloud. The dynamic and scalable nature of cloud environments demands automated security processes that can adapt to changes rapidly. Security automation involves the integration of security controls into the deployment pipeline, automated configuration management, and the use of infrastructure as code (IaC) to define and enforce security policies. Automated incident response workflows, security orchestration, and continuous monitoring are essential components of Security by Design that leverage automation to enhance the efficiency and effectiveness of security measures in the cloud.

Compliance is an integral consideration within Security by Design, ensuring that cloud architectures adhere to regulatory requirements, industry standards, and organizational policies. Security by Design promotes the proactive consideration of compliance requirements during the design and development phases, reducing the need for retroactive adjustments to meet regulatory mandates. By integrating compliance checks and audits into the automated deployment pipeline, organizations can ensure that security controls are aligned with regulatory frameworks, minimizing the risk of non-compliance and associated penalties.

Education and awareness are foundational aspects of Security by Design, recognizing that the effectiveness of security measures is contingent on the knowledge and vigilance of individuals involved in the development and operation of cloud architectures. Security awareness programs, training initiatives, and ongoing education efforts create a culture of security consciousness within organizations. By instilling a security mindset from the early stages of design, organizations empower individuals

to make informed security decisions, recognize potential risks, and contribute actively to the security posture of cloud architectures.

Collaboration is a core principle of Security by Design that extends beyond organizational boundaries. Cloud environments often involve collaboration with third-party vendors, cloud service providers, and other entities. Security by Design encourages collaborative efforts to share threat intelligence, best practices, and security insights. This collaborative approach extends to industry partnerships, information-sharing forums, and participation in security communities. By fostering a culture of collaboration, organizations benefit from a collective defense against emerging threats in the cloud landscape.

In conclusion, Security by Design represents a paradigm shift in the approach to building secure cloud architectures. By embedding security principles into the design and development processes from the outset, organizations can proactively address the unique challenges posed by the dynamic, scalable, and distributed nature of cloud environments. From identity and access management to encryption, network security, and container security, each component of Security by Design contributes to the establishment of a resilient security foundation. Through automation, compliance, education, and collaboration, Security by Design ensures that cloud architectures are not only secure by default but also adaptive and capable of evolving with the ever-changing threat landscape. In the era of cloud computing, where agility and security must coexist, Security by Design emerges as a guiding principle that aligns security measures with the transformative potential of the cloud.

Explore best practices for securing cloud networks.

Securing cloud networks entails a multifaceted approach that addresses the unique challenges and opportunities presented by cloud environments. Best practices for securing cloud networks are grounded in the principles of adaptability, visibility, control, and collaboration. One fundamental aspect is robust identity and access management (IAM). Adopting the principle of least privilege, organizations should ensure that users and applications have the minimum necessary permissions, reducing the risk of unauthorized access. Utilizing centralized IAM solutions, such as cloud directory services, facilitates consistent access control policies across diverse cloud resources, enhancing security.

Encryption is a cornerstone of cloud network security, safeguarding data both in transit and at rest. Implementing Transport Layer Security (TLS) or Secure Sockets Layer (SSL) protocols for data in transit ensures secure communication between users and cloud resources. Additionally, encrypting data at rest, whether stored in cloud databases or object storage, adds an extra layer of protection against unauthorized access. Organizations should manage encryption keys securely, leveraging key management services provided by cloud service providers or implementing dedicated key management solutions.

Network security in the cloud requires a paradigm shift from traditional on-premises approaches. Micro-segmentation is a best practice that involves dividing cloud networks into smaller, isolated segments to contain potential breaches. Cloud-native firewalls and web application firewalls (WAFs) should be deployed strategically to monitor and control traffic. Virtual Private Clouds (VPCs) contribute to network segmentation, isolating resources and controlling communication. By implementing these measures, organizations enhance network security in dynamic cloud environments where traditional perimeter-based defenses may fall short.

Continuous monitoring and auditing are indispensable components of best practices for securing cloud networks. Real-time visibility into network activities, configurations, and user behaviors allows organizations to promptly detect and respond to security incidents. Security Information and Event Management (SIEM) systems, combined with cloud-native monitoring solutions, facilitate centralized log management and analysis. Regular audits of network configurations, access controls, and security policies ensure ongoing compliance, identify security gaps, and provide insights for continuous improvement.

Vulnerability management should be an integral part of securing cloud networks. Automated scanning tools and regular vulnerability assessments help identify and remediate weaknesses in cloud systems and applications. Continuous monitoring and real-time vulnerability detection contribute to a proactive defense against potential exploits. Embracing a DevSecOps approach integrates security into the development pipeline, ensuring that vulnerabilities are addressed early in the software development lifecycle.

Cloud-native security services and features offered by cloud providers play a crucial role in enhancing network security. Leveraging services such as AWS GuardDuty, Azure Security Center, or Google Cloud Security Command Center provides automated threat detection, incident response, and security intelligence. Cloud providers also offer DDoS protection services, mitigating the risk of distributed denial-of-service attacks. By utilizing these cloud-native security features, organizations can augment their network defenses and benefit from the expertise and scale of their cloud providers.

Container security is a growing concern in cloud environments where microservices architectures and containerization technologies are prevalent. Implementing best practices for container security involves secure image registries, scanning container images for vulnerabilities, and ensuring secure runtime configurations. Container orchestration platforms like Kubernetes should be configured securely, and organizations should adopt container-specific security tools to monitor and protect containerized applications.

Automation is a key enabler of efficient and effective network security in the cloud. Automated workflows for incident response, threat detection, and vulnerability management streamline security processes and adapt to the dynamic nature of cloud environments. Infrastructure as Code (IaC) allows organizations to define and deploy network configurations programmatically, ensuring consistency and reducing the risk of misconfigurations. By automating routine security tasks, organizations enhance their ability to respond rapidly to security incidents and maintain a consistent and secure network environment.

Collaboration and information sharing are integral aspects of best practices for securing cloud networks. Organizations should actively participate in industry forums, Information Sharing and Analysis Centers (ISACs), and collaborative initiatives to share threat intelligence and best practices. Collaboration extends to partnerships with cloud service providers, third-party vendors, and peers in the industry. By fostering a culture of collaboration, organizations can benefit from collective insights, enhance their threat intelligence capabilities, and strengthen their overall network security posture.

Compliance with regulatory requirements, industry standards, and internal policies is a foundational element of best practices for securing cloud networks. Organizations must stay informed about relevant regulations, such as GDPR, HIPAA, or PCI DSS, and ensure that their cloud network configurations and security measures align with these mandates. Implementing automated compliance checks within the deployment pipeline helps maintain adherence to regulatory frameworks, reducing the risk of non-compliance and associated consequences.

User and entity behavior analytics (UEBA) contribute to best practices for securing cloud networks by leveraging machine learning algorithms to analyze patterns of behavior. UEBA tools establish baselines for normal user and entity behavior, enabling the identification of anomalous activities that may indicate security incidents. By detecting deviations from established behavioral patterns, organizations can proactively respond to potential insider threats, compromised accounts, or other malicious activities within the cloud.

In conclusion, best practices for securing cloud networks encompass a comprehensive and dynamic set of measures that align with the characteristics of cloud environments. From robust identity and access management to encryption, network segmentation, continuous monitoring, and automation, each practice contributes to building a resilient and secure network foundation. Embracing cloud-native security services, addressing container security, fostering collaboration, and ensuring compliance further enhance the overall security posture. In the rapidly evolving landscape of cloud computing, where agility and security are paramount, organizations that implement and adapt these best practices are better equipped to navigate the complexities and challenges of securing their cloud networks.

Discuss physical and virtual security measures for data centers in the cloud.

Securing data centers in the cloud involves a comprehensive approach that combines physical and virtual security measures to safeguard critical infrastructure, sensitive data, and ensure the uninterrupted operation of services. Physical security constitutes the foundation of data center protection, encompassing measures to safeguard the physical premises, facilities, and hardware. Access controls are crucial, beginning with secure perimeter fencing, access gates, and entry points. Biometric authentication, card readers, and surveillance cameras enhance the authentication process, ensuring that only authorized personnel gain entry to the data center facility.

Within the physical space, implementing secure server racks and cabinets adds an additional layer of protection. Locking mechanisms, such as biometric or electronic locks, prevent unauthorized access to individual servers. Additionally, the physical layout of the data center can contribute to security. Redundant systems, such as power and cooling, should be geographically separated to mitigate the risk of a single point of failure. Climate control and fire suppression systems are also essential to maintain optimal operating conditions while mitigating the risk of overheating or fire incidents.

Environmental controls extend beyond temperature and humidity management to include protection against environmental threats such as floods or earthquakes. Elevating critical infrastructure above potential flood levels and employing seismic-resistant designs in earthquake-prone regions are examples of physical measures to safeguard against natural disasters. Disaster recovery and business continuity planning are integral components of physical security, ensuring that data centers can recover swiftly from unforeseen events with minimal disruption.

In conjunction with physical security, virtual security measures are critical to protecting data within cloud data centers. Network security forms a central pillar, involving measures such as firewalls, intrusion detection and prevention systems, and virtual private networks (VPNs). Micro-segmentation is an advanced virtual security practice that involves dividing the network into smaller, isolated segments, restricting lateral movement and containing potential breaches. Virtual firewalls and cloud-based security services are essential components to defend against cyber threats within the virtual environment.

Identity and access management (IAM) are foundational virtual security measures, governing user access to cloud resources and data.

Multi-factor authentication (MFA) adds an extra layer of identity verification, mitigating the risk of unauthorized access due to compromised credentials. IAM policies should adhere to the principle of least privilege, ensuring that users have only the necessary permissions to perform their specific roles within the cloud environment.

Data encryption is paramount in virtual security, safeguarding data both in transit and at rest. Transport Layer Security (TLS) or Secure Sockets Layer (SSL) protocols encrypt data during transmission, ensuring secure communication between users and cloud resources. At rest, encryption protects stored data, particularly when managed by cloud service providers. Key management practices are critical in virtual security, ensuring secure storage and rotation of encryption keys to prevent unauthorized access.

Endpoint security is a crucial consideration in virtual security measures, as endpoints such as user devices and servers can be vulnerable entry points for cyber threats. Endpoint protection solutions, including antivirus software, endpoint detection and response (EDR) tools, and mobile device management (MDM) systems, enhance the overall security posture. Regular software updates and patch management are essential in addressing vulnerabilities that could be exploited by malicious actors.

Container security is a specialized area of virtual security that gains prominence in cloud data centers leveraging containerization technologies. Securing containerized applications involves scanning container images for vulnerabilities, implementing secure runtime configurations, and employing container orchestration platforms, such as Kubernetes, with secure configurations. Container security measures should address the unique challenges introduced by microservices architectures within cloud environments.

Security information and event management (SIEM) systems contribute to the virtual security of cloud data centers by aggregating and analyzing logs from various sources. SIEM tools enable real-time monitoring, correlation of security events, and proactive threat detection. Advanced SIEM solutions leverage machine learning and artificial intelligence to identify patterns indicative of potential security incidents, providing a proactive defense mechanism against cyber threats within the virtual environment.

Cloud-native security services offered by cloud providers are integral components of virtual security for data centers in the cloud. Platforms such as AWS GuardDuty, Azure Security Center, and Google Cloud Security Command Center provide automated threat detection, incident response, and security intelligence. Leveraging these services enables organizations to benefit from the scale and expertise of their cloud providers, enhancing the overall virtual security posture.

Continuous monitoring and auditing are essential practices in virtual security, providing visibility into network activities, configurations, and user behaviors. Regular security audits of cloud configurations, access controls, and virtual security policies ensure ongoing compliance, identify security gaps, and provide insights for continuous improvement. Automated monitoring solutions contribute to the early detection of security incidents, reducing the dwell time of potential threats within the virtual environment.

Collaboration and information sharing are crucial aspects of virtual security for cloud data centers. Organizations should actively participate in industry forums, Information Sharing and Analysis Centers (ISACs), and collaborative initiatives to share threat intelligence and best practices. Collaboration extends to partnerships with cloud service providers, third-party vendors, and peers in the industry. By fostering a culture of collaboration, organizations can benefit from collective insights, enhance their threat intelligence capabilities, and strengthen their overall virtual security posture.

Compliance with regulatory requirements, industry standards, and internal policies is a foundational element of virtual security for data centers in the cloud. Organizations must stay informed about relevant regulations, such as GDPR, HIPAA, or PCI DSS, and ensure that their virtual security measures align with these mandates. Implementing automated compliance checks within the deployment pipeline helps maintain adherence to regulatory frameworks, reducing the risk of non-compliance and associated consequences.

User and entity behavior analytics (UEBA) leverage machine learning algorithms to analyze patterns of behavior within the virtual environment. UEBA tools establish baselines for normal user and entity behavior, enabling the identification of anomalous activities that may indicate security incidents. By detecting deviations from established behavioral patterns, organizations can proactively respond to potential insider threats, compromised accounts, or other malicious activities within the virtual environment.

In conclusion, securing data centers in the cloud necessitates a holistic integration of physical and virtual security measures. The physical security of the facility, infrastructure, and environmental controls creates a secure foundation, while virtual security measures within the cloud environment address cyber threats, data protection, and access controls. The combination of robust physical and virtual security practices ensures that organizations can safeguard their data, maintain operational resilience, and navigate the complexities of securing data centers in the dynamic landscape of cloud computing.

Address the challenges and solutions related to securing endpoints in a cloud environment.

Securing endpoints in a cloud environment presents a unique set of challenges and demands a comprehensive approach to address the evolving threat landscape. One of the primary challenges is the proliferation of diverse devices accessing cloud resources, including traditional laptops, desktops, mobile devices, and Internet of Things (IoT) devices. The heterogeneity of these endpoints introduces complexities in enforcing consistent security policies and ensuring the uniform application of security controls across various platforms. In response, organizations must adopt device-agnostic security solutions capable of protecting endpoints regardless of their form factor or operating system, fostering a unified security posture in the cloud.

A significant challenge in securing cloud endpoints is the rise of remote work and the subsequent increase in the number of off-premises devices connecting to cloud services. The shift to remote work introduces new attack vectors, as endpoints may connect from unsecured networks, posing an increased risk of exposure to malicious activities. Implementing solutions such as virtual private networks (VPNs), secure remote access tools, and zero-trust security frameworks becomes essential to secure communications and authenticate users and devices connecting to cloud resources remotely. The zero-trust model, in particular, assumes that every user and device, even if inside the corporate network, should be treated as potentially untrusted, enforcing granular access controls and continuous authentication.

Another challenge is the dynamic nature of cloud environments, where endpoints may scale up or down rapidly based on demand. Traditional endpoint security measures that rely on static configurations and periodic updates may struggle to adapt to the dynamic nature of cloud infrastructure. Adopting cloud-native security solutions capable of auto-scaling, self-updating, and seamlessly integrating with cloud orchestration platforms ensures that security measures keep pace with the agility and scalability of cloud environments.

Endpoint visibility poses a significant challenge in cloud environments, where traditional network perimeters are dissolved, and resources are distributed across diverse cloud services. Traditional endpoint security relies on network-based visibility, but in the cloud, endpoints may connect directly to cloud services without traversing corporate networks. Implementing cloud-native security information and event management (SIEM) solutions and endpoint detection and response (EDR) tools capable of monitoring cloud-native logs and activities provides the necessary visibility to detect and respond to security incidents involving endpoints in the cloud.

The diversity of applications and services in the cloud introduces challenges in securing endpoints against various attack vectors. Cloud-native applications often leverage microservices architectures, containers, and serverless computing, each with its unique security considerations. Endpoint security solutions must evolve to protect against threats targeting specific cloud-native technologies, such as container vulnerabilities, serverless function exploits, or API-based attacks. Adopting specialized security tools designed for cloud-native environments, including container security platforms and serverless security solutions, helps organizations tailor their endpoint security measures to the intricacies of cloud architectures.

Data protection is a paramount concern in cloud environments, especially as endpoints interact with sensitive information stored in cloud repositories. Securing data on endpoints requires robust encryption mechanisms, data loss prevention (DLP) solutions, and secure file transfer protocols. Organizations must enforce encryption for data in transit and at rest on endpoints, ensuring that even if a device is compromised, the data remains protected. Additionally, implementing DLP policies that prevent unauthorized data transfers and integrating with cloud access security brokers (CASBs) enhances control over data interactions on endpoints.

The increased sophistication of cyber threats, including ransomware, phishing, and advanced persistent threats (APTs), poses a continuous challenge to endpoint security in the cloud. Traditional antivirus solutions may struggle to keep pace with polymorphic malware and targeted attacks. Organizations should augment their endpoint security measures with advanced threat detection technologies, such as behavioral analytics, machine learning, and threat intelligence integration. These technologies enable proactive identification of suspicious activities, rapid response to potential threats, and the continuous adaptation of security measures to emerging attack vectors.

The decentralized nature of cloud environments challenges the traditional concept of a centralized security perimeter. Endpoints in the cloud may not necessarily connect to a corporate network, and the lack of a well-defined perimeter complicates the application of traditional security controls. Embracing a zero-trust security model, where each endpoint is treated as untrusted regardless of its location, becomes essential. Zero-trust frameworks implement rigorous access controls, multi-factor authentication, and continuous monitoring to mitigate the risk of lateral movement and unauthorized access within cloud environments.

Shadow IT, where employees use unauthorized cloud applications and services, poses a significant challenge to endpoint security. End-users may unknowingly introduce security vulnerabilities by adopting unsanctioned cloud tools for collaboration, file sharing, or other purposes. Establishing a comprehensive cloud security policy, educating employees about the risks of shadow IT, and implementing cloud access security brokers (CASBs) help organizations regain visibility and control over endpoints interacting with cloud services, ensuring that only approved and secure applications are used.

Endpoint patch management is a critical yet challenging aspect of security in cloud environments. Traditional patch management approaches may struggle to keep up with the rapid release cycles of cloud-native applications and services. Organizations should adopt automated patch management solutions that integrate seamlessly with cloud orchestration platforms, ensuring timely and consistent application of security patches to endpoints. Additionally, leveraging infrastructure as code (IaC) principles enables organizations to define and deploy secure configurations programmatically, reducing the manual effort and improving the overall security posture.

Securing endpoints in the cloud requires effective incident response and management capabilities. The dynamic nature of cloud environments demands agile incident response workflows, playbooks, and coordination with cloud service providers. Automated incident response tools and cloud-native SIEM solutions enable organizations to detect and respond swiftly to security incidents involving endpoints. Collaboration with external incident response providers, threat intelligence sharing communities, and regulatory bodies enhances organizations' ability to respond effectively to advanced and persistent threats targeting cloud endpoints.

User awareness and training are crucial components of endpoint security in the cloud. End-users play a pivotal role in recognizing and mitigating security threats, especially in scenarios like phishing attacks or social engineering attempts. Regular training programs that educate users about secure cloud practices, the importance of strong passwords, and the recognition of suspicious activities contribute to building a resilient human firewall. Organizations should foster a security-aware culture where employees understand their role in safeguarding endpoints and are empowered to report potential security incidents promptly.

In conclusion, securing endpoints in a cloud environment is a multifaceted challenge that demands a holistic and adaptive approach. From addressing the diversity of devices and applications to mitigating the risks associated with remote work, dynamic cloud environments, and evolving cyber threats, organizations must continuously refine their endpoint security measures. Adopting cloud-native security solutions, leveraging advanced threat detection technologies, embracing a zero-trust model, and prioritizing user awareness contribute to building a robust defense against the complexities of securing endpoints in the dynamic landscape of cloud computing.

Explore the principles of IAM in cloud security.

Identity and Access Management (IAM) lies at the core of cloud security, serving as a foundational framework to manage and govern user identities and their access to resources within cloud environments. In the dynamic landscape of cloud computing, where agility and scalability are paramount, IAM principles provide the necessary controls to ensure that only authorized entities can interact with sensitive data, applications, and services. A fundamental principle of IAM is the concept of identity lifecycle management, encompassing the entire span of an identity's existence—from creation to modification, and ultimately to deactivation. This principle ensures that user identities are created with the appropriate permissions, updated as roles change, and deactivated promptly when no longer needed, reducing the risk of unauthorized access.

Authentication is a pivotal aspect of IAM, ensuring that entities accessing cloud resources are who they claim to be. In the cloud, where users can connect from diverse devices and locations, implementing strong authentication mechanisms becomes imperative. Multi-Factor Authentication (MFA) is a key principle that enhances traditional username/password authentication by requiring users to provide additional forms of verification, such as a code sent to their mobile device. By adopting MFA, organizations add an extra layer of security, mitigating the risk of unauthorized access resulting from compromised credentials, a common attack vector in cloud environments.

Authorization, the principle governing access permissions, is a critical IAM element that ensures users have the appropriate level of access to resources based on their roles and responsibilities. The principle of least privilege is integral to IAM authorization, advocating for granting the minimum necessary permissions for users to perform their specific functions. This principle reduces the attack surface, limiting the potential impact of a security breach. Cloud IAM solutions often provide fine-grained access controls, enabling organizations to implement granular permissions and adhere closely to the principle of least privilege.

Centralized Identity Management is a foundational principle of IAM in the cloud, emphasizing the importance of managing identities from a single, authoritative source. Cloud environments often involve multiple services and platforms, and a centralized identity management system ensures consistency and coherence across these diverse ecosystems. Integration with identity providers, such as Active Directory or LDAP, allows organizations to extend their existing identity management practices seamlessly into the cloud, streamlining the onboarding and offboarding of users while maintaining a unified view of identity information.

Role-Based Access Control (RBAC) is a key IAM principle that aligns access permissions with job responsibilities. RBAC ensures that users are assigned roles based on their functions within the organization, and each role is associated with specific access rights. This principle simplifies access management by grouping users into roles, enabling organizations to apply and manage permissions at a role level rather than individually for each user. Cloud IAM platforms often support RBAC, allowing organizations to define and enforce access controls consistently across various cloud services.

Policy-Based Access Control extends IAM principles by incorporating fine-grained access policies that specify conditions and constraints for access permissions. This principle enables organizations to define access rules based on contextual factors such as time of day, geographic location, or device type. By implementing policy-based access controls, organizations tailor access permissions dynamically, aligning with the evolving requirements of the business. Cloud IAM solutions often offer robust policy engines that allow organizations to enforce access controls based on a wide range of contextual criteria.

Audit and Monitoring are integral IAM principles designed to provide visibility into user activities and access patterns. Comprehensive logging and monitoring of IAM events enable organizations to track user interactions with cloud resources, detect anomalous behavior, and generate audit trails for compliance purposes. By adopting these principles, organizations gain insights into potential security incidents, unauthorized access attempts, or deviations from established IAM policies. Cloud IAM platforms often include features for real-time monitoring, log aggregation, and integration with Security Information and Event Management (SIEM) systems.

Immutable Identity is a contemporary IAM principle that aligns with the dynamic and ephemeral nature of cloud environments. In traditional IT landscapes, user identities may persist for extended periods, even after changes in roles or responsibilities. In the cloud, where resources are ephemeral and frequently provisioned and deprovisioned, the principle of immutable identity emphasizes that once an identity is assigned certain permissions, those permissions should not change retroactively. This principle ensures that users retain their assigned access rights even as resources evolve, providing consistency and predictability in IAM practices within the dynamic cloud ecosystem.

Federated Identity is a collaborative IAM principle that enables users to access resources seamlessly across multiple cloud environments and services using a single set of credentials. Federated identity systems allow organizations to establish trust relationships with external identity providers, enabling users to log in with their credentials from a trusted source. This principle enhances user experience by eliminating the need for separate credentials for each cloud service, and it simplifies identity management for organizations with a diverse cloud ecosystem.

Automated Provisioning and Deprovisioning is an efficiency-driven IAM principle designed to streamline the onboarding and offboarding processes. In the cloud, where resources can be provisioned and deprovisioned rapidly, automating identity lifecycle management becomes crucial. Automated IAM workflows enable organizations to provision user accounts, assign appropriate roles and permissions, and revoke access promptly when users no longer require it. This principle enhances operational efficiency, reduces the risk of human error, and ensures that IAM practices align with the agility of cloud environments.

Security by Design is an overarching IAM principle that emphasizes the proactive integration of security considerations into every phase of the software development lifecycle and system architecture. This principle recognizes that security is not an add-on but an integral part of IAM practices. By embedding security from the outset, organizations can ensure that IAM implementations are robust, resilient, and capable of addressing emerging threats. Security by Design aligns IAM principles with the evolving threat landscape, fostering a security-conscious culture within organizations and promoting continuous improvement in IAM practices.

Adaptive Authentication is a modern IAM principle that acknowledges the need for context-aware authentication mechanisms. In the cloud, where users access resources from diverse locations and devices, adaptive authentication adapts the level of authentication based on contextual factors such as user behavior, device characteristics, and location. This principle enhances security by dynamically adjusting authentication requirements, allowing for a seamless user experience while maintaining a strong security posture. Adaptive authentication aligns IAM practices with the dynamic and user-centric nature of cloud environments.

Collaborative IAM is a principle that extends beyond organizational boundaries, emphasizing the importance of cooperation in identity and access management. In cloud environments, where collaborations with external entities are common, organizations should establish federated identity relationships, share threat intelligence, and participate in industry-wide IAM standards. Collaborative IAM fosters a collective defense against emerging threats, promotes the exchange of best practices, and enables organizations to navigate the complexities of IAM in the interconnected and collaborative landscape of the cloud.

In conclusion, IAM principles are the bedrock of cloud security, providing the framework for managing identities and controlling access to resources in dynamic and diverse cloud environments. From identity lifecycle management and authentication to RBAC, policy-based access controls, and adaptive authentication, each principle contributes to building a robust IAM foundation. As organizations navigate the challenges of securing identities and access in the cloud, adherence to these principles ensures a secure, efficient, and adaptable IAM framework that aligns with the transformative potential of cloud computing.

Discuss the role of automation in improving security operations.

Automation plays a pivotal role in transforming security operations, offering a paradigm shift in how organizations detect, respond to, and mitigate security threats. In the complex and dynamic landscape of cybersecurity, automation is a force multiplier that empowers security teams to enhance their efficiency, accuracy, and agility. One of the key contributions of automation to security operations is in the realm of threat detection. Automated tools and systems can continuously monitor vast amounts of data, including logs, network traffic, and user behavior, enabling the rapid identification of anomalies and potential security incidents. By employing machine learning algorithms and behavioral analytics, automation aids in recognizing patterns indicative of malicious activities, reducing the reliance on manual monitoring and enhancing the ability to detect sophisticated threats in real-time.

Automated incident response is another critical aspect of leveraging automation in security operations. When a security incident is identified, automation enables the execution of predefined response actions without human intervention. This not only accelerates the response time but also ensures consistency in the application of security protocols. Automated incident response workflows can include actions such as isolating affected systems, blocking malicious IP addresses, or initiating remediation procedures. By automating these routine and time-sensitive tasks, security teams can focus their expertise on more complex and strategic aspects of incident investigation and resolution.

Security orchestration and automation platforms are central to streamlining and integrating security processes. These platforms provide a centralized framework for designing, executing, and managing automated workflows across diverse security tools and technologies. Security orchestration enables seamless collaboration between different security solutions, allowing them to work in concert to respond to threats comprehensively. Automation within orchestration platforms extends beyond incident response to include tasks such as vulnerability management, threat hunting, and compliance monitoring. This holistic approach to security operations enables organizations to build a cohesive and coordinated defense against evolving cyber threats.

Automation is particularly instrumental in vulnerability management, where the identification and remediation of vulnerabilities are critical to maintaining a secure environment. Automated vulnerability scanning tools can continuously assess systems, applications, and networks for known vulnerabilities, providing real-time insights into the security posture. Integration with patch management systems allows for the automated deployment of security patches, reducing the window of exposure to potential exploits. Automation in vulnerability management not only enhances the speed of remediation but also supports organizations in prioritizing and addressing the most critical vulnerabilities based on risk assessments.

The role of automation extends to threat intelligence analysis and integration. Automated tools can aggregate, analyze, and correlate threat intelligence feeds from various sources, providing security teams with actionable insights into emerging threats. By automating the ingestion of threat intelligence data, organizations can enhance their ability to proactively identify potential threats and vulnerabilities relevant to their specific environment. Automated threat intelligence sharing platforms further enable collaboration between organizations, facilitating the timely exchange of information about new threats and attack techniques.

Automated log management and analysis contribute significantly to improving security operations. Security Information and Event Management (SIEM) systems, enhanced by automation, can aggregate and analyze logs from diverse sources, correlating events to identify potential security incidents. Automated log analysis tools can detect patterns indicative of malicious activities, enabling security teams to prioritize and investigate incidents efficiently. Moreover, automation in log management aids in compliance monitoring by generating reports and alerts based on predefined security policies and regulatory requirements.

Cloud security, with its dynamic and scalable nature, benefits immensely from automation in security operations. Automated provisioning and deprovisioning of user accounts, coupled with identity and access management (IAM) automation, ensures that access controls align with the rapidly changing cloud environment. Automated configuration management tools help enforce security baselines and compliance standards consistently across cloud instances. Continuous monitoring and automated responses to changes in cloud infrastructure contribute to maintaining a secure and resilient cloud environment.

Automation is a linchpin in the domain of Security Operations Centers (SOCs), where the volume of security alerts and incidents can be overwhelming. Automated security orchestration enables SOCs to manage alerts efficiently, categorize them based on severity, and automate response actions. Security analysts can leverage automation to create playbooks that codify response procedures, allowing for consistent and rapid incident resolution. Furthermore, automation aids in the enrichment of security alerts with additional context, such as threat intelligence data and historical incident information, facilitating more informed decision-making by analysts.

Security automation also plays a crucial role in log retention and archiving, ensuring that organizations maintain comprehensive records of security events for compliance, forensic analysis, and incident response purposes. Automated log archiving solutions can categorize and store logs securely, with the ability to retrieve and analyze historical data when investigating security incidents. This level of automation in log management not only aids in meeting regulatory requirements but also enhances the effectiveness of retrospective analysis to identify patterns and trends.

A significant advantage of automation in security operations is the ability to create and enforce security policies consistently across an organization's IT infrastructure. Automated policy enforcement ensures that security controls, such as firewall rules, access permissions, and encryption settings, are applied uniformly. This is particularly crucial in large and complex environments where manual enforcement may lead to inconsistencies and oversights. Automation not only strengthens the security posture but also simplifies the management of security policies, reducing the risk of configuration errors.

Automated threat hunting is emerging as a proactive approach to identifying threats that may evade traditional security measures. Security teams can leverage automation to continuously search for indicators of compromise, suspicious patterns, or anomalous behaviors within the network. Automated threat hunting tools enable organizations to stay ahead of evolving threats by proactively seeking out potential security risks. This proactive stance aligns with the evolving nature of cyber threats, allowing organizations to detect and neutralize threats before they escalate.

Security automation is instrumental in managing the human element in security operations. By automating routine and repetitive tasks, security teams can allocate their time and expertise more effectively, focusing on strategic initiatives, threat analysis, and proactive security measures. This not only enhances the job satisfaction of security professionals but also addresses the perennial challenge of cybersecurity talent shortages. Automated incident response, in particular, allows organizations to respond rapidly to security incidents, reducing the burden on analysts and enabling them to concentrate on high-value tasks.

While automation contributes significantly to improving security operations, it is crucial to recognize that it is not a one-size-fits-all solution. Effective implementation requires thoughtful consideration of the organization's specific security needs, the integration of diverse security tools, and ongoing fine-tuning of automated workflows. Additionally, organizations must balance automation with human expertise, recognizing that certain aspects of security operations, such as complex threat analysis and decision-making, may require human intuition and contextual understanding. Striking the right balance between automation and human intervention ensures that security operations remain agile, adaptive, and resilient in the face of evolving cyber threats.

In conclusion, automation is a game-changer in the realm of security operations, offering a transformative approach to detecting, responding to, and mitigating security threats. From threat detection and incident response to vulnerability management, threat intelligence analysis, and log management, automation enhances the efficiency, accuracy, and agility of security operations. As organizations continue to grapple with the complexities of the cyber threat landscape, the strategic integration of automation into security operations emerges as a fundamental pillar for building a robust and resilient cybersecurity posture.

Explain the importance of continuous monitoring for identifying and responding to security threats.

Continuous monitoring is a cornerstone of modern cybersecurity strategies, playing a pivotal role in identifying and responding to security threats in a dynamic and ever-evolving threat landscape. The importance of continuous monitoring stems from the recognition that traditional, periodic security assessments are insufficient in the face of rapidly advancing cyber threats. In essence, continuous monitoring represents a shift from a reactive to a proactive security posture, enabling organizations to detect and respond to security incidents in near real-time, minimizing the impact of potential breaches.

One key aspect of the importance of continuous monitoring lies in its ability to provide organizations with an ongoing, comprehensive view of their IT environments. Traditional point-in-time assessments may miss emerging threats or changes in the network that occur between assessment intervals. Continuous monitoring, on the other hand, offers a continuous stream of data and insights into the organization's systems, networks, and applications, allowing security teams to maintain a constant awareness of their cybersecurity posture.

Continuous monitoring facilitates early threat detection by actively scanning for anomalies and deviations from established baselines. This proactive approach involves the use of automated tools and technologies to analyze vast amounts of data, including network traffic, system logs, and user behavior. By leveraging machine learning algorithms and behavioral analytics, continuous monitoring can identify patterns indicative of potential security threats, ranging from suspicious activities and unauthorized access attempts to abnormal data exfiltration. This early detection capability is crucial in today's threat landscape, where cyber adversaries employ increasingly sophisticated tactics to evade traditional security measures.

The real-time nature of continuous monitoring enables organizations to respond promptly to security incidents, reducing the dwell time of threats within their environments. Traditional incident response approaches, often initiated after periodic assessments, may result in delayed detection and response, allowing attackers to move laterally within the network and escalate their activities. Continuous monitoring shortens the response time by providing immediate alerts when anomalous activities are detected. This swift response is essential in mitigating the impact of security incidents, preventing data breaches, and minimizing the potential damage to the organization's reputation.

The importance of continuous monitoring is further underscored by its role in supporting compliance with regulatory requirements and industry standards. Many regulatory frameworks mandate the implementation of continuous monitoring practices to ensure the ongoing security and compliance of systems and data. Continuous monitoring helps organizations demonstrate their commitment to cybersecurity best practices, providing auditors with a real-time view of security controls, risk management activities, and incident response capabilities. This not only helps organizations meet compliance obligations but also enhances their overall cybersecurity posture.

In the context of network security, continuous monitoring is indispensable for identifying vulnerabilities and potential points of exploitation. Automated vulnerability scanning tools can continuously assess systems, applications, and network infrastructure for known vulnerabilities, allowing organizations to address security gaps promptly. The ability to detect and remediate vulnerabilities in near real-time is critical in a landscape where cyber threats exploit newly discovered weaknesses rapidly. Continuous monitoring supports organizations in maintaining a resilient security posture by preventing the exploitation of known vulnerabilities.

Continuous monitoring is equally essential in the realm of insider threat detection. Malicious insiders or compromised user accounts can pose significant risks to organizations, and continuous monitoring provides a means to detect anomalous user behavior indicative of insider threats. By establishing baselines for normal user activities and employing behavioral analytics, continuous monitoring can identify deviations that may suggest unauthorized access or malicious intent. This proactive approach enables organizations to address insider threats promptly, mitigating the risk of data breaches and protecting sensitive information.

The dynamic nature of cloud environments further underscores the importance of continuous monitoring. In cloud computing, where resources are provisioned and deprovisioned rapidly, traditional periodic assessments may struggle to keep pace with changes in the environment. Continuous monitoring solutions designed for cloud environments provide real-time visibility into the security posture of cloud-based assets, including virtual machines, containers, and serverless functions. This real-time visibility enables organizations to detect and respond to security threats across their entire hybrid and multi-cloud infrastructures.

Continuous monitoring contributes significantly to incident response capabilities by providing security teams with detailed information about the nature and scope of security incidents. The ability to correlate data from various sources, including logs, network traffic, and endpoint activities, allows security analysts to reconstruct the timeline of events leading up to and during a security incident. This contextual information is invaluable in understanding the tactics, techniques, and procedures employed by adversaries, facilitating more effective incident response strategies and threat mitigation efforts.

Automation is a key enabler of effective continuous monitoring, allowing organizations to analyze vast datasets and generate real-time alerts without overwhelming security teams with manual tasks. Automated monitoring tools can perform continuous vulnerability assessments, threat hunting, and log analysis, freeing up human resources to focus on strategic decision-making, incident response planning, and the development of proactive security measures. The synergy between automation and continuous monitoring empowers organizations to harness the full potential of real-time threat intelligence and data analysis.

The importance of continuous monitoring extends beyond traditional network security to encompass endpoint security. As organizations embrace remote work and mobile devices, continuous monitoring becomes instrumental in tracking and securing endpoints. Automated endpoint detection and response (EDR) tools can continuously monitor endpoints for signs of malicious activities, unauthorized access, or anomalous behavior. This level of endpoint visibility is crucial in a landscape where endpoints serve as common entry points for cyber threats. Continuous monitoring of endpoints enhances organizations' ability to identify and respond to security incidents involving user devices promptly.

In conclusion, the importance of continuous monitoring in identifying and responding to security threats cannot be overstated. In a threat landscape characterized by complexity, sophistication, and rapid evolution, continuous monitoring provides organizations with the agility and resilience needed to safeguard their digital assets. From early threat detection and real-time incident response to supporting compliance efforts and addressing vulnerabilities, continuous monitoring is a linchpin in the modern cybersecurity strategy.

As organizations navigate the challenges of securing their IT environments, the strategic implementation of continuous monitoring emerges as a foundational element for building a proactive and adaptive cybersecurity posture.

Address the challenges and strategies associated with third-party security in the cloud.

The integration of third-party services in cloud environments introduces a myriad of challenges and complexities, necessitating a strategic and comprehensive approach to ensure the security of sensitive data and critical systems. One of the primary challenges associated with third-party security in the cloud is the inherent loss of direct control over infrastructure and data. When organizations leverage third-party services, they relinquish certain aspects of control, relying on service providers for the management and security of the underlying infrastructure. This loss of control poses a risk, as organizations may have limited visibility into the security measures employed by third-party providers, potentially exposing them to vulnerabilities and threats that are beyond their immediate oversight.

Ensuring the security and compliance of third-party services becomes paramount, especially in regulated industries where stringent data protection requirements must be met. Service providers may operate in different regions, each subject to varying regulatory frameworks, making it challenging for organizations to navigate and align with diverse compliance standards. The absence of a unified global regulatory framework for cloud services exacerbates this challenge, requiring organizations to engage in thorough due diligence when selecting third-party providers and ensuring that contractual agreements explicitly address compliance obligations.

The shared responsibility model, a fundamental concept in cloud security, introduces complexities in delineating security responsibilities between the cloud service provider and the customer. While cloud providers typically manage the security of the infrastructure, customers are responsible for securing their data, applications, and access controls. In the context of third-party services, this model becomes more intricate, as organizations need to clearly define the security responsibilities pertaining to the integration of external services. Ambiguities or misalignments in the shared responsibility model may lead to security gaps, with potential repercussions for data integrity, confidentiality, and overall system resilience.

Identity and access management (IAM) challenges amplify when dealing with third-party services in the cloud. Integrating external services often requires granting specific permissions and access rights to the third party, introducing the risk of over-permissioning or misconfigurations. Inadequate IAM practices may result in unauthorized access, data exposure, or compromise of critical systems. Organizations must adopt a least-privilege principle, ensuring that third-party services only have access to the minimum resources necessary for their functionalities. Implementing robust IAM policies, regular audits, and automated controls can mitigate the risks associated with misconfigured access permissions.

Vendor lock-in is a strategic concern in third-party security within the cloud. Organizations may become heavily dependent on a specific third-party service, limiting their flexibility and ability to switch providers if needed. This dependence may stem from proprietary interfaces, data formats, or unique features offered by the third party. To address this challenge, organizations should adopt interoperable standards, ensure data portability, and incorporate exit strategies in their contracts to mitigate the risks of vendor lock-in. Planning for flexibility and scalability in third-party integrations becomes essential to avoid potential challenges in the long run.

The dynamic nature of cloud environments introduces challenges related to monitoring and visibility when integrating third-party services. Traditional security tools may not seamlessly integrate with external services, leading to gaps in monitoring and threat detection. A lack of visibility into the security events and activities of third-party services can impede the timely detection of anomalies or malicious activities. Implementing cloud-native security solutions that support the integration of third-party logs, events, and activities into centralized monitoring systems helps address this challenge. Continuous monitoring practices enhance the organization's ability to detect and respond promptly to security incidents involving third-party services.

The growing complexity of supply chains and ecosystems in the cloud amplifies the risks associated with third-party security. Many organizations rely on a multitude of third-party services, each introducing its own set of security considerations. Assessing and managing the security posture of multiple third-party providers demand a holistic and scalable approach. Organizations should implement standardized security assessments, conduct regular audits, and establish a robust vendor risk management program to evaluate the security practices of their third-party partners. Collaborative industry initiatives and standards for third-party security assessments can further streamline this process.

The threat landscape in the cloud is dynamic, with adversaries constantly evolving their tactics to exploit vulnerabilities. Third-party services may become attractive targets for attackers seeking to compromise organizations indirectly. A security incident affecting a third-party service can have cascading effects on interconnected systems. To mitigate this risk, organizations should conduct thorough risk assessments, including evaluating the security postures of their third-party providers. Collaborative threat intelligence sharing within industry sectors can enhance the collective defense against emerging threats, enabling organizations to proactively adapt their security measures.

As organizations adopt multi-cloud or hybrid cloud strategies, the complexity of third-party integrations increases. Each cloud environment may have its own set of security controls, identity management mechanisms, and compliance requirements. Harmonizing security practices across diverse cloud providers becomes challenging, especially when integrating third-party services that interact with multiple clouds. Implementing a unified security framework, leveraging cloud-agnostic security solutions, and ensuring consistent security policies across different cloud environments help organizations navigate the complexities of multi-cloud security and third-party integrations.

Strategies for addressing the challenges of third-party security in the cloud encompass a combination of proactive measures, robust governance, and collaborative efforts. Conducting thorough due diligence during the selection of third-party providers is foundational. Organizations should prioritize security assessments, evaluate compliance postures, and engage in open dialogues with potential providers to ensure alignment with security objectives and standards. Clear contractual agreements that explicitly define security responsibilities, compliance obligations, and incident response procedures are essential to establish a solid foundation for a secure third-party integration.

Implementing a risk-based approach to third-party security involves categorizing third-party services based on their criticality and the sensitivity of the data they handle. This approach allows organizations to prioritize security measures, allocate resources efficiently, and tailor security controls to the level of risk associated with each third-party integration. Continuous monitoring practices, including real-time threat detection, automated log analysis, and behavioral analytics, contribute to maintaining visibility and responsiveness to security events involving third-party services.

Collaboration and information sharing within industry sectors play a pivotal role in addressing common challenges and threats associated with third-party security. Organizations can benefit from collective intelligence, sharing insights, and best practices for managing the security risks introduced by third-party integrations. Industry forums, consortiums, and collaborative initiatives facilitate the exchange of threat intelligence, enabling organizations to stay ahead of emerging threats and collectively enhance the security posture of third-party services.

Embracing a zero-trust security model is integral to mitigating the risks associated with third-party integrations. Instead of relying solely on perimeter defenses, a zero-trust approach assumes that every entity, including third-party services, is potentially untrusted. Implementing strong access controls, continuous authentication, and encryption helps organizations enforce the principle of least privilege and limit the potential impact of security incidents involving third-party services. Zero-trust frameworks provide an adaptive and context-aware security posture that aligns with the dynamic nature of cloud environments.

Education and awareness within organizations are critical components of third-party security strategies. Employees and stakeholders should be informed about the potential risks associated with third-party integrations and educated on security best practices. Establishing a culture of security awareness and accountability ensures that individuals responsible for managing third-party relationships understand the importance of security considerations, adhere to policies, and actively participate in ongoing risk management efforts.

In conclusion, addressing the challenges and strategies associated with third-party security in the cloud requires a multifaceted and proactive approach. Organizations must navigate complexities related to control, compliance, shared responsibility, and the dynamic nature of cloud environments. By implementing robust security practices, conducting thorough due diligence, fostering collaboration within industries, and embracing a zero-trust mindset, organizations can enhance the security posture of their third-party integrations and ensure the resilience of their overall cloud ecosystem. As the cloud landscape continues to evolve, a strategic and adaptive approach to third-party security becomes indispensable for organizations seeking to harness the benefits of external services while effectively managing associated risks.

Explore how security infrastructure can adapt to the dynamic nature of cloud environments.

Adapting security infrastructure to the dynamic nature of cloud environments is a complex and ongoing challenge that requires a holistic approach, combining technological innovation, strategic planning, and a fundamental shift in mindset. One of the key characteristics of cloud environments is their dynamic and elastic nature, where resources are provisioned, scaled, and deprovisioned rapidly to meet changing demands. Traditional security models designed for static, on-premises environments may struggle to keep pace with the agility and scale of cloud infrastructures. Therefore, security in the cloud must be designed to embrace and adapt to this dynamic landscape, ensuring that protective measures are seamlessly integrated into every facet of the cloud environment.

One foundational aspect of adapting security infrastructure to the cloud is the adoption of a proactive and continuous security posture. Unlike traditional environments where security was often seen as a perimeter-based approach, cloud security requires a shift towards a zero-trust model. In a zero-trust framework, trust is never assumed, and every entity, whether internal or external, is treated as potentially untrusted. This approach aligns with the dynamic nature of cloud environments, emphasizing granular access controls, continuous monitoring, and adaptive authentication. Implementing a zero-trust architecture ensures that security is not solely dependent on perimeter defenses but is distributed throughout the cloud infrastructure, making it resilient to the dynamic nature of resource provisioning and deprovisioning.

Cloud-native security tools and technologies play a crucial role in adapting security infrastructure to the cloud's dynamic nature. Traditional security solutions designed for static data centers may lack the agility and scalability required in cloud environments. Cloud-native security tools, on the other hand, are specifically crafted to operate seamlessly within dynamic and distributed cloud infrastructures. These tools often leverage Application Programming Interfaces (APIs) provided by cloud service providers to integrate with and gain insights into the dynamic aspects of cloud resources. Cloud-native security solutions include features such as auto-scaling, self-healing, and automation, aligning with the dynamic provisioning and workload changes inherent in cloud environments.

Automation is a linchpin in adapting security infrastructure to the dynamic nature of the cloud. With the rapid pace of resource provisioning and deprovisioning in the cloud, manual security processes become a bottleneck and may lead to oversights and misconfigurations. Automation enables security teams to implement consistent and rapid security measures, such as automated provisioning of security controls, continuous vulnerability scanning, and real-time incident response. By leveraging Infrastructure as Code (IaC) and configuration management tools, organizations can automate the deployment and configuration of security controls, ensuring that security policies are consistently applied as cloud resources evolve.

Visibility and monitoring are critical components of adapting security infrastructure to the dynamic nature of the cloud. The ephemeral nature of cloud resources, including virtual machines, containers, and serverless functions, requires a shift from traditional logging and monitoring approaches. Cloud environments generate vast amounts of data, and continuous monitoring is essential for detecting and responding to security incidents promptly. Cloud-native Security Information and Event Management (SIEM) solutions, integrated with cloud service provider APIs, provide real-time visibility into the security posture of cloud resources. These solutions enable security teams to correlate and analyze events across the dynamic cloud environment, enhancing their ability to identify and respond to security threats.

Identity and access management (IAM) is a cornerstone of adapting security infrastructure to the dynamic nature of cloud environments. In the cloud, where users, applications, and services interact from diverse locations and devices, traditional IAM models may fall short. Cloud IAM solutions offer adaptive and context-aware authentication mechanisms, ensuring that access controls align with the dynamic nature of user interactions. Implementing Identity as a Service (IDaaS) solutions enables organizations to manage identities, access permissions, and authentication centrally, providing a unified and scalable IAM approach that adapts to the dynamic provisioning and deprovisioning of users and resources.

The integration of DevOps practices and security, often referred to as DevSecOps, is pivotal in adapting security infrastructure to the dynamic nature of cloud environments. DevOps methodologies emphasize collaboration, automation, and continuous integration/continuous deployment (CI/CD) pipelines. By embedding security into the DevOps lifecycle, organizations can ensure that security measures are seamlessly integrated into the rapid development and deployment cycles of cloud-native applications. DevSecOps practices facilitate the automation of security testing, code analysis, and compliance checks, allowing security to keep pace with the dynamic evolution of cloud-based applications.

Microservices architecture, commonly employed in cloud-native applications, presents both opportunities and challenges for security infrastructure adaptation. Microservices enable the decomposition of monolithic applications into smaller, independently deployable services. While this architecture enhances agility and scalability, it introduces complexities in securing the interactions between microservices. Implementing service mesh technologies, such as Istio or Linkerd, becomes crucial for securing communication between microservices. These technologies provide features like mutual TLS, access controls, and observability, allowing organizations to adapt their security infrastructure to the dynamic and distributed nature of microservices.

Containers, another integral component of cloud-native applications, bring their own set of security considerations. Container orchestration platforms, like Kubernetes, are widely used for managing containerized applications at scale. Adapting security infrastructure to the dynamic nature of containers involves implementing container security tools that integrate with orchestration platforms. These tools enable organizations to enforce security policies, conduct vulnerability scanning, and monitor the runtime behavior of containers. Implementing container security as code and integrating it into CI/CD pipelines ensures that security measures are applied consistently as containers are deployed and scaled.

Serverless computing, exemplified by functions as a service (FaaS), further challenges traditional security models. In a serverless environment, organizations do not manage the underlying infrastructure, and functions are executed on-demand. Adapting security infrastructure to serverless computing involves implementing security controls at the application and function level. Cloud providers offer serverless security services that enable organizations to apply fine-grained access controls, monitor function execution, and detect anomalous behavior. Serverless security requires a shift in mindset, focusing on application-level security and leveraging cloud-native security services.

Encryption is fundamental in adapting security infrastructure to the dynamic nature of cloud environments. End-to-end encryption ensures the confidentiality and integrity of data as it traverses dynamic cloud infrastructures. Implementing encryption for data at rest, in transit, and during processing safeguards sensitive information regardless of the dynamic state of cloud resources. Cloud providers offer native encryption services, such as Key Management Services (KMS), enabling organizations to manage encryption keys centrally and consistently across dynamic cloud environments. Encryption also serves as a crucial component of a data-centric security strategy, ensuring that data remains protected regardless of its location or the dynamic nature of the cloud.

Security orchestration and automation platforms contribute significantly to adapting security infrastructure to the dynamic nature of the cloud. These platforms provide a centralized framework for orchestrating and automating security workflows across diverse cloud environments. By integrating with cloud-native APIs and security tools, orchestration platforms enable organizations to automate incident response, threat hunting, and vulnerability remediation. Security orchestration facilitates a coordinated and adaptive response to security incidents, aligning with the dynamic nature of cloud environments and the evolving threat landscape.

Collaboration and information sharing within the cybersecurity community are crucial in adapting security infrastructure to the dynamic nature of the cloud. Threat intelligence sharing, industry collaborations, and participation in security communities provide organizations with insights into emerging threats and best practices. By staying informed about the latest security trends, vulnerabilities, and attack techniques, organizations can proactively adapt their security infrastructure to mitigate evolving risks. Collaborative efforts also play a role in shaping industry standards and guidelines for cloud security, fostering a collective defense against common challenges.

In conclusion, adapting security infrastructure to the dynamic nature of cloud environments requires a comprehensive and agile approach that aligns with the principles of cloud-native computing. From embracing a zero-trust model and leveraging automation to implementing cloud-native security tools and collaborating within the cybersecurity community, organizations must continually evolve their security strategies to address the challenges posed by dynamic and distributed cloud infrastructures. As cloud technologies continue to advance, organizations that prioritize adaptive security measures will be better positioned to navigate the complexities of the cloud landscape and safeguard their digital assets in an ever-changing threat environment.

Chapter 3: Encryption Essentials: Safeguarding Your Data

Provide a comprehensive overview of encryption principles.
Encryption, a fundamental pillar of modern cybersecurity, is a complex and nuanced set of principles and techniques aimed at safeguarding sensitive information from unauthorized access or interception. At its core, encryption is a process of transforming plaintext, or human-readable data, into ciphertext, which is unintelligible without the appropriate decryption key. The overarching goal is to ensure the confidentiality, integrity, and authenticity of data, whether at rest, in transit, or during processing.

Symmetric encryption, one of the foundational encryption principles, employs a single secret key for both encryption and decryption. The challenge lies in securely distributing and managing this shared key among communicating parties. Advanced Encryption Standard (AES), a widely adopted symmetric encryption algorithm, exemplifies the strength and versatility of symmetric cryptography. AES operates on fixed-size blocks of data and supports key lengths of 128, 192, or 256 bits. The robustness of AES has made it the de facto standard for securing a myriad of applications and communication channels.

Asymmetric encryption, also known as public-key cryptography, introduces the concept of two mathematically related keys: a public key for encryption and a private key for decryption. The security of asymmetric encryption relies on the computational difficulty of certain mathematical problems, such as factoring large prime numbers.

The RSA algorithm, a prominent example of asymmetric encryption, leverages the challenge of factoring the product of two large prime numbers to establish the security of the system. Asymmetric encryption addresses the key distribution challenge inherent in symmetric encryption, as users can freely share their public keys while keeping their private keys confidential.

Hybrid encryption represents a fusion of symmetric and asymmetric encryption, capitalizing on the strengths of both. In a hybrid scheme, data is encrypted with a symmetric key, and this key is then encrypted using the recipient's public key. This approach combines the efficiency of symmetric encryption for bulk data with the key distribution and management benefits of asymmetric encryption. Hybrid encryption is widely employed in secure communication protocols, ensuring the confidentiality and integrity of data exchanges.

End-to-end encryption (E2EE) is a concept applied in communication scenarios where only the communicating users can read the messages. In E2EE systems, data is encrypted on the sender's device and decrypted on the recipient's device, with the keys typically residing solely with the users. Messaging applications like Signal and WhatsApp implement E2EE to provide users with a high level of privacy and security, preventing even service providers from accessing the content of communications.

Quantum computing introduces unique challenges to traditional encryption methods. Algorithms such as Shor's algorithm, when executed on a sufficiently powerful quantum computer, can efficiently factor large numbers, compromising the security of widely used asymmetric encryption algorithms. To address this threat, post-quantum cryptography explores alternative mathematical structures, such as lattice-based or hash-based cryptography, that are believed to be resistant to quantum attacks. The cryptographic community is actively researching and developing post-quantum algorithms to ensure the continued security of encrypted communication in the quantum era.

In the context of data at rest, encryption plays a crucial role in protecting information stored on devices, databases, or other storage media. Full disk encryption (FDE) is a method where the entire storage device is encrypted, ensuring that all data, including the operating system and system files, is protected. BitLocker for Windows and FileVault for macOS are examples of FDE implementations. Additionally, file-level encryption allows for the selective encryption of individual files or directories, providing more granular control over data protection.

Data in transit, as it traverses networks or communication channels, is particularly susceptible to interception. Transport Layer Security (TLS) and its predecessor, Secure Sockets Layer (SSL), are cryptographic protocols that secure data in transit by encrypting the communication between clients and servers. TLS utilizes both symmetric and asymmetric encryption, with the symmetric key negotiated during the initial phase of the communication. This ensures the confidentiality and integrity of data exchanged over the internet, safeguarding sensitive information during online transactions, email communication, and other data transfers.

Public Key Infrastructure (PKI) is a comprehensive framework that underlies many encryption applications, providing a system for managing digital keys and certificates. PKI employs asymmetric encryption to establish the authenticity of public keys, typically through the use of digital certificates issued by trusted entities known as certificate authorities (CAs). This infrastructure supports secure communication, digital signatures, and the verification of the identity of communication partners in various online applications.

Hash functions, while distinct from encryption, are integral to cryptographic principles. Hash functions generate fixed-size outputs, or hash values, from variable-size inputs. Unlike encryption, hashing is a one-way process, making it computationally infeasible to reverse the transformation and derive the original input from the hash value. Hash functions are employed in various cryptographic applications, including the creation of digital signatures, password storage, and data integrity verification. Commonly used hash functions include SHA-256 and SHA-3.

Digital signatures leverage asymmetric encryption to provide a mechanism for verifying the authenticity and integrity of digital messages or documents. The sender uses their private key to create a digital signature, which is then verified by recipients using the sender's public key. Digital signatures ensure that a message has not been tampered with during transit and that it was indeed generated by the claimed sender. This principle is foundational to secure communication, electronic transactions, and the establishment of trust in digital interactions.

Key management is a critical aspect of encryption principles, encompassing the secure generation, distribution, storage, and disposal of cryptographic keys. The strength of an encryption system relies not only on the complexity of the encryption algorithms but also on the effectiveness of key management practices. Key generation must use truly random processes, and keys must be securely distributed to authorized users. Key rotation and secure storage mechanisms are essential to mitigate the risk associated with compromised keys over time. Effective key management is a continuous process that ensures the ongoing security of encrypted data.

Forward secrecy, also known as perfect forward secrecy (PFS), is an encryption principle that enhances the security of communication by generating unique session keys for each session. Even if a long-term private key is compromised, forward secrecy ensures that past communications remain secure, as the compromise does not affect the confidentiality of past sessions. Protocols like the Diffie-Hellman key exchange, specifically its ephemeral variants, are employed to achieve forward secrecy. Forward secrecy is particularly crucial in environments where long-term key compromises are a significant concern.

Homomorphic encryption is an advanced cryptographic technique that allows computations to be performed on encrypted data without decrypting it first. This property is invaluable in scenarios where sensitive data needs to be processed by third-party services or in cloud computing environments. Homomorphic encryption enables privacy-preserving data analytics and computations, as the data remains encrypted throughout the processing steps, and only the final result is decrypted. While computationally intensive, ongoing research aims to enhance the efficiency of homomorphic encryption for broader practical applications.

Side-channel attacks represent a category of attacks that exploit information leaked during the execution of cryptographic algorithms. Unlike traditional attacks that target the algorithm itself, side-channel attacks focus on unintended information leakage, such as timing variations, power consumption, or electromagnetic emanations. Countermeasures against side-channel attacks involve implementing algorithms and implementations that minimize or eliminate the information leakage, ensuring that cryptographic processes are not vulnerable to these indirect forms of attack.

In conclusion, encryption principles form the bedrock of modern cybersecurity, providing the means to secure sensitive information across various contexts and applications. Whether applied to protect data at rest, in transit, or during processing, encryption techniques address the ever-present threat of unauthorized access and interception. As the digital landscape evolves, encryption continues to play a pivotal role in ensuring the confidentiality, integrity, and authenticity of information, adapting to emerging technologies and threats while upholding the principles of privacy and security.

Differentiate between symmetric and asymmetric encryption methods.

Symmetric and asymmetric encryption methods represent two fundamental approaches to securing information in the field of cryptography, each with its own set of characteristics, use cases, and strengths. Symmetric encryption, also known as secret-key or private-key encryption, relies on a single secret key for both the encryption and decryption of data. The key is shared between communicating parties, and the security of the system hinges on the confidentiality of this shared secret. Symmetric encryption algorithms, such as the Advanced Encryption Standard (AES), are highly efficient and well-suited for bulk data encryption, making them a preferred choice for scenarios where speed and computational efficiency are paramount.

In symmetric encryption, the same secret key is used by both the sender and the recipient to transform plaintext into ciphertext and vice versa. This simplicity contributes to the speed and efficiency of symmetric encryption, making it ideal for applications where computational resources are constrained, such as in embedded systems or resource-limited devices. However, the Achilles' heel of symmetric encryption lies in the secure distribution of the shared key. As both parties need to possess the key for secure communication, a secure and confidential channel is required to exchange the key initially. The challenge of key distribution becomes increasingly complex as the number of communicating parties grows, making symmetric encryption less practical for large-scale, multi-user scenarios.

On the other hand, asymmetric encryption, also known as public-key cryptography, introduces a pair of mathematically related keys: a public key and a private key. Unlike symmetric encryption, where the same key is used for both encryption and decryption, asymmetric encryption utilizes a different key for each operation. The public key, as the name suggests, can be freely shared, while the private key must be kept confidential. The security of asymmetric encryption relies on mathematical problems that are computationally difficult to solve, such as factoring large prime numbers or solving discrete logarithm problems.

Asymmetric encryption offers a powerful solution to the key distribution challenge inherent in symmetric encryption. In a typical scenario, anyone can use the public key to encrypt a message, but only the possessor of the corresponding private key can decrypt and access the original plaintext. This paradigm enables secure communication between parties without the need for a shared secret key. The widely used RSA (Rivest-Shamir-Adleman) and Elliptic Curve Cryptography (ECC) are examples of asymmetric encryption algorithms.

While the key distribution problem is mitigated by asymmetric encryption, it comes with its own set of trade-offs. Asymmetric encryption tends to be computationally more intensive than symmetric encryption, making it less suitable for bulk data encryption. Therefore, a common practice is to use asymmetric encryption to establish a secure communication channel and exchange a shared symmetric key, which is then used for the actual data encryption using symmetric encryption. This hybrid approach combines the efficiency of symmetric encryption with the key distribution benefits of asymmetric encryption.

Another crucial distinction between symmetric and asymmetric encryption lies in their application to specific use cases. Symmetric encryption excels in scenarios where speed, efficiency, and resource constraints are critical factors. It is commonly employed in applications like data encryption for storage, secure communication within a closed system, and encryption of sensitive information on resource-constrained devices. The efficiency of symmetric encryption makes it well-suited for high-performance computing environments, such as securing network traffic and data stored on servers.

Conversely, asymmetric encryption is often chosen for scenarios where secure key exchange and digital signatures are essential. The use of public and private key pairs enables functionalities such as digital signatures, where the private key is used to sign a message, and the corresponding public key is used to verify the authenticity of the signature. This is particularly valuable in applications like secure email communication, digital signatures for document verification, and establishing secure connections on the internet, as seen in the Transport Layer Security (TLS) and Secure Sockets Layer (SSL) protocols.

Key management is a critical aspect that differentiates symmetric and asymmetric encryption. In symmetric encryption, the challenge lies in securely distributing and managing the shared secret key among all communicating parties. The compromise of the shared key jeopardizes the security of all communications. Key distribution is typically handled through secure channels or through physical means to prevent interception. Key rotation practices are essential to periodically change the shared key, reducing the risk associated with a compromised key.

Asymmetric encryption simplifies key management by eliminating the need for a shared secret key. Each user possesses a unique pair of public and private keys, and secure communication is achieved by using the recipient's public key to encrypt a message. The private key, held exclusively by the recipient, is then used for decryption. This decentralization of keys simplifies key management and eliminates the need for secure key distribution channels. However, managing key pairs at scale, especially in environments with numerous users, necessitates robust key management practices, including key revocation and certificate management.

The concept of trust is intrinsic to both symmetric and asymmetric encryption but manifests in different ways. In symmetric encryption, trust relies heavily on the secure distribution and protection of the shared secret key. As long as the key remains confidential, the parties can trust the security of their communication. However, the challenge arises when dealing with a large number of users, each requiring the shared key. Establishing and maintaining trust in the confidentiality of the key becomes increasingly complex.

Asymmetric encryption introduces the concept of a trust anchor, typically in the form of a certificate authority (CA). The CA verifies the identity of entities and issues digital certificates containing public keys. Users can trust the authenticity of a public key if it is associated with a valid digital certificate issued by a trusted CA. This hierarchical trust model is fundamental to the security of asymmetric encryption and forms the basis for secure communication on the internet. However, the trust in asymmetric encryption relies on the assumption that private keys are adequately protected and that the CA infrastructure is secure.

In summary, the choice between symmetric and asymmetric encryption depends on the specific requirements of the application, the computational resources available, and the key management considerations. Symmetric encryption excels in scenarios where efficiency and speed are paramount, making it suitable for high-performance computing and resource-constrained devices. Asymmetric encryption, with its ability to address the key distribution challenge and support functionalities like digital signatures, is instrumental in securing communication on the internet and applications that demand secure key exchange. In practice, a hybrid approach often combines the strengths of both symmetric and asymmetric encryption to achieve a balance between efficiency and key distribution security. Ultimately, both encryption methods play pivotal roles in the diverse landscape of modern cryptography, contributing to the confidentiality, integrity, and authenticity of information in various digital environments.

Explore the importance of end-to-end encryption in securing communication channels.

End-to-end encryption (E2EE) stands as a cornerstone in the realm of cybersecurity, playing a pivotal role in securing communication channels and safeguarding sensitive information exchanged between users. At its essence, E2EE is a cryptographic principle that ensures that only the communicating users can read the messages, preventing third parties, including service providers and potential adversaries, from accessing the content of the communication. This level of privacy and security is achieved by encrypting the data on the sender's device and decrypting it on the recipient's device, with cryptographic keys residing solely with the end-users. The significance of E2EE becomes pronounced in an era where digital communication is ubiquitous and the need for privacy, confidentiality, and data protection is paramount.

One of the fundamental contributions of E2EE lies in its ability to mitigate the risk of unauthorized access and interception of communication. In traditional communication models, where data is often transmitted in plaintext or can be accessed at intermediary points, the potential for eavesdropping and data interception is a persistent concern. E2EE addresses this vulnerability by ensuring that even if the communication is intercepted during transit, the intercepted data remains encrypted and indecipherable without the proper cryptographic keys. This capability enhances the overall security posture of digital communication, especially in scenarios where the sensitivity of the information being exchanged demands the highest level of protection.

Secure messaging applications, such as Signal and WhatsApp, exemplify the practical implementation of E2EE to ensure private and confidential communication. In these applications, messages are encrypted on the sender's device using a unique encryption key, and the ciphertext is transmitted to the recipient. The recipient's device then uses its private key to decrypt the message, restoring the original plaintext. This entire process occurs seamlessly in the background, preserving the user experience while offering robust security against unauthorized access. By adopting E2EE, these applications provide users with a level of assurance that their messages remain confidential and are visible only to the intended recipients.

In addition to preventing unauthorized access, E2EE also safeguards against the potential compromise of communication service providers. In scenarios where the communication service provider stores or processes user data, there is an inherent risk of data breaches or unauthorized access by employees. E2EE shifts the trust model by ensuring that the service provider does not have access to the plaintext content of the communication. Even if the service provider's systems were to be compromised, the encrypted data would remain unreadable without the cryptographic keys held by the end-users. This heightened level of protection aligns with the growing awareness and concern for user privacy in the digital landscape.

Furthermore, E2EE plays a crucial role in protecting user data from legal or government requests for information. In jurisdictions where privacy laws are stringent, service providers may be compelled to disclose user data to law enforcement agencies. E2EE acts as a safeguard by ensuring that even if the service provider were to comply with legal requests, the information disclosed would be encrypted and unintelligible without the corresponding keys held by the end-users. This not only preserves user privacy but also aligns with the principle of user control over their own data.

E2EE is particularly instrumental in securing sensitive communication in professional and business contexts. Industries such as healthcare, finance, and legal services, where the exchange of confidential information is routine, benefit significantly from the robust protection provided by E2EE. Medical professionals sharing patient information, financial analysts discussing sensitive transactions, and legal practitioners communicating about privileged matters all rely on E2EE to ensure the confidentiality and integrity of their communication. In these sectors, where regulatory compliance and data protection are paramount, E2EE becomes an indispensable tool for meeting stringent security requirements.

Despite the numerous advantages of E2EE, its adoption and implementation have faced challenges, particularly in the context of balancing security with usability. The seamless user experience that many individuals have come to expect from modern communication applications often involves some level of compromise on security. For instance, cloud-based messaging services that synchronize messages across multiple devices may sacrifice end-to-end encryption for the sake of convenience. Striking the right balance between security and usability remains an ongoing challenge for developers and service providers seeking to implement E2EE in a way that meets user expectations.

The increasing awareness of privacy concerns and the value placed on individual control over personal data have prompted a growing demand for E2EE in various communication platforms. Users are increasingly prioritizing applications that provide robust encryption mechanisms, recognizing the importance of protecting their sensitive conversations from unauthorized access. This shift in user preferences has influenced the industry, leading to a broader adoption of E2EE across various platforms and services, from email providers to collaborative tools.

E2EE is not without its criticisms and debates, especially in the context of law enforcement and national security concerns. While it is essential for protecting user privacy, the same features that make E2EE robust against unauthorized access can also pose challenges for legitimate investigations. The tension between privacy rights and the needs of law enforcement to access certain information for public safety purposes is an ongoing debate that requires careful consideration and a nuanced approach to striking the right balance.

As technology continues to evolve, so do the threats and challenges to digital communication. The rise of sophisticated cyber threats, state-sponsored hacking, and malicious actors seeking to exploit vulnerabilities necessitate a proactive and adaptive approach to security. E2EE, with its focus on user-centric security and the principle of minimal trust, becomes a vital component of

this defense strategy. It empowers users to take control of their digital conversations and ensures that the confidentiality of their communication is not contingent on the trustworthiness of intermediaries.

In conclusion, the importance of end-to-end encryption in securing communication channels cannot be overstated in a digital landscape where privacy is a fundamental right and the protection of sensitive information is paramount. E2EE serves as a robust mechanism for safeguarding communication against unauthorized access, protecting user data from potential compromises, and preserving user privacy in the face of evolving cybersecurity threats. As the digital ecosystem continues to advance, the adoption of E2EE is not just a technological choice but a reflection of societal values and expectations regarding the protection of personal information in the digital age.

Discuss strategies and best practices for encrypting data stored in the cloud.

Encrypting data stored in the cloud is a critical aspect of securing sensitive information and maintaining the confidentiality and integrity of digital assets. As organizations increasingly leverage cloud services for storage and processing, adopting robust encryption strategies becomes imperative to mitigate the risks associated with unauthorized access, data breaches, and compliance violations. A comprehensive approach to encrypting data in the cloud involves a combination of encryption techniques, key management practices, and adherence to established security best practices.

One fundamental strategy for encrypting data in the cloud is to implement encryption at rest. This involves encrypting data when it is stored in storage repositories, such as cloud-based databases or object storage services. Cloud service providers often offer native encryption features that allow organizations to encrypt entire volumes or specific data objects. For example, Amazon S3 provides server-side encryption to automatically encrypt objects upon storage, while Azure Storage offers similar capabilities with Azure Storage Service Encryption (SSE). This approach ensures that even if unauthorized parties gain access to the physical storage infrastructure, the stored data remains encrypted and unreadable without the appropriate decryption keys.

In addition to encryption at rest, encrypting data in transit is crucial to protect information as it moves between the user's device and the cloud storage. Secure data transmission protocols, such as Transport Layer Security (TLS) or its predecessor Secure Sockets Layer (SSL), should be enforced to encrypt data during transit. Cloud providers often support these protocols for communication with their services, ensuring that data is encrypted as it travels over the internet. Encrypting data in transit safeguards against interception, eavesdropping, and Man-in-the-Middle (MitM) attacks, providing a comprehensive layer of protection for data throughout its lifecycle.

A pivotal consideration in encrypting data in the cloud is the choice between symmetric and asymmetric encryption. Symmetric encryption, where the same key is used for both encryption and decryption, is efficient and well-suited for bulk data encryption. Cloud services may utilize symmetric encryption for encrypting data at rest, employing strong algorithms like Advanced Encryption Standard (AES). Asymmetric encryption, which involves a pair of public and private keys, is often employed for secure key exchange and digital signatures. Striking a balance between the efficiency of symmetric encryption and the key distribution benefits of asymmetric encryption is a best practice in cloud data encryption.

Key management is a foundational element of any encryption strategy, particularly in the cloud. Effectively managing encryption keys involves secure generation, storage, distribution, rotation, and, if necessary, destruction of cryptographic keys. Cloud service providers typically offer Key Management Services (KMS) or Hardware Security Modules (HSMs) to facilitate key management. AWS Key Management Service (KMS) and Azure Key Vault are examples of such services. Implementing a robust key management strategy ensures that encryption keys are well-protected, and access is tightly controlled, reducing the risk of unauthorized key exposure.

Another critical consideration is the lifecycle management of encryption keys, encompassing key rotation and key revocation. Regularly rotating encryption keys helps mitigate the impact of compromised keys, especially in situations where an attacker gains access over an extended period. Cloud providers often support automated key rotation, enabling organizations to update encryption keys without disruption to services. Additionally, key revocation mechanisms are essential for promptly invalidating compromised or deprecated keys, ensuring that access to encrypted data is restricted only to entities with valid and authorized keys.

When encrypting data in the cloud, organizations must consider the balance between security and usability. Client-side encryption provides an approach where data is encrypted on the client's side before it is sent to the cloud. This ensures that the cloud service provider has no access to the plaintext data or encryption keys. Tools like AWS Key Management Service (KMS) and Azure Key Vault can be leveraged for client-side key management. While client-side encryption enhances security, it can introduce challenges in terms of key management, user experience, and the potential loss of some cloud-based functionalities that rely on access to plaintext data.

Tokenization represents an alternative strategy for protecting sensitive data in the cloud. Instead of encrypting the actual data, tokenization involves replacing sensitive elements with tokens or references that are meaningless to unauthorized users. Tokenization is often applied to payment card data or personally identifiable information (PII). Cloud providers and third-party tokenization services can assist in implementing tokenization strategies, offering an added layer of security without the need for direct access to the encryption keys. While not a traditional encryption method, tokenization complements encryption strategies and is particularly useful in scenarios where preserving the format and structure of the data is essential.

Homomorphic encryption, an advanced cryptographic technique, allows computations to be performed on encrypted data without decrypting it first. This innovative approach enables secure data processing in the cloud without exposing the plaintext information to the cloud service provider. While homomorphic encryption is computationally intensive and may not be suitable for all use cases, it represents a cutting-edge strategy for securing data during processing in cloud environments where data privacy is a paramount concern.

Cloud Access Security Brokers (CASBs) play a significant role in enhancing the security of data in the cloud by providing visibility, control, and security features. CASBs can enforce encryption policies, ensuring that data is encrypted before it is stored in the cloud and decrypted only when accessed by authorized users. Additionally, CASBs offer functionalities such as data loss prevention (DLP), threat detection, and access controls, enhancing the overall security posture of cloud-stored data.

Data classification and segmentation are integral components of a comprehensive data encryption strategy. By classifying data based on sensitivity and implementing segmentation controls, organizations can apply different encryption measures based on the importance and risk associated with the data. For example, highly sensitive financial data may require stronger encryption measures compared to non-sensitive information. This tailored approach enables organizations to allocate resources judiciously, focusing encryption efforts on the most critical and sensitive data.

Regularly auditing and monitoring encrypted data in the cloud is crucial for identifying anomalous activities, potential security incidents, or unauthorized access. Cloud providers often offer logging and monitoring services that capture events related to data access, key management, and encryption activities. Leveraging these logs for continuous monitoring allows organizations to detect and respond to security threats promptly. Security Information and Event Management (SIEM) solutions can also be integrated to provide a centralized view of security events and facilitate real-time incident response.

Collaboration and adherence to industry standards and compliance requirements are essential aspects of cloud data encryption. Different industries and regions have specific regulations governing the protection of sensitive data. For example, the General Data Protection Regulation (GDPR) in Europe mandates stringent data protection measures, while the Health Insurance Portability and Accountability Act (HIPAA) in the United States imposes specific requirements on the protection of healthcare data. Aligning encryption strategies with regulatory requirements ensures that organizations not only meet legal obligations but also bolster the overall security posture of their cloud-stored data.

Educating employees and end-users about the importance of data encryption, security best practices, and their role in maintaining a secure cloud environment is paramount. Human factors remain a significant challenge in cybersecurity, and organizations must invest in training programs to raise awareness about the risks of data exposure and the proper use of encryption tools. Establishing a culture of security awareness contributes to a proactive defense against insider threats and inadvertent data exposures.

In conclusion, encrypting data stored in the cloud requires a multifaceted approach that encompasses encryption at rest and in transit, robust key management practices, consideration of key rotation and revocation, and the adoption of innovative encryption techniques like homomorphic encryption. The balance between security and usability, the use of client-side encryption, tokenization, and the integration of CASBs contribute to a comprehensive encryption strategy. Regular auditing, monitoring, and compliance with industry standards enhance the overall security posture, while educating employees about the importance of encryption establishes a proactive defense against evolving cybersecurity threats. As organizations navigate the complexities of cloud environments, a thoughtful and adaptive approach to data encryption is essential to safeguard sensitive information and maintain trust in the integrity of cloud-based services.

Explain the significance of effective key management in encryption.

Effective key management is a cornerstone in the realm of encryption, playing a pivotal role in the security and integrity of sensitive information across various digital environments. At its core, key management encompasses the entire lifecycle of cryptographic keys—those essential elements that underpin encryption algorithms, ensuring the confidentiality and integrity of data. The significance of effective key management becomes increasingly pronounced as organizations grapple with the growing complexity of cybersecurity threats, the widespread adoption of encryption, and the need to safeguard digital assets in an ever-evolving threat landscape.

One fundamental aspect of effective key management lies in the secure generation of cryptographic keys. The strength of an encryption system hinges on the randomness and unpredictability of its keys. Cryptographically secure random number generators are employed to generate keys that resist statistical analysis and provide a high level of entropy. This initial step is critical in ensuring that the keys used for encryption are robust and resistant to brute-force attacks or other attempts to compromise their confidentiality.

Secure key distribution is another paramount component of key management. In scenarios where multiple parties need access to encrypted information, ensuring the secure and confidential exchange of keys is a complex challenge. Symmetric encryption, where the same key is used for both encryption and decryption, requires a secure channel for key distribution. Asymmetric encryption, which involves a pair of public and private keys, mitigates the challenge by allowing the public key to be freely shared while keeping the private key confidential. Secure key distribution mechanisms are essential to prevent unauthorized parties from gaining access to the cryptographic keys, as the compromise of keys poses a severe risk to the security of the encrypted data.

The secure storage of cryptographic keys is a critical consideration in effective key management. Keys must be stored in a manner that protects them from unauthorized access, theft, or tampering. Hardware Security Modules (HSMs) represent a secure enclave for storing cryptographic keys in a dedicated hardware device, providing both physical and logical protection. Cloud-based Key Management Services (KMS) offered by cloud service providers offer a virtualized solution for secure key storage, leveraging the provider's infrastructure while maintaining stringent security controls.

Effective key management encompasses robust key rotation practices. Over time, cryptographic keys may become susceptible to various attacks or vulnerabilities due to advances in computing power or the discovery of new cryptographic weaknesses. Key rotation involves periodically replacing existing keys with new ones, ensuring that even if a key is compromised, the window of vulnerability is limited. Automated key rotation mechanisms streamline this process, enabling organizations to regularly update keys without disrupting their cryptographic systems.

The concept of key revocation is a crucial element in effective key management. In situations where a key is compromised, lost, or no longer trusted, it must be promptly revoked to prevent its unauthorized use. Key revocation lists or mechanisms within a Key Management System (KMS) enable organizations to invalidate compromised keys, ensuring that they are no longer accepted for encryption or decryption operations. The timely revocation of keys is essential for minimizing the potential impact of key compromises and maintaining the overall security of the cryptographic system.

A nuanced aspect of key management involves considering the impact of quantum computing on existing cryptographic algorithms. Quantum computers, when sufficiently advanced, could potentially break widely used asymmetric encryption algorithms, such as RSA and ECC, by efficiently solving mathematical problems like factoring large numbers. Post-quantum cryptography explores alternative cryptographic algorithms that are believed to be resistant to quantum attacks. Effective key management in the era of quantum computing involves preparing for the transition to post-quantum algorithms and ensuring that systems are equipped to adapt to the changing landscape of cryptographic security.

Forward secrecy, also known as perfect forward secrecy (PFS), is an advanced key management concept that enhances the security of communication channels. In scenarios where long-term keys are used for encryption, the compromise of a single key could potentially expose all past communication encrypted with that key. Forward secrecy mitigates this risk by generating unique session keys for each session, ensuring that even if a long-term key is compromised, the confidentiality of past sessions remains intact. Protocols like the

Diffie-Hellman key exchange, specifically its ephemeral variants, are employed to achieve forward secrecy, adding an additional layer of protection to encrypted communication.

The advent of cloud computing introduces new dimensions to key management challenges. Cloud environments often involve shared infrastructure, and organizations must navigate the complexities of securing keys in a multi-tenant and distributed setting. Cloud-based Key Management Services (KMS) offered by major cloud providers, including AWS Key Management Service and Azure Key Vault, provide tools for organizations to manage encryption keys securely in the cloud. Effective key management in the cloud involves understanding the shared responsibility model, where cloud providers manage the security of the cloud infrastructure, and organizations are responsible for securing their data and access controls, including the management of encryption keys.

In the context of effective key management, organizations must adopt a proactive stance toward auditing and monitoring key-related activities. Logging key management events, such as key generation, distribution, rotation, and revocation, provides a trail of activities that can be invaluable for forensic analysis and incident response. Integrating Key Management Systems (KMS) with Security Information and Event Management (SIEM) solutions allows organizations to centralize and correlate key-related events, enabling real-time monitoring and alerting for potential security incidents. Regularly reviewing key management logs contributes to a comprehensive security strategy, helping organizations identify anomalous activities and respond promptly to potential threats.

Human factors remain a significant challenge in key management. Human errors, such as accidental key disclosure or improper handling of cryptographic material, can compromise the security of encryption systems. Educating employees about the importance of key management, the risks associated with key exposure, and the proper handling of cryptographic keys is essential. Security awareness training and ongoing education programs contribute to building a security-conscious culture within an organization, reducing the likelihood of human-related security incidents.

The regulatory landscape also plays a crucial role in shaping effective key management practices. Different industries and regions have specific regulations governing the protection of sensitive data, and adherence to these regulations often requires robust key management measures. For instance, the General Data Protection Regulation (GDPR) in Europe mandates stringent data protection measures, including encryption, as part of the broader framework for safeguarding personal data. Effective key management not only aligns with regulatory requirements but also demonstrates a commitment to data privacy and security.

Collaboration within the cybersecurity community is essential for advancing effective key management practices. Sharing insights, best practices, and lessons learned among industry professionals and researchers contributes to a collective understanding of evolving threats and effective mitigation strategies. Standardization efforts, such as those led by organizations like the National Institute of Standards and Technology (NIST), provide frameworks and guidelines for cryptographic key management, promoting consistency and interoperability across diverse systems and applications.

In conclusion, the significance of effective key management in encryption cannot be overstated in the digital age where the confidentiality and integrity of data are paramount. Robust key generation, secure distribution, careful storage, and the implementation of key rotation and revocation practices are foundational elements of key management. The advent of quantum computing and the complexities of cloud environments introduce additional dimensions to key management challenges, necessitating a forward-looking and adaptable approach. Forward secrecy, auditing, monitoring, and addressing human factors contribute to a comprehensive key management strategy. As organizations navigate the intricacies of securing cryptographic keys, effective key management emerges as a linchpin in the broader framework of cybersecurity, ensuring that encryption remains a robust defense against evolving threats in the dynamic landscape of digital security.

Explore how encryption is applied to secure cloud storage services.

The application of encryption to secure cloud storage services is a critical aspect of safeguarding sensitive data in an era where organizations increasingly rely on cloud platforms for storing and managing their digital assets. Encryption serves as a fundamental tool in mitigating the risks associated with unauthorized access, data breaches, and compliance violations in cloud storage environments. At its core, cloud storage encryption involves the use of cryptographic techniques to transform data into a secure and unintelligible form, ensuring that even if the stored information is accessed without proper authorization, it remains protected and unreadable.

One primary dimension of cloud storage encryption is the concept of encryption at rest, where data is encrypted when it is stored in the cloud. This ensures that even if unauthorized parties gain access to the physical storage infrastructure, the stored data remains encrypted and indecipherable without the appropriate decryption keys. Cloud service providers often offer native encryption features that allow organizations to enable encryption at rest for their stored data. For instance, Amazon S3 provides server-side encryption options, including SSE-S3, SSE-KMS, and SSE-C, allowing users to choose the level of control and management they want over their encryption keys.

Symmetric encryption algorithms, such as the Advanced Encryption Standard (AES), are commonly employed for encrypting data at rest in cloud storage. In this approach, the same secret key is used for both encryption and decryption, ensuring efficiency and computational speed. The cloud storage service, or the organization itself, is responsible for managing and safeguarding the encryption keys securely. Symmetric encryption is well-suited for scenarios where the primary concern is the protection of data at rest, and the performance impact of encryption and decryption operations needs to be minimized.

In addition to encryption at rest, securing data in transit is crucial for maintaining the integrity of information as it moves between the user's device and the cloud storage service. Transport Layer Security (TLS) or its predecessor Secure Sockets Layer (SSL) are cryptographic protocols that encrypt data during transit, preventing unauthorized interception, eavesdropping, or tampering. Cloud storage providers typically enforce these secure transmission protocols for communication with their services, ensuring that data is encrypted while traversing the internet. The combination of encryption at rest and in transit forms a comprehensive strategy for protecting data stored in the cloud throughout its entire lifecycle.

Key management is a foundational aspect of applying encryption to secure cloud storage services. The secure generation, storage, distribution, rotation, and, if necessary, revocation of cryptographic keys are critical components of a robust key management strategy. Cloud service providers offer Key Management Services (KMS) or integrate with Hardware Security Modules (HSMs) to assist organizations in managing their encryption keys securely. AWS Key Management Service (KMS), Azure Key Vault, and Google Cloud Key Management Service are examples of cloud-based key management solutions that facilitate the secure storage and management of encryption keys.

Symmetric key management involves securing the shared secret key used for both encryption and decryption. In the cloud storage context, organizations must ensure that these keys are generated securely, distributed to authorized users, and stored in a manner that protects them from unauthorized access. Regular key rotation practices are employed to update encryption keys periodically, reducing the risk associated with a compromised key. Automated key rotation mechanisms provided by cloud service providers streamline this process, ensuring that organizations can maintain a high level of security without disrupting their cloud storage operations.

Asymmetric encryption, which involves a pair of public and private keys, introduces additional considerations to key management in cloud storage. The public key can be freely shared, while the private key must be kept confidential. Organizations utilizing asymmetric encryption for secure key exchange or digital signatures must carefully manage their key pairs to prevent unauthorized access to the private keys. Secure generation, storage, and distribution of key pairs, along with periodic key rotation and key revocation practices, are essential for maintaining the security of asymmetric encryption in cloud storage environments.

Client-side encryption represents a paradigm shift in how encryption is applied to secure cloud storage services. In this approach, data is encrypted on the client's side before it is transmitted to the cloud. The cloud storage service has no access to the plaintext data or the encryption keys used for the encryption process. This model empowers users with greater control over their data and enhances the overall security of cloud storage. However, client-side encryption introduces challenges in terms of key management, user experience, and the potential loss of some cloud-based functionalities that rely on access to plaintext data.

Cloud Access Security Brokers (CASBs) play a significant role in enhancing the security of data in cloud storage by providing additional layers of control, visibility, and security features. CASBs can enforce encryption policies, ensuring that data is encrypted before it is stored in the cloud and decrypted only when accessed by authorized users. CASBs also offer functionalities such as data loss prevention (DLP), threat detection, and access controls, contributing to an enhanced security posture for cloud-stored data.

Tokenization is an alternative approach to securing sensitive data in cloud storage services. Instead of encrypting the actual data, tokenization involves replacing sensitive elements with tokens or references that are meaningless to unauthorized users. Tokenization is often applied to specific types of data, such as payment card information or personally identifiable information (PII). Cloud providers and third-party tokenization services can assist in implementing tokenization strategies, offering an added layer of security without the need for direct access to encryption keys.

Homomorphic encryption, an advanced cryptographic technique, allows computations to be performed on encrypted data without decrypting it first. While not yet widely adopted due to its computational intensity, homomorphic encryption holds promise for securing data in cloud storage environments where data privacy is a paramount concern. It enables secure processing of encrypted data in the cloud without exposing the plaintext information to the cloud service provider.

Effective key management practices are particularly crucial when applying encryption to secure cloud storage services. The shared responsibility model in cloud computing necessitates a clear understanding of the division of responsibilities between the cloud service provider and the organization. While the provider manages the security of the cloud infrastructure, organizations are responsible for securing their data and access controls, including the management of encryption keys. Ensuring that encryption keys are well-protected, regularly rotated, and promptly revoked in case of compromise contributes to the overall security of cloud-stored data.

Regulatory compliance further shapes the landscape of applying encryption in cloud storage services. Different industries and regions have specific regulations governing the protection of sensitive data. Adherence to these regulations often requires organizations to

implement encryption as part of a broader framework for data protection. The General Data Protection Regulation (GDPR) in Europe, for example, mandates stringent measures for safeguarding personal data, including encryption. Effectively applying encryption in cloud storage services helps organizations align with regulatory requirements and demonstrates a commitment to data privacy and security.

In conclusion, the application of encryption to secure cloud storage services is a multifaceted endeavor that involves encryption at rest and in transit, key management practices, and consideration of various encryption models, including symmetric, asymmetric, client-side, and tokenization. The choice of encryption strategy depends on factors such as the nature of the data, user requirements, and regulatory considerations. The evolving landscape of cloud computing, advancements in encryption techniques, and the need for user-centric security continue to shape the ways in which organizations secure their data in cloud storage. As cloud environments become integral to modern IT infrastructures, the effective application of encryption stands as a foundational element in maintaining trust, confidentiality, and integrity in the storage and management of digital assets.

Address challenges and solutions for implementing encryption in multi-cloud scenarios.

Implementing encryption in multi-cloud scenarios presents a unique set of challenges and complexities, requiring organizations to navigate a landscape where data is distributed across multiple cloud service providers (CSPs). The adoption of multi-cloud architectures offers benefits such as redundancy, resilience, and flexibility, but it also introduces intricacies related to key management, interoperability, and consistency in encryption practices. One of the primary challenges lies in achieving a unified and consistent encryption strategy across different cloud environments. Each CSP may have its own set of encryption services, key management practices, and nuances in implementation. This diversity demands a careful evaluation of the encryption capabilities of each cloud provider and the development of a cohesive strategy that aligns with organizational security policies.

Key management emerges as a central challenge when implementing encryption in a multi-cloud environment. With data dispersed across multiple CSPs, managing encryption keys in a secure and standardized manner becomes complex. Organizations need to establish a centralized key management approach that spans across cloud providers, ensuring consistent key generation, distribution, rotation, and revocation practices. The use of cloud-agnostic key management services or the integration of Hardware Security Modules (HSMs) can help organizations maintain control over encryption keys and enforce a uniform key management policy across diverse cloud environments.

Interoperability is another significant challenge in multi-cloud encryption. Cloud providers may offer proprietary encryption services, making it challenging to implement a solution that seamlessly integrates with multiple platforms. This challenge requires organizations to adopt encryption standards and protocols that are widely supported across different CSPs. Embracing industry-standard encryption algorithms, such as Advanced Encryption Standard (AES), and utilizing interoperable key exchange mechanisms, such as Key Management Interoperability Protocol (KMIP), fosters compatibility and facilitates a consistent encryption approach in a multi-cloud setting.

The dynamic nature of multi-cloud environments introduces challenges related to data movement and migration. Data may flow across different cloud platforms, and organizations must ensure that encryption remains effective during these transitions. Implementing encryption in a way that is agnostic to the physical location of data and remains intact during migration processes is essential. Solutions such as client-side encryption, where data is encrypted on the client's side before being transmitted to the cloud, can provide a level of data independence from the underlying cloud infrastructure, ensuring that encryption persists during data transfers between clouds.

Ensuring the security of data in a multi-cloud environment requires addressing the challenge of managing access controls and user identities consistently. Different CSPs may have distinct Identity and Access Management (IAM) systems, making it challenging to enforce uniform access policies across the multi-cloud ecosystem. Organizations must adopt strategies that centralize identity management and access controls, ensuring that users and applications have consistent and secure access to encrypted data, regardless of the cloud provider hosting the information. Federation services and identity management platforms that span multiple clouds can contribute to a cohesive and secure access control framework.

The regulatory landscape adds an additional layer of complexity to implementing encryption in multi-cloud scenarios. Different regions and industries have specific data protection and privacy regulations that organizations must adhere to. Ensuring compliance with these regulations while utilizing encryption across multiple clouds requires a thorough understanding of the legal and regulatory requirements in each jurisdiction. Organizations may need to customize their encryption implementations based on regional regulations, adopting a flexible yet compliant approach that aligns with diverse legal frameworks.

In the context of multi-cloud encryption, the challenge of auditing and monitoring becomes critical for maintaining visibility into security events and potential threats. Each CSP may provide its own set of logging and monitoring tools, and integrating these disparate sources of information into a centralized Security Information and Event Management (SIEM) system is essential. A unified approach to auditing enables organizations to detect anomalous activities, monitor key management events, and respond promptly to security incidents across the multi-cloud environment. Regularly reviewing logs and conducting comprehensive audits contribute to a proactive security posture.

The intricacies of multi-cloud encryption extend to the selection of encryption models that align with diverse use cases and requirements. Determining whether to implement encryption at the application layer, the database layer, or through the use of storage services depends on factors such as performance, data sensitivity, and the specific services offered by each cloud provider. Striking the right balance between security and operational efficiency becomes crucial in multi-cloud environments, where different applications and workloads may demand varied encryption strategies.

Addressing the challenge of secure collaboration and data sharing in a multi-cloud setting requires thoughtful implementation of encryption mechanisms. Organizations may need to share encrypted data across clouds while ensuring that authorized parties can access and decrypt the information. Implementing secure key exchange mechanisms, leveraging techniques like hybrid encryption, and establishing trust frameworks for cross-cloud collaboration contribute to secure data sharing practices in multi-cloud scenarios. Balancing the need for collaboration with the imperative of maintaining data confidentiality becomes pivotal in architecting effective multi-cloud encryption solutions.

A notable challenge in multi-cloud encryption involves the potential impact on performance and latency. Encrypting and decrypting data can introduce computational overhead, and organizations must carefully assess the trade-offs between security and performance. Adopting encryption models that align with the specific performance requirements of each application and workload helps strike a balance. Additionally, leveraging hardware-based encryption acceleration, when available, can mitigate the performance impact and ensure that encryption does not compromise the responsiveness of applications in a multi-cloud environment.

The emergence of quantum computing adds a layer of complexity to multi-cloud encryption strategies. Quantum computers have the potential to break widely used asymmetric encryption algorithms, necessitating a transition to quantum-resistant cryptographic approaches. Organizations operating in multi-cloud environments must plan for the long-term security of their encrypted data by adopting encryption algorithms that are resilient to quantum attacks. This forward-looking approach involves staying informed about developments in post-quantum cryptography and preparing for the eventual integration of

quantum-resistant encryption schemes into multi-cloud architectures.

A critical aspect of multi-cloud encryption involves preparing for incident response and recovery. Organizations must develop comprehensive incident response plans that account for security incidents occurring in any of the cloud environments. This includes scenarios such as key compromises, unauthorized access, or data breaches. Ensuring that incident response processes are tailored to the multi-cloud landscape, with clear communication and coordination across cloud providers, helps minimize the impact of security incidents and facilitates a swift recovery.

In conclusion, implementing encryption in multi-cloud scenarios requires organizations to navigate a complex landscape of challenges related to key management, interoperability, data movement, access controls, regulatory compliance, auditing, encryption models, collaboration, performance, quantum computing, and incident response. Addressing these challenges demands a holistic and strategic approach that considers the unique characteristics of each cloud environment while adhering to consistent and standardized encryption practices. The evolving nature of multi-cloud architectures and the dynamic cybersecurity landscape underscore the importance of continuous adaptation and a proactive stance toward security in the multi-cloud era. As organizations embrace the benefits of multi-cloud environments, the effective implementation of encryption becomes a cornerstone in safeguarding data, ensuring privacy, and maintaining the trustworthiness of digital assets across diverse cloud platforms.

Introduce the potential impact of quantum computing on traditional encryption methods.

The advent of quantum computing heralds a paradigm shift in the field of cryptography, posing unprecedented challenges to traditional encryption methods that have long served as the bedrock of digital security. Quantum computers leverage the principles of quantum mechanics to perform computations at speeds exponentially faster than classical computers, thereby threatening the security assumptions underlying widely-used cryptographic algorithms. One of the most prominent impacts of quantum computing on encryption lies in its potential to undermine asymmetric encryption algorithms, such as RSA and ECC, which rely on the difficulty of certain mathematical problems for their security.

The security of asymmetric encryption methods hinges on the mathematical complexity of tasks like factoring large integers or solving discrete logarithm problems, which classical computers find computationally infeasible within a reasonable timeframe. However, quantum computers, specifically those employing Shor's algorithm, have demonstrated the capability to solve these problems exponentially faster. This implies that the widely-deployed public-key cryptographic systems, where a pair of public and private keys are used for encryption and decryption, could be vulnerable to rapid decryption by a quantum adversary. The ramifications of this vulnerability extend across a spectrum of applications, from securing communication channels to protecting digital signatures and facilitating secure key exchanges.

In the realm of secure communication, the potential impact of quantum computing on traditional encryption methods is profound. Protocols like the Transport Layer Security (TLS), which rely on asymmetric encryption for key exchange and establishing secure communication channels, could face vulnerabilities in a post-quantum era. The confidentiality of data transmitted over the internet, safeguarded by protocols like HTTPS, could be compromised as quantum adversaries may decrypt intercepted communications retrospectively. The robustness of secure email communication, online banking transactions, and various e-commerce activities, all of which rely on public-key cryptography, could be fundamentally challenged, necessitating a paradigm shift in cryptographic strategies to address the quantum threat.

Digital signatures, a fundamental component of ensuring data integrity and authenticity, are also vulnerable to the disruptive power of quantum computing. Signature schemes based on the mathematical properties of elliptic curves, such as ECDSA (Elliptic Curve Digital Signature Algorithm), may be rendered obsolete by quantum adversaries capable of efficiently solving the underlying mathematical problems. The repercussions of compromised digital signatures extend across domains critical to digital trust, including authentication, non-repudiation, and the integrity of software updates. In a post-quantum landscape, reassessing and transitioning to quantum-resistant signature schemes becomes imperative to maintain the integrity of digital communications and transactions.

Quantum computing's impact on encryption is not confined to the compromise of specific algorithms; it extends to the very foundations of secure communication. The Diffie-Hellman key exchange, a cornerstone of secure key establishment in cryptographic protocols, is vulnerable to quantum attacks. Quantum computers can efficiently solve the discrete logarithm problem, undermining the security assurances provided by Diffie-Hellman-based key exchange mechanisms. Consequently, the confidentiality of symmetric encryption keys exchanged using protocols like TLS could be compromised, unraveling the security assurances that these protocols currently provide.

Post-quantum cryptography emerges as a field of study and development aiming to address the vulnerabilities introduced by quantum computing. Researchers are exploring cryptographic algorithms that remain secure even in the face of quantum adversaries. Lattice-based cryptography, hash-based cryptography, code-based cryptography, and multivariate polynomial cryptography are among the promising candidates for post-quantum cryptographic schemes. These approaches leverage mathematical problems that are believed to be hard for quantum computers to solve efficiently, offering a potential avenue for securing communication channels and data in the quantum era.

Lattice-based cryptography, in particular, has gained prominence as a leading contender for post-quantum security. The hardness of lattice problems, such as the Learning With Errors (LWE) problem, forms the basis of cryptographic schemes resistant to quantum attacks. Lattice-based cryptography offers a diverse set of cryptographic primitives, including encryption, digital signatures, and key exchange protocols, making it a versatile candidate for transitioning to a quantum-safe cryptographic infrastructure. The ongoing research and standardization efforts in the post-quantum cryptography community aim to provide viable alternatives to the cryptographic algorithms currently in use, facilitating a seamless transition to quantum-resistant security measures.

While the advent of quantum computing presents a formidable challenge to existing cryptographic paradigms, it also opens avenues for new cryptographic techniques that harness the unique properties of quantum mechanics. Quantum key distribution (QKD) is one such approach that leverages the principles of quantum superposition and entanglement to establish secure communication channels. QKD offers a theoretically secure method for key exchange, with the security guarantees rooted in the principles of quantum mechanics. As quantum computers threaten existing key exchange mechanisms, QKD represents a potential solution for achieving quantum-safe key distribution and preserving the confidentiality of symmetric encryption keys.

However, the practical implementation and widespread adoption of QKD face significant challenges, including the vulnerability of current QKD systems to certain types of quantum attacks and the need for specialized infrastructure. The feasibility of deploying QKD at scale in the context of existing communication networks remains an active area of research and development. Despite these challenges, QKD exemplifies the interdisciplinary nature of quantum cryptography, where advancements in quantum information science converge with the field of cryptography to chart new directions in securing digital communication.

The transition to quantum-resistant cryptographic systems requires a coordinated and proactive approach across various stakeholders, including standardization bodies, industry, and governmental entities. The National Institute of Standards and Technology (NIST) is playing a pivotal role in this transition by leading the Post-Quantum Cryptography Standardization project. The project involves the evaluation and standardization of candidate algorithms submitted by the cryptographic community, with the goal of establishing a set of quantum-resistant cryptographic standards for future use. NIST's efforts underscore the collaborative nature of addressing the quantum threat, emphasizing the need for a collective response to ensure the resilience of digital security in the quantum era.

In conclusion, the potential impact of quantum computing on traditional encryption methods transcends the realm of theoretical speculation, posing tangible threats to the security foundations that underpin digital communication and data protection. The vulnerabilities introduced by quantum computers to widely-used asymmetric encryption algorithms necessitate a strategic and collaborative response from the cybersecurity community. Post-quantum cryptography and quantum-resistant algorithms represent a beacon of hope in mitigating these vulnerabilities, offering the prospect of maintaining the confidentiality, integrity, and authenticity of digital information in the face of quantum advancements. As the quantum era unfolds, the resilience of cryptographic systems will be defined by the ability of researchers, industry leaders, and policymakers to navigate the complexities of quantum-resistant cryptography and secure the digital landscape for generations to come.

Explore how encryption aligns with regulatory requirements in various industries.

Encryption plays a crucial role in aligning with regulatory requirements across various industries, serving as a fundamental tool to safeguard sensitive information and maintain compliance with data protection standards. In the financial sector, for instance, regulations such as the Payment Card Industry Data Security Standard (PCI DSS) mandate the use of encryption to secure payment transactions and protect cardholder data. This ensures that financial institutions adhere to stringent security measures, reducing the risk of data breaches and unauthorized access.

Healthcare, another highly regulated industry, relies on encryption to uphold the Health Insurance Portability and Accountability Act (HIPAA). This legislation demands the protection of patients' electronic protected health information (ePHI), emphasizing the necessity of encryption to safeguard medical records, ensuring confidentiality and integrity. By encrypting data both in transit and at rest, healthcare organizations comply with HIPAA regulations, mitigating the potential impact of unauthorized access and data breaches.

In the realm of telecommunications, encryption aligns with regulations such as the Communications Assistance for Law Enforcement Act (CALEA). While CALEA focuses on enabling lawful interception of communication, encryption is vital to protecting the privacy of users and maintaining the security of communications. Striking a balance between regulatory compliance and user privacy, encryption in telecommunications ensures that sensitive information remains confidential while still allowing lawful authorities to access relevant data when required.

Government agencies globally recognize the importance of encryption in safeguarding national security and sensitive information. Various regulations, such as the Federal Risk and Authorization Management Program (FedRAMP) in the United States, mandate encryption as part of the cybersecurity requirements for cloud services used by government entities. Encryption becomes a critical component in securing classified information, communications, and critical infrastructure, aligning with the stringent security measures needed to protect against cyber threats.

In the legal sector, where confidentiality is paramount, encryption aligns with regulations and ethical standards that govern the protection of client-attorney privileged information. Legal professionals must adhere to guidelines that require the implementation of encryption to ensure the confidentiality and integrity of legal documents and communications. By doing so, legal entities comply with regulations, build trust with clients, and uphold the ethical principles of the legal profession.

The retail industry, which handles vast amounts of customer data and payment information, is subject to regulations like the General Data Protection Regulation (GDPR) in Europe and similar data protection laws globally. Encryption is a cornerstone for GDPR compliance, helping retailers protect the personal data of individuals and avoid hefty fines. By encrypting customer information and ensuring secure payment processes, retailers align with regulatory requirements, fostering consumer trust in an era of increasing concerns about data privacy.

In the education sector, where student records and sensitive information are prevalent, encryption aligns with regulations such as the Family Educational Rights and Privacy Act (FERPA) in the United States. FERPA mandates the protection of students' educational records, and encryption plays a pivotal role in securing this information. Educational institutions employ encryption to ensure the confidentiality of student data, aligning with FERPA requirements and creating a secure learning environment.

The energy and utilities sector, with its critical infrastructure, faces unique challenges in terms of cybersecurity and regulatory compliance. Regulations like the North American Electric Reliability Corporation Critical Infrastructure Protection (NERC CIP) standards mandate encryption to protect the grid's critical assets and sensitive information. Encryption helps mitigate the risk of cyber threats and unauthorized access, aligning with regulatory frameworks that prioritize the security of energy infrastructure.

In the evolving landscape of technology and digital services, the General Data Protection Regulation (GDPR) in Europe serves as a comprehensive framework governing data protection and privacy. Organizations across industries, irrespective of their geographical location, are compelled to adhere to GDPR standards when handling the personal data of EU residents. Encryption emerges as a central element in GDPR compliance, enabling organizations to protect personal data, uphold privacy rights, and avoid severe penalties.

In conclusion, encryption stands as a linchpin in aligning with regulatory requirements across diverse industries, playing a pivotal role in safeguarding sensitive information, ensuring data integrity, and mitigating the risks associated with unauthorized access and data breaches. As regulations continue to evolve to address the challenges of the digital age, the adoption of robust encryption measures becomes imperative for organizations seeking to navigate the complex landscape of compliance while upholding the highest standards of data security and privacy.

Emphasize the role of user awareness in maintaining the effectiveness of encryption.

User awareness is a critical factor in maintaining the effectiveness of encryption, serving as a frontline defense against potential security vulnerabilities and ensuring the proper implementation of encryption protocols. In the digital age, where individuals are integral participants in the exchange and protection of sensitive information, understanding the role and importance of encryption is paramount. Users need to be cognizant of the potential threats to their data and the security measures in place, fostering a proactive approach to cybersecurity.

Educating users about the basics of encryption is essential to demystify the technical aspects and promote a sense of responsibility. By grasping the concept that encryption transforms readable data into an unreadable format, users gain an appreciation for the security layers protecting their information. This awareness lays the foundation for individuals to comprehend the significance of encryption in safeguarding their personal and sensitive data from unauthorized access.

Furthermore, user awareness plays a pivotal role in ensuring the correct utilization of encryption tools and technologies. Users need to be well-versed in employing encryption features in communication platforms, email services, and other applications they regularly use. Understanding how to activate and manage encryption settings enhances the overall security posture, preventing unintentional data exposure and mitigating risks associated with human error.

In the context of password management, user awareness becomes a linchpin in fortifying encryption. Users must be educated on the importance of strong, unique passwords and the role they play in the encryption process. A weak password undermines the efficacy of encryption, as it becomes an easily penetrable gateway for cyber adversaries. Through awareness programs and training initiatives, users can adopt robust password practices, complementing the protective measures encryption affords.

Moreover, phishing attacks and social engineering exploits underscore the need for heightened user awareness. Individuals must be vigilant in recognizing phishing attempts that seek to compromise their credentials or deceive them into divulging sensitive information. Understanding the tactics employed by cybercriminals empowers users to discern malicious intent, reinforcing the encryption barriers that protect against unauthorized access and data breaches.

In the workplace, organizations must prioritize cybersecurity awareness training to instill a culture of responsibility among employees. This includes educating staff on the significance of encryption in protecting corporate assets, customer data, and intellectual property. An informed workforce becomes a formidable defense against insider threats, as employees understand their role in upholding encryption practices and maintaining the overall security posture of the organization.

Beyond the workplace, personal devices and the increasing trend of remote work introduce additional dimensions to user awareness. Individuals need to comprehend the importance of encrypting their devices, securing Wi-Fi connections, and implementing virtual private networks (VPNs) for secure communication. This extends the protective umbrella of encryption to the personal and professional spheres, creating a holistic approach to data security.

Additionally, user awareness is crucial in navigating the balance between convenience and security. While encryption provides robust protection, users must understand that convenience features like auto-fill and password-saving functionalities may introduce vulnerabilities. Educating users about the potential risks associated with these features enables them to make informed decisions, striking a balance that aligns with their security preferences and organizational policies.

As technology evolves, staying informed about emerging encryption standards and best practices is an ongoing responsibility for users. Whether it involves adopting the latest encryption algorithms or understanding the implications of quantum computing on current encryption methods, user awareness ensures that individuals remain proactive in adapting to evolving cybersecurity landscapes. Organizations should facilitate continuous education and awareness programs to keep users abreast of advancements and emerging threats, fostering a resilient defense against potential vulnerabilities.

The interconnected nature of digital ecosystems emphasizes the collective responsibility of users in maintaining the effectiveness of encryption. Whether through social media platforms, online banking, or email communications, individuals contribute to the broader cybersecurity landscape. Recognizing the shared responsibility in safeguarding digital assets fosters a sense of community awareness, where users actively participate in creating a secure online environment.

In conclusion, user awareness is indispensable in preserving the effectiveness of encryption as a foundational element of cybersecurity. Through education, training, and ongoing awareness initiatives, users become empowered stakeholders in the protection of their data and contribute to the overall resilience of digital ecosystems. As encryption continues to play a pivotal role in securing information in the digital age, the synergy between robust technical measures and an informed user base becomes paramount in addressing the dynamic challenges of cyberspace.

Chapter 4: Identity Management in the Cloud Era

Highlight the central role of identity management in cloud security.

Identity management stands as the linchpin in ensuring the security of cloud environments, playing a central role in safeguarding digital assets, data, and applications. As organizations increasingly transition to cloud-based infrastructures, the dynamic nature of these environments demands a robust and comprehensive approach to identity management. At its core, identity management in the cloud revolves around authenticating, authorizing, and managing the identities of users and entities accessing resources, regardless of their location or device. This process is foundational to establishing trust and controlling access, forming the backbone of cloud security protocols.

Authentication, the initial step in identity management, verifies the identity of users and devices seeking access to cloud resources. Cloud environments commonly employ multi-factor authentication (MFA) to enhance security, requiring users to provide multiple forms of identification such as passwords, biometrics, or security tokens. By implementing strong authentication measures, organizations fortify their defenses against unauthorized access and mitigate the risk of compromised credentials, a prevalent attack vector in the digital landscape.

Authorization, the subsequent facet of identity management, governs the permissions and privileges granted to authenticated users. Role-based access control (RBAC) is a prevalent authorization model in cloud security, assigning roles to users based on their responsibilities and restricting access accordingly. Effective authorization ensures that users have the appropriate level of access to perform their tasks while preventing unauthorized activities, thereby mitigating the potential for data breaches and unauthorized modifications.

Identity management also extends its reach to encompass the entire lifecycle of user identities, from onboarding to offboarding. Provisioning and de-provisioning mechanisms ensure that users gain timely access to the resources they need upon joining an organization and lose access promptly upon departure. Automating these processes enhances efficiency, reduces the risk of human error, and ensures compliance with security policies, maintaining a tight grip on access controls throughout an individual's tenure.

In the cloud, where scalability is a defining characteristic, identity management adapts to accommodate the fluid nature of resources and workloads. Identity as a Service (IDaaS) solutions emerges as a key enabler, providing cloud-based identity management services that facilitate secure access to applications and data from any location. This approach streamlines identity management processes, allowing organizations to scale their operations seamlessly while maintaining a centralized and standardized approach to security.

Furthermore, Single Sign-On (SSO) solutions contribute to the efficiency of identity management in the cloud. SSO enables users to access multiple applications with a single set of credentials, reducing the need for multiple logins and simplifying the user experience. This not only enhances productivity but also strengthens security by minimizing the chances of weak password practices, as users need to remember and manage fewer credentials.

As organizations embrace multi-cloud and hybrid cloud architectures, identity management becomes paramount in orchestrating secure interactions across diverse environments. Federation services facilitate seamless and secure authentication and authorization processes between different cloud platforms and on-premises systems. This interoperability ensures a cohesive identity management strategy, enabling organizations to leverage the benefits of varied cloud services without compromising on security.

Identity management plays a pivotal role in compliance adherence, especially in industries subject to stringent regulatory frameworks. Cloud security standards such as the Health Insurance Portability and Accountability Act (HIPAA) and the General Data Protection Regulation (GDPR) mandate robust identity management practices to protect sensitive data and ensure privacy. By aligning identity management protocols with regulatory requirements, organizations demonstrate their commitment to safeguarding information and mitigate the risk of legal consequences.

In the context of DevOps and continuous integration/continuous deployment (CI/CD) pipelines, identity management becomes integral to maintaining a secure software development lifecycle. By integrating identity management solutions with DevOps processes, organizations ensure that only authorized individuals and systems contribute to code repositories, access development environments, and deploy applications. This cohesive approach fosters a culture of security throughout the development lifecycle, minimizing vulnerabilities and enhancing overall resilience.

Identity management also addresses the evolving threat landscape by incorporating risk-based authentication. Analyzing contextual factors such as device type, geolocation, and user behavior allows organizations to adapt their authentication mechanisms dynamically. In the face of anomalous activities, the system can prompt for additional verification, providing an adaptive and proactive response to potential security threats. This risk-based approach enhances the effectiveness of identity management in identifying and mitigating security risks promptly.

Collaboration tools and cloud-based productivity suites have become integral to modern work environments. Identity management extends its influence to these collaboration platforms, ensuring secure and controlled access to communication and collaboration tools. By integrating identity management with collaboration platforms, organizations strike a balance between fostering collaborative work practices and maintaining stringent security measures, safeguarding sensitive information shared within these digital ecosystems.

The integration of artificial intelligence (AI) and machine learning (ML) technologies further augments the capabilities of identity management in the cloud. These technologies enable proactive threat detection by analyzing patterns of user behavior and identifying deviations that may indicate potential security risks. By leveraging AI and ML, identity management systems can adapt and respond to emerging threats, enhancing the overall resilience of cloud security postures.

In conclusion, identity management stands as the cornerstone of cloud security, orchestrating the complex dance of authentication, authorization, and lifecycle management in dynamic and interconnected cloud environments. As organizations navigate the complexities of digital transformation, the efficacy of their identity management practices determines the strength of their defense against cyber threats. By adopting a comprehensive and adaptive approach to identity management, organizations not only fortify their cloud security but also lay the groundwork for a resilient and scalable digital future.

Explain the concept of SSO and its benefits in cloud environments.

Single Sign-On (SSO) is a fundamental authentication and access management concept that streamlines user experiences and enhances security in cloud environments. At its core, SSO allows users to access multiple applications and services with a single set of credentials, eliminating the need to remember and manage numerous usernames and passwords for each application. This not only simplifies the user experience but also contributes significantly to security by reducing the likelihood of weak passwords and streamlining the management of access controls.

In the context of cloud environments, where organizations increasingly rely on a multitude of applications and services, SSO emerges as a key solution to address the complexities associated with user authentication. Cloud computing has transformed the way businesses operate, leading to the adoption of various cloud-based applications, platforms, and services. These may include communication tools, collaboration platforms, productivity suites, and specialized business applications, each requiring separate login credentials. SSO consolidates these authentication processes, providing users with seamless access to diverse resources using a unified set of credentials.

One of the primary benefits of SSO in cloud environments is the enhancement of user productivity. By eliminating the need to remember and enter multiple sets of credentials, SSO streamlines the login process, saving users time and reducing the frustration associated with managing numerous passwords. Users can seamlessly move between different applications and services without the interruption of repeated logins, fostering a more efficient and user-friendly experience. This improved productivity is particularly valuable in workplaces where individuals interact with a diverse array of cloud-based tools throughout their daily tasks.

Security is a paramount concern in any cloud environment, given the potential risks associated with unauthorized access and data breaches. SSO contributes to the overall security posture by minimizing the human factor in password management. Users, freed from the burden of remembering multiple passwords, are less likely to resort to weak or easily guessable credentials. Additionally, organizations can enforce stronger password policies and implement multi-factor authentication (MFA) more effectively when managing a unified authentication system through SSO. This, in turn, bolsters the security of cloud-based resources and protects sensitive data from unauthorized access.

The centralization of user authentication through SSO also facilitates more robust access control mechanisms. Administrators can efficiently manage and enforce user permissions, roles, and entitlements across various applications from a centralized identity management platform. This not only simplifies the task of access governance but also ensures that users have the appropriate levels of access based on their roles and responsibilities. The granular control afforded by SSO aids organizations in adhering to security best practices and regulatory compliance requirements, fostering a more secure and auditable environment.

As organizations increasingly adopt hybrid and multi-cloud architectures, SSO becomes a crucial component in ensuring a seamless and secure user experience across diverse cloud platforms. With SSO, users can navigate between on-premises and cloud-based applications without encountering authentication barriers. This interoperability is particularly beneficial for businesses leveraging a combination of public cloud services, private cloud infrastructure, and legacy systems. SSO solutions that support federation protocols enable organizations to establish trust relationships between identity providers and service providers, facilitating secure and standardized authentication across heterogeneous environments.

Furthermore, the adoption of mobile devices and the prevalence of remote work highlight the importance of SSO in providing secure and convenient access to cloud resources. Users accessing cloud applications from various devices, locations, and networks can benefit from the streamlined authentication process facilitated by SSO. This accessibility is essential for modern work environments, where flexibility and mobility are key considerations. SSO ensures that users can securely connect to cloud services without compromising on convenience, striking a balance between user experience and security.

The cost-effectiveness of SSO implementation in cloud environments is another compelling aspect. While there are upfront investments in deploying and integrating SSO solutions, the long-term benefits in terms of reduced helpdesk requests for password resets, increased user productivity, and enhanced security outweigh the initial costs. The efficiency gained through simplified authentication processes and centralized access management contributes to a more streamlined IT infrastructure, ultimately leading to cost savings and operational efficiencies.

Moreover, SSO aligns with the principles of Zero Trust security models by continuously verifying the identity of users and devices, regardless of their location or network. With SSO, organizations can implement adaptive authentication mechanisms that assess contextual factors, such as device type, geolocation, and user behavior, to dynamically adjust the level of authentication required. This risk-based approach enhances the security posture by detecting and responding to anomalous activities, minimizing the potential impact of security threats.

In conclusion, Single Sign-On is a foundational concept that plays a pivotal role in enhancing user experience and strengthening security in cloud environments. By simplifying the authentication process, centralizing access management, and promoting interoperability across diverse platforms, SSO addresses the complexities of modern IT landscapes. As organizations continue to embrace cloud computing, SSO stands as a valuable tool in optimizing productivity, fortifying security, and ensuring a seamless and secure user experience in the dynamic and interconnected world of cloud technology.

Explore the significance of MFA in enhancing identity verification.

Multi-Factor Authentication (MFA) stands as a critical and robust mechanism in enhancing identity verification across various digital platforms. As the digital landscape evolves, traditional username and password combinations have proven susceptible to breaches and unauthorized access. MFA addresses this vulnerability by introducing additional layers of verification beyond the conventional username and password, significantly bolstering the security of identity verification processes.

One of the primary strengths of MFA lies in its ability to provide an extra layer of defense against unauthorized access. By requiring users to provide multiple forms of identification, MFA mitigates the risks associated with compromised credentials, phishing attacks, and brute-force attempts. Even if an attacker manages to obtain a user's password, the additional authentication factors act as a formidable barrier, ensuring that unauthorized individuals are unable to gain access to sensitive accounts and information.

The effectiveness of MFA is particularly evident in the financial sector, where securing access to online banking and financial transactions is of paramount importance. Banking institutions widely implement MFA to safeguard customer accounts and prevent fraudulent activities. Users are often required to provide something they know (password), something they have (a mobile device or security token), and sometimes something they are (biometric data). This multifaceted approach significantly enhances the assurance of a user's identity, reducing the risk of financial fraud and unauthorized fund transfers.

Moreover, MFA plays a crucial role in protecting sensitive personal and corporate information. As organizations migrate to cloud-based services and adopt digital collaboration tools, the need for robust identity verification becomes increasingly vital. MFA adds an extra layer of security to cloud platforms, email services, and collaboration tools, ensuring that only authorized individuals with the correct credentials and additional authentication factors can access sensitive data. This is particularly relevant in industries handling confidential information, such as healthcare and legal sectors, where compliance with data protection regulations necessitates stringent identity verification measures.

In the realm of healthcare, where patient confidentiality is paramount, MFA becomes an indispensable tool. Electronic Health Records (EHRs) contain sensitive medical information, and unauthorized access can have severe consequences. MFA adds an extra layer of security to healthcare systems, requiring healthcare professionals and staff to provide multiple forms of identification before accessing patient records. This not only protects patient privacy but also aligns with healthcare regulations that mandate stringent security measures to safeguard electronic health information.

The use of MFA is also prevalent in government and defense sectors, where the protection of classified information and national security is paramount. Government agencies often implement MFA to secure access to sensitive databases, communication systems, and critical infrastructure. By requiring multiple authentication factors, MFA helps prevent unauthorized individuals, including malicious actors and foreign entities, from gaining access to classified information, ensuring the integrity and security of government operations.

MFA's significance extends to the education sector, where institutions manage vast amounts of student and faculty information. With the increasing adoption of online learning platforms and digital collaboration tools, protecting student records and educational resources becomes crucial. MFA adds an extra layer of security to educational systems, ensuring that only authorized users with the correct credentials and additional verification measures can access academic databases, learning management systems, and other sensitive information.

Additionally, the advent of remote work and the rise of Bring Your Own Device (BYOD) policies further underscore the importance of MFA in identity verification. As employees access corporate networks and sensitive data from various devices and locations, the risk of unauthorized access escalates. MFA acts as a powerful deterrent, preventing unauthorized individuals from exploiting weak or stolen passwords to gain entry. This is especially relevant in the current era, where the boundaries of the traditional office have expanded, and the security perimeter has become more fluid.

Biometric authentication, a common component of MFA, introduces a unique and personal aspect to identity verification. Biometric factors such as fingerprints, facial recognition, and iris scans provide a high level of assurance in confirming an individual's identity. The use of biometrics in MFA not only enhances security but also offers a convenient and user-friendly experience. As technology advances, biometric authentication becomes more sophisticated and reliable, further strengthening the overall efficacy of MFA in identity verification.

In the context of e-commerce and online transactions, where financial transactions and personal information are exchanged, MFA serves as a safeguard against fraudulent activities. Users are often required to provide additional verification, such as a one-time password (OTP) sent to their mobile device, to confirm their identity during online transactions. This adds an extra layer of security, protecting both consumers and businesses from unauthorized access, payment fraud, and identity theft.

The regulatory landscape also reinforces the significance of MFA in enhancing identity verification. Data protection regulations, such as the General Data Protection Regulation (GDPR) in Europe and the Health Insurance Portability and Accountability Act (HIPAA) in the United States, emphasize the importance of robust security measures to protect personal and sensitive information. MFA aligns with these regulatory requirements, providing organizations with a framework to implement strong identity verification processes and demonstrating a commitment to safeguarding user privacy.

As organizations increasingly adopt a Zero Trust security model, which assumes that threats may exist both outside and inside the network, MFA becomes a foundational element in enforcing this approach. Zero Trust principles advocate for continuous verification of user identities and devices, irrespective of their location or network. MFA, with its multifaceted authentication factors, aligns seamlessly with the Zero Trust philosophy, ensuring that access is granted only after rigorous and ongoing identity verification.

In conclusion, Multi-Factor Authentication (MFA) holds immense significance in enhancing identity verification across diverse sectors and digital platforms. Its multifaceted approach, combining something the user knows, something the user has, and sometimes something the user is, adds layers of security that are crucial in the face of evolving cyber threats. As organizations and individuals navigate an increasingly interconnected and digital world, the adoption of MFA emerges as a proactive and effective strategy to fortify identity verification processes, protect sensitive information, and mitigate the risks of unauthorized access and cyberattacks.

Discuss the challenges and solutions for identity federation in a multi-cloud environment.

Identity federation in a multi-cloud environment introduces a complex set of challenges that organizations must navigate to ensure seamless and secure access across diverse cloud platforms. One of the primary challenges stems from the heterogeneity of identity systems and protocols employed by different cloud service providers. Each cloud provider may have its own authentication and authorization mechanisms, making it challenging to establish a unified identity federation framework. This heterogeneity can lead to interoperability issues, making it difficult for organizations to implement a standardized and consistent approach to identity federation.

To address the challenge of varying identity protocols in a multi-cloud environment, organizations often adopt standards-based approaches such as Security Assertion Markup Language (SAML) or OpenID Connect. These protocols provide a common language for identity assertions, enabling interoperability across different cloud platforms. By implementing standardized protocols, organizations can establish a foundation for identity federation that facilitates the secure exchange of authentication and authorization information between different cloud providers.

Another challenge in identity federation within a multi-cloud environment is the need for a centralized and robust identity management system. In a multi-cloud scenario, users may need to access resources and applications across different cloud platforms, each with its own user directory and access policies. A centralized identity management system helps streamline user provisioning, de-provisioning, and access control, ensuring that users have consistent and secure access to resources across the multi-cloud landscape.

One solution to the challenge of decentralized identity management is the adoption of Identity as a Service (IDaaS) platforms. IDaaS platforms provide cloud-based identity management services, allowing organizations to centralize user identities and access policies. These platforms often offer features such as single sign-on (SSO), multi-factor authentication (MFA), and user provisioning, providing a comprehensive solution for identity federation in a multi-cloud environment. By leveraging IDaaS, organizations can simplify the management of user identities and enhance the overall security of their multi-cloud deployments.

Interoperability is a critical aspect of identity federation, and challenges arise when integrating on-premises identity systems with cloud-based ones. Many organizations maintain legacy identity infrastructure on-premises, and transitioning to a multi-cloud environment requires seamless integration with cloud-based identity systems. Compatibility issues, differences in authentication mechanisms, and data synchronization challenges can impede the smooth integration of on-premises and cloud-based identity systems.

To overcome interoperability challenges, organizations may implement identity federation gateways or brokers. These components act as intermediaries, translating authentication and authorization requests between on-premises and cloud-based identity systems. By introducing a federated identity layer, organizations can bridge the gap between different environments, ensuring that users can seamlessly authenticate and access resources regardless of their location or the underlying identity infrastructure.

The dynamic nature of cloud environments introduces challenges related to scalability and flexibility in identity federation. As organizations scale their operations or adopt new cloud services, the identity federation solution must be able to adapt and accommodate changes efficiently. Traditional identity federation models that rely on static trust relationships between identity providers and service providers may struggle to keep pace with the dynamic nature of multi-cloud environments.

To address scalability challenges, organizations are increasingly adopting decentralized and token-based approaches to identity federation. Technologies such as JSON Web Tokens (JWT) and OAuth 2.0 provide a lightweight and scalable framework for secure identity assertions. These token-based approaches allow for dynamic and fine-grained access control, enabling organizations to scale their identity federation solutions while maintaining flexibility in accommodating changes in the multi-cloud landscape.

Security and privacy concerns represent significant challenges in identity federation within a multi-cloud environment. The exchange of identity information across different cloud platforms introduces potential risks, including the exposure of sensitive user attributes and the possibility of unauthorized access. Ensuring the confidentiality, integrity, and privacy of identity information becomes paramount, especially when dealing with compliance requirements and regulations governing the protection of personal data.

To address security and privacy challenges, organizations must implement robust encryption mechanisms for the transmission and storage of identity information during the federation process. Additionally, the use of secure identity protocols, such as OAuth 2.0 and OpenID Connect, incorporates industry best practices for securing identity assertions. Regular security audits, monitoring, and compliance checks further enhance the overall security posture of identity federation in a multi-cloud environment, ensuring that sensitive information remains protected and regulatory requirements are met.

Compliance with regulatory frameworks represents a unique challenge in identity federation, as different regions and industries may have specific requirements regarding the handling of identity information. Multi-cloud environments often involve the processing and exchange of user data across geographic boundaries, necessitating adherence to data protection laws such as the General Data Protection Regulation (GDPR) in Europe or the Health Insurance Portability and Accountability Act (HIPAA) in the United States.

To navigate the complex landscape of regulatory compliance, organizations must implement identity federation solutions that provide granular control over data access and usage. Role-based access control (RBAC), fine-grained authorization policies, and audit trails help organizations demonstrate compliance with data protection regulations. Additionally, organizations may opt for identity federation solutions that offer jurisdiction-aware capabilities, allowing them to align with regional data protection requirements while ensuring seamless access for users across the multi-cloud environment.

In conclusion, identity federation in a multi-cloud environment presents multifaceted challenges that demand strategic planning and innovative solutions. Addressing issues related to varying identity protocols, decentralized identity management, interoperability, scalability, security, and regulatory compliance requires a holistic approach. By leveraging standardized protocols, adopting IDaaS platforms, implementing token-based approaches, addressing interoperability with gateways, ensuring robust security measures, and prioritizing regulatory compliance, organizations can establish a resilient identity federation framework that empowers users with secure and seamless access across diverse cloud platforms.

Explain the principles of RBAC and its application in cloud security.

Role-Based Access Control (RBAC) is a fundamental and widely adopted security model that governs access to resources based on users' roles within an organization. RBAC is grounded in the principle of granting permissions and privileges to users based on their assigned roles and responsibilities, rather than specifying access rights individually for each user. This approach simplifies access management, enhances security, and fosters a more scalable and manageable security framework. In the context of cloud security, RBAC becomes a cornerstone in orchestrating access controls across diverse cloud environments.

The key principle of RBAC is the notion of defining roles that correspond to specific job functions within an organization. Each role is associated with a set of permissions that delineate the actions a user with that role can perform. For instance, an organization might define roles such as "administrator," "developer," or "analyst," each equipped with distinct permissions aligned with the respective responsibilities of individuals in those roles. This abstraction enables organizations to structure access control in a way that mirrors their organizational hierarchy and operational workflows.

In cloud security, RBAC addresses the challenges of managing access to a myriad of resources and services across multiple cloud platforms. Cloud environments are characterized by their dynamic nature, with resources being provisioned, modified, and decommissioned dynamically. RBAC provides a scalable approach to access management in such dynamic environments by allowing organizations to define roles and associated permissions that align with the ever-evolving needs of users interacting with cloud resources.

RBAC is particularly advantageous in cloud environments where the adoption of Infrastructure as a Service (IaaS), Platform as a Service (PaaS), and Software as a Service (SaaS) models introduces a diverse array of resources and services. In an IaaS scenario, RBAC can be applied to control access to virtual machines, storage, and networking components. In a PaaS context, RBAC helps regulate access to development and deployment tools, databases, and application hosting services. For SaaS applications, RBAC ensures that users have appropriate access to functionalities and data within the cloud-based applications.

One of the key benefits of RBAC in cloud security is its ability to streamline access management by avoiding the intricacies of managing permissions for individual users. As organizations scale their cloud operations, managing access on a per-user basis becomes impractical and error-prone. RBAC provides a more systematic and efficient approach, where users are assigned roles based on their job functions, and permissions associated with those roles are consistently applied. This simplifies the onboarding and offboarding processes, ensuring that users are granted the necessary access when they join the organization and have their access promptly revoked when they depart.

Moreover, RBAC supports the principle of least privilege, a fundamental security concept advocating for granting users the minimum level of access required to perform their job functions. By assigning roles with specific permissions, RBAC aligns with the principle of least privilege, mitigating the risk of unauthorized access and limiting the potential impact of security incidents. This is particularly crucial in cloud environments where the shared responsibility model underscores the importance of organizations controlling access to their cloud resources.

RBAC also enhances the auditability and accountability of access controls in cloud environments. With roles clearly defining the permissions associated with specific job functions, organizations can readily audit who has access to what resources and services. This audit trail aids in compliance efforts, ensuring that organizations can demonstrate adherence to regulatory requirements and internal security policies. RBAC's transparency in access management contributes to robust security postures in cloud environments, fostering trust and accountability.

In multi-cloud and hybrid cloud architectures, where organizations leverage multiple cloud service providers or maintain a combination of on-premises and cloud resources, RBAC provides a consistent and standardized approach to access control. This is particularly valuable in environments where different cloud providers may have varying access management mechanisms. RBAC serves as a unifying framework, allowing organizations to define roles and associated permissions consistently across diverse cloud platforms, promoting interoperability and reducing complexity in access management.

To implement RBAC effectively in cloud security, organizations often leverage identity and access management (IAM) solutions that support RBAC principles. These IAM solutions provide the necessary infrastructure to define roles, associate permissions, and manage user access within the cloud environment. Cloud providers offer native IAM services that facilitate RBAC implementation, allowing organizations to create, modify, and revoke roles seamlessly. Additionally, third-party IAM solutions may offer extended capabilities and integration with other security tools, enhancing the overall effectiveness of RBAC in cloud security.

Challenges in RBAC implementation in cloud environments include the need for careful role design, regular reviews of access policies, and the complexity introduced by dynamic resource provisioning. Designing roles that accurately reflect job functions while adhering to the principle of least privilege requires a nuanced understanding of organizational workflows and potential security risks. Regular reviews and audits of access policies are essential to ensure that roles and permissions remain aligned with evolving organizational requirements and industry best practices.

In conclusion, RBAC is a foundational principle in cloud security that aligns access management with organizational structures and operational workflows. Its application in cloud environments provides a scalable, systematic, and transparent approach to access control. By defining roles and associated permissions, RBAC streamlines access management, enhances security postures, and contributes to the auditability and accountability of access controls. As organizations continue to embrace the agility and flexibility of cloud computing, RBAC stands as a key mechanism to ensure that users have appropriate access to cloud resources while maintaining the principles of security and compliance.

Discuss the importance of efficient user provisioning and de-provisioning processes.

Efficient user provisioning and de-provisioning processes are crucial components of identity and access management (IAM) systems, playing a pivotal role in ensuring the security, productivity, and compliance of organizations. User provisioning involves the creation and assignment of user accounts, along with associated access rights and permissions, when individuals join an organization or require access to new systems or resources. On the other hand, de-provisioning encompasses the systematic removal or modification of user accounts and access privileges when individuals leave the organization, change roles, or no longer require specific access. The importance of these processes extends across various facets of organizational operations, cybersecurity, and regulatory compliance.

One of the primary reasons for emphasizing efficient user provisioning is to enhance organizational productivity and agility. As businesses evolve and adapt to changing requirements, the ability to quickly and accurately provision user accounts and access privileges becomes a critical success factor. Efficient user provisioning ensures that new employees can swiftly access the tools and resources necessary to perform their roles, minimizing delays in onboarding processes. This agility is particularly crucial in dynamic industries where rapid response to market demands and changes in workforce composition is essential for maintaining competitiveness.

Furthermore, streamlined user provisioning contributes to improved user experiences within an organization. When individuals are granted timely access to the systems and applications they need, frustration is minimized, and productivity is maximized. Efficient provisioning processes also foster a positive onboarding experience for new employees, setting the tone for their engagement and satisfaction within the organization. This positive user experience, coupled with quick and hassle-free access to resources, promotes a collaborative and efficient work environment.

From a cybersecurity perspective, the importance of efficient user provisioning cannot be overstated. Delays or inaccuracies in setting up user accounts may result in security vulnerabilities, as employees may resort to workarounds or temporary solutions to access essential resources. Robust user provisioning processes help ensure that access rights are aligned with individuals' job responsibilities, reducing the likelihood of overprivileged accounts that could be exploited by malicious actors. It serves as a foundational element in enforcing the principle of least privilege, where individuals are granted only the minimum level of access necessary to perform their job functions, minimizing the attack surface.

Efficient user provisioning is particularly crucial in the context of cloud computing, where the dynamic and scalable nature of cloud environments requires organizations to adapt quickly to changing demands. Automated provisioning solutions and cloud-native identity management tools play a pivotal role in ensuring that users gain access to cloud resources seamlessly. This not only enhances the overall security of cloud deployments but also contributes to the optimization of resource utilization, cost management, and the scalability of cloud operations.

On the flip side, effective de-provisioning processes are equally essential in maintaining a robust security posture. When individuals leave an organization, change roles, or no longer require certain access rights, prompt and accurate de-provisioning is necessary to revoke their access privileges. Failure to de-provision accounts in a timely manner poses significant security risks, as former employees or individuals with outdated roles may retain access to sensitive information, systems, or applications. This represents a potential insider threat and exposes the organization to the risk of unauthorized access or data breaches.

Moreover, efficient de-provisioning is vital for compliance with regulatory requirements and industry standards. Many regulations, such as the Health Insurance Portability and Accountability Act (HIPAA) and the General Data Protection Regulation (GDPR), mandate organizations to implement robust processes for managing user access and ensuring that individuals have access only to the data and systems necessary for their roles. In the event of an audit or compliance check, organizations must be able to demonstrate that they have effective de-provisioning mechanisms in place to revoke access promptly when needed.

Timely de-provisioning also contributes to cost management and resource optimization. When user accounts are deactivated promptly upon departure or role changes, organizations can avoid unnecessary licensing costs, reduce the risk of inactive accounts being exploited, and ensure that resources are allocated efficiently. From a broader operational standpoint, efficient de-provisioning aligns with the principles of good governance and risk management, reducing the attack surface, and mitigating potential security incidents associated with unauthorized access.

Automation plays a critical role in enhancing the efficiency of both user provisioning and de-provisioning processes. Automated provisioning ensures consistency and accuracy by systematically applying access policies based on predefined rules and role assignments. It reduces the likelihood of human errors and accelerates the onboarding of new employees or the provisioning of access to additional resources. Similarly, automated de-provisioning helps organizations enforce timely account terminations and access revocations, mitigating the risks associated with human delays or oversights in the de-provisioning workflow.

The significance of efficient user provisioning and de-provisioning processes becomes even more pronounced in the context of remote work and the increasing reliance on cloud-based services. In distributed work environments, where employees may access corporate resources from various locations and devices, the need for agile and secure access management is heightened. Efficient IAM processes, including user provisioning and de-provisioning, contribute to a seamless and secure remote work experience, ensuring that individuals have the appropriate access regardless of their physical location.

In conclusion, efficient user provisioning and de-provisioning processes are integral to organizational productivity, cybersecurity, and regulatory compliance. These processes not only enable organizations to respond quickly to changes in workforce composition and operational requirements but also contribute to a positive user experience. With the evolving landscape of work environments, the role of automated provisioning and de-provisioning becomes increasingly critical, providing organizations with the tools needed to maintain security, optimize resource utilization, and ensure compliance in a dynamic and interconnected digital landscape.

Explore how identity governance ensures compliance with security policies.

Identity governance plays a paramount role in ensuring compliance with security policies within organizations. It encompasses a comprehensive set of processes, policies, and technologies that facilitate the management of user identities, their access rights, and the enforcement of security policies governing those access rights. As organizations grapple with evolving regulatory landscapes, increased cyber threats, and the complexity of modern IT environments, identity governance emerges as a linchpin for maintaining a secure and compliant infrastructure.

A core aspect of identity governance revolves around identity lifecycle management, encompassing user onboarding, changes, and offboarding. During the onboarding phase, identity governance ensures that individuals receive the appropriate access rights and permissions necessary to perform their job functions. This process aligns with the principle of least privilege, granting users the minimum access required for their roles, thus minimizing potential security risks. Identity governance provides a structured framework for defining and enforcing access policies during the onboarding process, ensuring that security policies are embedded in the identity provisioning workflow.

In the context of compliance, identity governance addresses the imperative to adhere to industry-specific regulations, international data protection laws, and internal security policies. For instance, regulatory frameworks such as the General Data Protection Regulation

(GDPR) and the Health Insurance Portability and Accountability Act (HIPAA) mandate stringent controls over the access and handling of personal and sensitive information. Identity governance ensures that access to such data is governed by well-defined policies, and organizations can demonstrate compliance through robust reporting and auditing mechanisms. These mechanisms, integral to identity governance platforms, provide transparency into user access, changes, and activities, offering organizations the means to validate adherence to regulatory requirements.

A fundamental component of identity governance is the implementation of access controls and entitlement management. By defining and enforcing access policies based on job roles, responsibilities, and business processes, identity governance ensures that users have the necessary permissions to carry out their duties. This aligns with the concept of role-based access control (RBAC), where users are assigned roles with specific access rights, streamlining the access management process and reducing the risk of unauthorized access. Through identity governance, organizations can regularly review and recertify access entitlements, addressing the dynamic nature of business operations and ensuring that access policies remain up-to-date and compliant.

Effective identity governance incorporates automated workflows for access request and approval processes. This streamlines the access provisioning process, accelerates response times to access requests, and enforces consistent approval mechanisms. By automating these workflows, identity governance not only improves operational efficiency but also mitigates the risk of human errors and deviations from security policies. Additionally, automated access request and approval workflows contribute to compliance by providing a traceable and auditable record of access decisions, demonstrating adherence to security policies and regulatory requirements.

Identity governance also addresses the critical aspect of privileged access management (PAM). Privileged accounts, often targeted by cyber attackers, require heightened security measures to prevent unauthorized access and potential misuse. Identity governance incorporates PAM into its framework by defining and managing policies around privileged access. This includes monitoring and auditing privileged user activities, ensuring that privileged access is granted only when necessary, and implementing just-in-time access to minimize the exposure of privileged credentials. By integrating PAM into identity governance, organizations bolster their security postures, meet compliance requirements, and mitigate the risk of insider threats.

A noteworthy contribution of identity governance to compliance is the establishment of continuous monitoring and risk assessment mechanisms. Identity governance platforms often incorporate analytics and risk-based approaches to evaluate user behavior, access patterns, and deviations from established security policies. This proactive monitoring allows organizations to detect and respond to potential security threats promptly. By continuously assessing risks and adjusting access controls dynamically, identity governance not only enhances security but also ensures a responsive and adaptive compliance framework that aligns with the evolving threat landscape.

Furthermore, identity governance facilitates audit and reporting capabilities that are essential for compliance assessments and regulatory audits. Detailed reports on user access, changes, and activities enable organizations to provide evidence of adherence to security policies and regulatory requirements. Compliance audits often necessitate the ability to trace and document access permissions, modifications, and reviews. Identity governance platforms offer centralized and comprehensive reporting, aiding organizations in demonstrating their commitment to compliance and providing the necessary documentation to regulatory bodies.

In the realm of cloud computing and hybrid IT environments, identity governance extends its reach to cover the complexities associated with diverse platforms and services. As organizations leverage cloud-based applications, infrastructure, and services, identity governance ensures a consistent and unified approach to access management. This is particularly crucial in multi-cloud environments, where each cloud service may have its own identity and access management mechanisms. Identity governance integrates these disparate systems, offering a centralized view of user identities, access policies, and compliance status across the entire hybrid IT landscape.

The principles of identity governance align seamlessly with the Zero Trust security model, a paradigm that assumes no inherent trust and requires continuous verification of user identities and devices. Identity governance supports the implementation of Zero Trust by enforcing rigorous access controls, continuous monitoring, and risk-based assessments. This approach enhances security by minimizing the potential for unauthorized access, lateral movement within networks, and the impact of security incidents. In doing so, identity governance contributes not only to compliance but also to the establishment of a robust and adaptive security posture.

Challenges in identity governance and compliance often arise from the dynamic nature of modern organizations, where employees change roles, projects, and responsibilities frequently. Effective identity governance solutions must account for these changes, ensuring that access rights evolve accordingly and that users retain only the access necessary for their current roles. Additionally, organizations must grapple with the integration of identity governance across various systems, applications, and cloud platforms, necessitating interoperability and standardized approaches to access management.

In conclusion, identity governance serves as a linchpin for ensuring compliance with security policies in the complex and dynamic landscape of modern organizations. By incorporating principles such as access controls, entitlement management, continuous monitoring, and risk assessment, identity governance provides a robust framework that aligns with regulatory requirements, industry standards, and internal security policies. The integration of identity governance into the broader context of IAM not only enhances security postures but also contributes to the efficiency of access management processes. As organizations navigate the challenges of a digital and interconnected world, identity governance stands as a critical enabler for achieving and sustaining compliance with evolving security policies.

Explore the use of biometric authentication as an additional layer of identity verification.

Biometric authentication has emerged as a cutting-edge and secure method for verifying individuals' identities, adding a robust layer to conventional authentication mechanisms. Unlike traditional methods relying on passwords or PINs, biometric authentication leverages unique biological or behavioral characteristics, such as fingerprints, facial features, iris patterns, voiceprints, or even behavioral traits like keystroke dynamics. This approach not only enhances security but also offers a more user-friendly and seamless experience. As the digital landscape evolves, incorporating biometric authentication as an additional layer of identity verification addresses the limitations of traditional methods and fortifies the overall security posture.

One of the key advantages of biometric authentication lies in its inherent uniqueness and difficulty to replicate. Each individual possesses distinct biometric features that are difficult to forge or duplicate, providing a high level of certainty in verifying identity. For example, fingerprints, with their intricate ridges and patterns, are highly unique to each person. This distinctiveness makes it significantly challenging for unauthorized individuals to gain access by mimicking or impersonating someone else's biometric traits. As a result, biometric authentication serves as a potent deterrent against identity theft, a prevalent concern in the digital era.

Fingerprint recognition stands out as one of the most widely adopted forms of biometric authentication. The ridges and valleys on an individual's fingertips create a unique pattern that remains constant over time. Mobile devices, laptops, and even some payment cards now integrate fingerprint sensors, allowing users to unlock their devices, authorize transactions, or access sensitive information with a simple touch. This seamless integration into everyday devices enhances user convenience while bolstering security, as the likelihood of someone else having the same fingerprint is exceedingly low.

Facial recognition represents another prominent and increasingly prevalent form of biometric authentication. Leveraging advanced algorithms and artificial intelligence, facial recognition systems analyze the unique features of a person's face, such as the arrangement of eyes, nose, and mouth. Apple's Face ID and various security surveillance systems exemplify the widespread adoption of facial recognition technology. The non-intrusive nature of facial recognition, where users simply need to look at a device's camera, aligns with the growing demand for frictionless and user-friendly authentication methods.

Iris recognition, though less common than fingerprints or facial recognition, offers a highly accurate and secure biometric authentication method. The unique patterns in the iris, the colored part of the eye, are stable throughout an individual's life and provide a distinctive identifier. This form of biometric authentication is employed in high-security environments, such as government facilities and certain access control systems. While less prevalent in consumer devices, iris recognition exemplifies the versatility of biometrics in catering to various security needs.

Voice recognition represents a behavioral biometric authentication method, relying on the distinctive vocal characteristics of an individual. Factors such as pitch, tone, cadence, and even speech patterns contribute to the uniqueness of an individual's voiceprint. Voice recognition finds applications in phone-based authentication systems, virtual assistants, and customer service interactions. As with other biometric methods, the advantage lies in the difficulty of replicating an individual's voice accurately, enhancing the security of voice-based authentication.

Keystroke dynamics, a lesser-known but intriguing form of behavioral biometrics, involves analyzing the way individuals type on keyboards. Each person exhibits a unique typing rhythm, speed, and pressure, forming a behavioral pattern that can be used for identity verification. While not as widely adopted as fingerprint or facial recognition, keystroke dynamics can add an extra layer of security in scenarios where continuous user authentication is desirable, such as during online sessions or access to sensitive systems.

One of the notable benefits of incorporating biometric authentication is its potential to reduce reliance on passwords, which are susceptible to various security risks such as theft, hacking, or social engineering. Biometrics offer a more secure and convenient alternative, alleviating the need for users to remember complex passwords or frequently change them. The human factor in password-based authentication introduces vulnerabilities, as individuals often choose weak passwords, reuse them across multiple accounts, or fall victim to phishing attacks. Biometric authentication addresses these vulnerabilities by providing a unique and inherent means of verifying identity, mitigating the risks associated with password-based systems.

Biometric authentication's integration into mobile devices has become particularly prominent, exemplifying its widespread adoption and acceptance. Smartphones equipped with fingerprint sensors, facial recognition cameras, or even iris scanners have become ubiquitous, demonstrating the consumer appetite for convenient yet secure authentication methods. Mobile biometric authentication not only secures access to personal devices but also serves as a catalyst for broader applications, including mobile payments, secure app access, and the protection of sensitive data stored on mobile platforms.

In the financial sector, biometric authentication has gained traction as a means to enhance the security of transactions and account access. Biometrics provide an additional layer of identity verification, reducing the risk of fraudulent activities such as unauthorized fund transfers or identity theft. Financial institutions leverage biometrics, especially fingerprints and facial recognition, to authenticate users during mobile banking transactions or when accessing online banking platforms. This not only enhances security but also aligns with regulatory requirements for robust customer authentication in the financial industry.

The healthcare sector has also embraced biometric authentication to secure access to electronic health records (EHRs) and sensitive patient information. Healthcare professionals often use fingerprint or iris recognition to authenticate themselves before accessing patient records or medical systems. Biometric authentication in healthcare aligns with the Health Insurance Portability and Accountability Act (HIPAA) requirements for safeguarding patient information and ensures that only authorized personnel can access sensitive medical data.

The integration of biometric authentication into government initiatives has further underscored its significance in enhancing security and identity verification. Biometrics play a crucial role in national identity programs, border control systems, and secure access to government facilities. Countries worldwide have implemented biometric identification methods, such as fingerprint or facial recognition, in passports and national identity cards to strengthen border security and prevent identity fraud. The use of biometrics in government applications demonstrates its reliability in large-scale identity verification scenarios.

While the adoption of biometric authentication introduces numerous benefits, it is not without challenges and considerations. Privacy concerns represent a significant consideration, as biometric data is inherently sensitive and unique to individuals. The storage and protection of biometric information raise ethical and legal questions, necessitating robust security measures and compliance with data protection regulations. Striking a balance between enhanced security and safeguarding individuals' privacy is crucial for fostering trust in biometric authentication systems.

Another challenge lies in the potential vulnerabilities of biometric systems to spoofing or presentation attacks. Techniques such as using high-quality photos, 3D-printed masks, or deepfake videos pose risks to facial recognition systems. Similarly, fingerprint sensors may be susceptible to lifted prints or artificial replicas. Continuous advancements in biometric technology, including liveness detection and anti-spoofing measures, aim to address these concerns by ensuring that the biometric samples presented for authentication are from live and genuine sources.

In conclusion, the integration of biometric authentication as an additional layer of identity verification represents a paradigm shift in the way individuals authenticate and interact with digital systems. Its unique advantages, including inherent uniqueness, convenience, and resistance to traditional authentication vulnerabilities, make it a compelling choice in the evolving landscape of digital security. As biometric technology continues to advance and gain acceptance across various sectors, its role in enhancing security, user experience, and identity verification processes is poised to become even more prominent. While challenges such as privacy considerations and potential spoofing attacks persist, ongoing research and development in the field aim to address these issues, ensuring that biometric authentication remains a key enabler of secure and user-friendly digital interactions.

Address common challenges and pitfalls in cloud identity management.

Cloud identity management, while offering numerous benefits such as scalability, flexibility, and accessibility, introduces a set of common challenges and pitfalls that organizations must navigate to ensure a secure and efficient environment. One of the primary challenges is the complexity associated with managing identities across diverse cloud services and platforms. In a multi-cloud or hybrid cloud environment, organizations often leverage various cloud providers, each with its own identity and access management mechanisms. The lack of standardized protocols and interoperability among these systems can result in a fragmented identity landscape, making it challenging to enforce consistent access policies and maintain a unified view of user identities.

Interoperability challenges extend to the integration of cloud identity management with on-premises identity systems. Many organizations maintain legacy identity infrastructure on-premises, and the migration to cloud-based services necessitates seamless integration with existing identity systems. Compatibility issues, differences in authentication mechanisms, and data synchronization challenges can impede the smooth integration of on-premises and cloud-based identity systems, leading to inconsistencies and potential security gaps in identity management.

The dynamic nature of cloud environments introduces challenges related to scalability and adaptability in identity management. As organizations scale their operations or adopt new cloud services, the identity management solution must be able to adapt and accommodate changes efficiently. Traditional identity management models that rely on static configurations and trust relationships may struggle to keep pace with the dynamic nature of cloud environments, leading to delays in provisioning, de-provisioning, and access management.

Security and privacy concerns represent significant challenges in cloud identity management. The exchange of identity information across different cloud platforms introduces potential risks, including the exposure of sensitive user attributes and the possibility of unauthorized access. Ensuring the confidentiality, integrity, and privacy of identity information becomes paramount, especially when dealing with compliance requirements and regulations governing the protection of personal data. The use of secure identity protocols, encryption mechanisms, and regular security audits becomes essential to mitigate the risks associated with unauthorized access and data breaches.

One of the common pitfalls in cloud identity management is the mismanagement of user identities during the onboarding and offboarding processes. In the onboarding phase, organizations may face challenges in accurately provisioning user accounts and assigning appropriate access rights. Delays or inaccuracies in this process can lead to users lacking the necessary permissions to perform their job functions, hampering productivity and potentially causing frustration. On the other hand, the offboarding process, which involves de-provisioning user accounts and revoking access, poses the risk of overlooking terminated or departing employees, resulting in lingering access and potential security vulnerabilities.

Identity and access sprawl is another challenge in cloud identity management, particularly in environments where users have access to a multitude of cloud services and applications. Without proper governance and oversight, organizations may struggle to manage the proliferation of user accounts and permissions, leading to a lack of visibility and control over who has access to what resources. This identity sprawl can contribute to compliance violations, increase the attack surface, and create challenges in auditing and monitoring user activities across the cloud ecosystem.

The complexity of role management in cloud environments adds to the challenges organizations face in identity management. Cloud services often offer a wide array of granular permissions, and defining and managing roles in a way that aligns with organizational structures and compliance requirements can be intricate. Inconsistent role definitions, overly permissive roles, or difficulties in keeping roles up-to-date with evolving business needs can lead to security risks and compliance issues. Striking a balance between providing users with the necessary access and adhering to the principle of least privilege becomes a delicate task in the cloud identity management landscape.

Password-related challenges persist in cloud identity management, despite efforts to move towards more secure authentication methods. Users may still resort to weak passwords, reuse passwords across multiple services, or fall victim to phishing attacks. Additionally, enforcing strong password policies and ensuring regular password rotations can become cumbersome for administrators, impacting the overall security of cloud identities. The reliance on passwords as a primary authentication factor introduces vulnerabilities, necessitating a shift towards multifactor authentication (MFA) and other advanced authentication methods to enhance security.

Effective monitoring and auditing of user activities pose challenges in cloud identity management. In a dynamic and distributed cloud environment, tracking user actions, detecting anomalous behavior, and generating comprehensive audit logs become complex tasks. The lack of centralized visibility into user activities across various cloud services can hinder organizations in promptly identifying and responding to security incidents or policy violations. Establishing robust monitoring and auditing capabilities requires careful planning, the integration of security information and event management (SIEM) solutions, and the implementation of continuous monitoring practices.

Compliance with regulatory frameworks represents a unique challenge in cloud identity management, as different regions and industries may have specific requirements regarding the handling of identity information. Multi-cloud environments often involve the processing and exchange of user data across geographic boundaries, necessitating adherence to data protection laws such as the General Data Protection Regulation (GDPR) in Europe or the Health Insurance Portability and Accountability Act (HIPAA) in the United States. Ensuring that cloud identity management practices align with regional and industry-specific regulations requires a comprehensive understanding of legal requirements and the implementation of robust governance and control measures.

In conclusion, addressing the common challenges and pitfalls in cloud identity management demands a holistic approach that combines technological solutions, standardized processes, and proactive governance. Organizations must strive for interoperability among diverse cloud platforms, implement scalable and adaptive identity management solutions, prioritize security and privacy measures, and carefully manage the entire identity lifecycle. By focusing on effective onboarding and offboarding processes, mitigating identity and access sprawl, refining role management strategies, addressing password-related vulnerabilities, enhancing monitoring and auditing capabilities, and ensuring compliance with regulatory frameworks, organizations can navigate the complexities of cloud identity management and establish a secure and resilient identity infrastructure in the cloud.

Discuss emerging trends and technologies in cloud identity management.

Emerging trends and technologies in cloud identity management are reshaping the landscape of digital authentication, access control, and security. One notable trend is the increasing adoption of Zero Trust security models. Zero Trust challenges the traditional notion of trusting entities based on their location within a network, advocating for continuous verification of users and devices regardless of their location or network proximity. This paradigm shift aligns closely with the dynamic and distributed nature of cloud environments, where users access resources from various locations and devices. By implementing Zero Trust principles, organizations enhance their overall security postures, mitigating the risks associated with unauthorized access and insider threats.

Multifactor authentication (MFA) has become a cornerstone in cloud identity management, providing an additional layer of security beyond traditional username and password combinations. While MFA is not a new concept, its adoption has gained momentum as organizations recognize the limitations of password-based authentication. Emerging technologies in MFA include biometric authentication, contextual authentication, and adaptive authentication. Biometric methods, such as fingerprint recognition, facial recognition, and iris scanning, offer a more secure and user-friendly alternative to passwords. Contextual authentication considers various factors, such as the user's location, device, and behavior, to assess the risk level and adjust authentication requirements accordingly. Adaptive authentication dynamically adjusts the level of authentication based on real-time risk assessments, allowing organizations to balance security and user experience.

Blockchain technology is making inroads into cloud identity management, addressing challenges related to identity verification, data privacy, and decentralized identity. Blockchain's decentralized and tamper-resistant nature provides a secure foundation for managing digital identities. Users can control their identities through self-sovereign identity (SSI) solutions built on blockchain, allowing them to share only necessary information with service providers without compromising their privacy. Blockchain also facilitates secure and auditable identity verification processes, reducing the reliance on central authorities for identity validation. The integration of blockchain in cloud identity management holds the promise of enhancing security, transparency, and user control over personal data.

Another noteworthy trend is the convergence of identity and access management (IAM) with privileged access management (PAM). Traditionally treated as separate domains, IAM focuses on managing user identities and access, while PAM addresses the security of privileged accounts and credentials. The merging of IAM and PAM streamlines access management processes, offering a unified approach to governing both regular user access and privileged access. This convergence ensures consistent policies, improves visibility into access controls, and enhances the overall security posture by applying robust identity management principles to privileged accounts.

Continuous authentication is gaining prominence as a proactive approach to identity management. Traditional authentication methods often rely on a one-time validation during the login process. Continuous authentication, in contrast, continuously monitors user activities and behavior throughout a session, dynamically adjusting access controls based on risk assessments. This approach helps detect anomalous behavior, unauthorized access, or account takeover attempts in real-time. Continuous authentication aligns with the dynamic and evolving nature of cloud environments, where users' activities and access patterns may change rapidly, requiring adaptive security measures.

Identity as a Service (IDaaS) has emerged as a prominent trend, offering cloud-based solutions for identity management. IDaaS provides organizations with scalable and flexible identity management services without the need for extensive on-premises infrastructure. These services typically include authentication, authorization, user provisioning, and single sign-on (SSO) capabilities delivered through a cloud-based platform. IDaaS solutions simplify the deployment and management of identity services, catering to the needs of organizations seeking agility, cost-effectiveness, and rapid scalability in their identity management practices.

Machine learning and artificial intelligence (AI) are playing an increasingly significant role in cloud identity management. These technologies enhance the capabilities of authentication systems by analyzing vast amounts of data to detect patterns, anomalies, and potential security threats. AI-driven authentication solutions can adapt to changing user behaviors, identify suspicious activities, and trigger additional authentication measures when necessary. Machine learning algorithms also contribute to risk-based authentication, where the level of authentication is dynamically adjusted based on the perceived risk level, providing a balance between security and user convenience.

The concept of decentralized identity, often associated with blockchain, is gaining traction as a means to empower individuals with greater control over their digital identities. Decentralized identity solutions enable users to own and manage their identity information, eliminating the need for centralized identity providers. Users can selectively share specific attributes or credentials with service providers, enhancing privacy and reducing the reliance on a single, centralized authority for identity verification. Decentralized identity aligns with the principles of self-sovereign identity, where individuals have autonomy and control over how their digital identities are utilized across various online interactions.

Identity orchestration is emerging as a trend that focuses on streamlining the complexities of managing identity and access across diverse environments. With organizations increasingly adopting multi-cloud and hybrid cloud architectures, identity orchestration provides a centralized approach to defining, enforcing, and monitoring access policies. This trend involves the integration of various identity management components, including authentication, authorization, and policy enforcement, into a unified and orchestrated framework. Identity orchestration aims to simplify the management of identities across complex and distributed IT landscapes, ensuring consistency and adherence to security policies.

Privacy-enhancing technologies are gaining prominence in cloud identity management, addressing concerns related to the collection, storage, and processing of personal data. Privacy-preserving authentication methods, such as zero-knowledge proofs and homomorphic encryption, enable organizations to authenticate users without exposing sensitive information. These technologies contribute to the protection of user privacy while ensuring the necessary level of identity verification. As privacy regulations become more stringent, integrating privacy-enhancing technologies into identity management practices becomes essential for organizations seeking to comply with data protection requirements.

In conclusion, the evolving landscape of cloud identity management is shaped by several emerging trends and technologies that prioritize security, privacy, and adaptability. From the adoption of Zero Trust and multifactor authentication to the integration of blockchain, AI, and decentralized identity, organizations are leveraging innovative approaches to enhance the effectiveness and resilience of their identity management practices. Continuous authentication, the convergence of IAM and PAM, IDaaS solutions, and the use of machine learning further contribute to a dynamic and future-ready identity management ecosystem. As organizations continue to navigate the complexities of the digital landscape, staying abreast of these emerging trends and technologies in cloud identity management becomes imperative for fostering robust, user-centric, and secure identity practices.

Chapter 5: Securing Cloud Applications: Best Practices

Define the unique challenges and considerations in securing cloud-based applications.

Securing cloud-based applications presents a distinctive set of challenges and considerations that require a comprehensive and adaptive approach to address the complexities introduced by the dynamic nature of cloud environments. One of the primary challenges is the shared responsibility model inherent in cloud computing. While cloud service providers (CSPs) manage the security of the cloud infrastructure, customers are responsible for securing their applications and data within the cloud. This division of responsibilities necessitates a clear understanding of the security measures provided by the CSP and the customer's obligations in configuring, managing, and monitoring the security of their cloud-based applications.

The dynamic and scalable nature of cloud environments introduces challenges related to asset visibility and control. Traditional security measures, designed for static and on-premises environments, may struggle to keep pace with the rapid provisioning, de-provisioning, and scaling of resources in the cloud. Ensuring continuous visibility into the application landscape, identifying unauthorized changes, and maintaining control over access rights become intricate tasks. Adopting cloud-native security solutions that provide real-time visibility, automated asset discovery, and dynamic access controls helps organizations overcome these challenges and adapt to the agility of cloud-based applications.

Identity and access management (IAM) emerge as critical considerations in securing cloud-based applications, given the increased complexity of user interactions, access patterns, and the diversity of cloud services. Managing user identities, enforcing access controls, and ensuring the principle of least privilege require robust IAM strategies. Challenges arise in defining and maintaining consistent access policies across multiple cloud services, platforms, and environments. Integrating IAM solutions that support single sign-on (SSO), multifactor authentication (MFA), and role-based access control (RBAC) helps organizations streamline access management and mitigate the risks associated with unauthorized access or privilege escalation.

Data protection becomes a paramount concern in cloud-based applications, particularly in light of regulatory requirements and privacy concerns. The shared nature of cloud infrastructure introduces the need for robust encryption mechanisms to protect sensitive data both in transit and at rest. Challenges include selecting appropriate encryption methods, managing encryption keys securely, and ensuring compliance with data protection regulations such as the General Data Protection Regulation (GDPR) or the Health Insurance Portability and Accountability Act (HIPAA). Implementing data loss prevention (DLP) solutions, encryption protocols, and regular security audits helps organizations maintain the confidentiality and integrity of their data in cloud environments.

The increased reliance on application programming interfaces (APIs) in cloud-based architectures introduces security challenges related to API exposure, authentication, and authorization. APIs serve as the communication channels between different components of cloud applications, and their security is paramount in preventing unauthorized access and data breaches. Challenges include inadequate authentication mechanisms, improper handling of sensitive data in API calls, and the potential for API vulnerabilities. Implementing robust API security measures, such as proper authentication protocols, access controls, and regular security assessments, helps organizations fortify their cloud-based applications against API-related risks.

Network security considerations in cloud-based applications differ significantly from traditional on-premises environments. Cloud environments leverage virtualized networks, software-defined networking (SDN), and diverse connectivity options, introducing challenges in ensuring secure communication between application components. The dynamic nature of cloud-based networks requires organizations to adapt to changes in network configurations, maintain effective segmentation, and implement security controls to protect against network-based attacks. Deploying network security solutions, leveraging virtual private clouds (VPCs), and implementing network monitoring tools contribute to establishing a resilient network security posture in cloud environments.

The concept of shared tenancy, where multiple tenants share the same underlying infrastructure in a cloud environment, introduces challenges in achieving isolation between different applications and tenants. While CSPs implement robust measures to ensure logical separation, customers must consider the potential for side-channel attacks, shared resource vulnerabilities, and the impact of neighboring tenants on application performance and security. Implementing secure coding practices, conducting thorough vulnerability assessments, and leveraging containerization technologies contribute to enhancing isolation and security within cloud-based applications.

As organizations embrace DevOps practices and leverage continuous integration/continuous deployment (CI/CD) pipelines in cloud environments, the integration of security into the development lifecycle becomes crucial. The traditional approach of bolting on security measures after development may lead to delays, overlook vulnerabilities, and hinder the agility of cloud-based application development. Challenges include balancing speed and security, integrating security testing tools into CI/CD pipelines, and fostering a culture of collaboration between development and security teams. Implementing DevSecOps practices, where security is integrated throughout the development lifecycle, helps organizations proactively address security concerns and deliver secure and resilient cloud-based applications.

Visibility and monitoring in cloud environments pose challenges due to the distributed nature of resources, the variety of cloud services, and the sheer volume of data generated. Traditional monitoring tools designed for on-premises environments may not provide the required insights into the performance and security of cloud-based applications. Challenges include correlating and analyzing logs from diverse cloud services, detecting and responding to security incidents in real-time, and ensuring compliance with regulatory requirements for monitoring and auditing. Adopting cloud-native monitoring solutions, implementing security information and event management (SIEM) systems, and leveraging artificial intelligence (AI) for anomaly detection contribute to establishing effective visibility and monitoring in cloud environments.

The rapid evolution of cloud-based technologies introduces challenges related to staying abreast of security best practices, emerging threats, and evolving compliance requirements. Security teams must continuously update their skills, adapt security policies, and monitor industry developments to effectively secure cloud-based applications. Challenges include the need for ongoing training, understanding the unique security features offered by different CSPs, and aligning security practices with industry standards and regulations. Engaging in continuous education, participating in industry forums, and fostering a culture of continuous improvement within the security team help organizations navigate the dynamic landscape of cloud security.

Supply chain security represents an emerging consideration in the context of cloud-based applications. Organizations often rely on third-party vendors and services to enhance the functionality and features of their cloud applications. However, this reliance introduces challenges in assessing and ensuring the security posture of third-party components, APIs, and integrations. Challenges include vetting the security practices of external providers, managing the security of open-source components, and monitoring for vulnerabilities introduced by third-party dependencies. Implementing robust vendor risk management processes, conducting security assessments of external components, and maintaining visibility into the supply chain contribute to mitigating supply chain-related security risks in cloud-based applications.

In conclusion, securing cloud-based applications demands a holistic and adaptive approach that considers the unique challenges posed by the shared responsibility model, dynamic environments, diverse cloud services, and emerging technologies. Organizations must prioritize identity and access management, data protection, API security, network security, isolation, DevSecOps practices, visibility, and supply chain security to establish a comprehensive security posture. Addressing these considerations helps organizations navigate the complexities of securing cloud-based applications effectively, ensuring resilience, compliance, and protection against evolving cyber threats.

Explore the principles of incorporating security into the development process.

Incorporating security into the development process is a fundamental principle that aligns with the evolving landscape of software development, emphasizing proactive measures to identify and mitigate security risks throughout the entire development lifecycle. Adopting a security-first mindset requires integrating security practices seamlessly into each stage of the development process, from planning and design to coding, testing, deployment, and maintenance. This approach, commonly known as DevSecOps, represents a paradigm shift from traditional software development, where security considerations were often addressed as an afterthought or during the later stages of the development cycle.

The principles of incorporating security into the development process start with fostering a culture of collaboration between development, operations, and security teams. This collaborative approach breaks down silos and encourages cross-functional communication, ensuring that security considerations are not isolated to a particular phase but are woven into the fabric of the entire development lifecycle. By promoting a shared responsibility for security across teams, organizations create an environment where security is seen as an integral part of delivering high-quality software, rather than a hindrance to development speed.

In the planning phase, security considerations begin with threat modeling and risk assessments. Understanding the potential threats and vulnerabilities that may impact the application allows development teams to make informed decisions about the security controls and measures needed. Threat modeling involves identifying potential attack vectors, analyzing the impact of security weaknesses, and prioritizing mitigation strategies. By integrating threat modeling into the planning process, organizations can make risk-informed decisions, allocate resources efficiently, and set the foundation for a secure development process.

The design phase focuses on incorporating security features and controls into the architecture of the application. Security design principles, such as the principle of least privilege, defense in depth, and fail-safe defaults, guide the development of resilient and secure systems. Adopting secure coding practices and leveraging security libraries or frameworks specific to the programming language contribute to building a robust security foundation. Designing security controls at this stage ensures that security is not an add-on but an integral part of the application's structure, preventing vulnerabilities that may arise from poorly designed architectures.

As developers move to the coding phase, secure coding practices become imperative. This involves adhering to coding standards, avoiding common vulnerabilities such as injection attacks, ensuring input validation, and utilizing secure coding techniques. Automated code analysis tools and static code analysis play a crucial role in identifying security vulnerabilities during the coding phase. Continuous integration (CI) pipelines can be configured to run security scans automatically, providing real-time feedback to developers and enabling the early detection and remediation of security issues.

The testing phase is a critical juncture for validating the security posture of the application. Security testing encompasses various approaches, including static analysis, dynamic analysis, penetration testing, and security scanning. Static analysis examines the source code for vulnerabilities, dynamic analysis involves testing the application in runtime, and penetration testing simulates real-world attacks to identify potential weaknesses. Automated security testing tools integrated into the CI/CD pipeline enable developers to identify and address security issues rapidly, fostering a continuous feedback loop that aligns with the principles of agility and iterative development.

Continuous monitoring represents a key principle in the post-deployment phase, ensuring that the application's security is actively assessed in production environments. Monitoring tools, security information and event management (SIEM) systems, and log analysis contribute to detecting and responding to security incidents in real-time. Anomaly detection and behavior analysis help identify suspicious activities, potential breaches, or deviations from normal behavior. Continuous monitoring aligns with the principle of ongoing improvement, allowing organizations to adapt and respond to emerging threats and vulnerabilities throughout the application's lifecycle.

The principle of automation plays a pivotal role in incorporating security into the development process. Automation enables the consistent application of security controls, reduces the risk of human error, and accelerates the identification and remediation of security vulnerabilities. Automated security testing, code analysis, and deployment pipelines ensure that security measures are seamlessly integrated into the development workflow, aligning with the principles of agility and efficiency. Continuous integration and continuous deployment (CI/CD) pipelines, coupled with automated security checks, enable organizations to deliver secure software at a rapid pace without compromising on quality.

Education and training constitute a foundational principle in incorporating security into the development process. Developers and team members need to be equipped with the knowledge and skills necessary to identify and address security issues. Security awareness training, secure coding courses, and knowledge sharing sessions foster a culture of continuous learning, empowering development teams to make informed security decisions. Investing in the education of development teams aligns with the principle of building a security-conscious culture, where security is everyone's responsibility, not just the domain of dedicated security professionals.

Integrating security into the development process also requires a commitment to compliance with industry standards, regulations, and best practices. Understanding the specific security requirements relevant to the application's domain helps organizations establish a baseline for security controls. Compliance with standards such as the Payment Card Industry Data Security Standard (PCI DSS), Health Insurance Portability and Accountability Act (HIPAA), or General Data Protection Regulation (GDPR) ensures that the application meets the necessary security and privacy requirements. Aligning with compliance standards is a fundamental principle that reflects a commitment to governance, risk management, and adherence to industry-recognized security practices.

The principle of feedback and continuous improvement emphasizes the importance of learning from security incidents, vulnerabilities, and evolving threat landscapes. Organizations should establish mechanisms for collecting feedback from security incidents, post-mortem analyses, and lessons learned sessions. This feedback loop informs the refinement of security policies, the adjustment of security controls, and the enhancement of security awareness training. A culture of continuous improvement ensures that the development process remains adaptive to changing security challenges and fosters resilience against emerging threats.

Communication and transparency constitute integral principles in incorporating security into the development process. Open and transparent communication channels between development, operations, and security teams facilitate the sharing of security insights, challenges, and solutions. Regular security meetings, collaborative threat modeling sessions, and cross-functional collaboration contribute to breaking down communication barriers and ensuring that security considerations are woven into the fabric of the development process. Transparency fosters a shared understanding of security goals, risks, and priorities among team members, aligning with the principles of collaboration and shared responsibility.

In conclusion, incorporating security into the development process is not merely a set of practices but a set of principles that guide the entire lifecycle of software development. From planning and design to coding, testing, deployment, and maintenance, these principles emphasize collaboration, proactive risk management, education, compliance, and a commitment to continuous improvement. DevSecOps, as a cultural and procedural shift, encapsulates these principles, ensuring that security is not an impediment to development but an integral and seamless part of the process. As organizations embrace these principles, they establish a foundation for building secure, resilient, and high-quality software in today's dynamic and evolving threat landscape.

Explain the importance of securing application programming interfaces (APIs).

The importance of securing Application Programming Interfaces (APIs) has become increasingly critical in the digital era, as APIs serve as the connective tissue of modern software architectures, facilitating seamless communication and interaction between diverse applications, services, and systems. APIs play a pivotal role in enabling the interoperability of software components, allowing them to share data and functionality. However, this interconnectedness also introduces a myriad of security challenges, making the robust protection of APIs imperative for the overall security posture of applications and the broader digital ecosystem.

One primary facet of the importance of securing APIs lies in their role as gateways to sensitive data and business logic. APIs often expose access to valuable resources, databases, and functionalities that power various applications and services. Inadvertent exposure or exploitation of inadequately secured APIs can lead to unauthorized access, data breaches, and compromise of critical business information. Consequently, organizations must implement robust authentication and authorization mechanisms to ensure that only authorized users or systems can access and interact with APIs, mitigating the risk of unauthorized data access or manipulation.

The ubiquity of APIs in modern software development introduces a significant attack surface that malicious actors can exploit. API endpoints, often exposed over the internet, are susceptible to a range of security threats, including injection attacks, cross-site scripting (XSS), and cross-site request forgery (CSRF). Securing APIs requires implementing input validation, proper sanitization of user input, and adherence to secure coding practices to thwart these common web application vulnerabilities. Failure to address these threats may expose APIs to exploitation, leading to potential data breaches, service disruptions, and compromise of user privacy.

The importance of securing APIs is further underscored by the rise of mobile and cloud computing. Mobile applications frequently rely on APIs to retrieve data and deliver dynamic content, while cloud services leverage APIs for seamless integration with third-party applications. In these scenarios, APIs become the linchpin of functionality, making them attractive targets for attackers seeking to compromise mobile apps, cloud services, or the underlying infrastructure. Security measures such as encryption, secure communication protocols, and thorough API security assessments are essential to safeguard against potential threats in these dynamic computing environments.

The increasing adoption of microservices architecture amplifies the significance of API security. Microservices, by design, encourage the decomposition of complex applications into smaller, independently deployable services that communicate via APIs. While this architectural approach enhances scalability and agility, it also necessitates robust API security measures to mitigate the risks associated with inter-service communication. Protecting APIs within a microservices architecture involves implementing authentication, authorization, and encryption at each communication point, ensuring that the compromise of one service does not lead to cascading vulnerabilities across the entire application landscape.

Securing APIs is crucial for safeguarding sensitive user data, especially in applications that involve user authentication and authorization. Many applications, including those in the realms of finance, healthcare, and e-commerce, rely on APIs to manage user accounts, process transactions, and access sensitive information. Inadequate security measures, such as weak authentication mechanisms or insufficient data encryption, can expose users to identity theft, financial fraud, or unauthorized access to personal health information. Consequently, API security becomes integral to protecting the privacy and trust of users, forming a foundational component of compliance with data protection regulations.

The importance of securing APIs extends beyond traditional web applications to include the Internet of Things (IoT) ecosystem. IoT devices often communicate with cloud services or other devices through APIs, creating a network of interconnected endpoints. Insecure APIs in IoT environments pose significant risks, allowing attackers to manipulate device functionalities, compromise privacy, or even gain unauthorized access to critical infrastructure. Implementing API security measures tailored to the unique characteristics of IoT, such as device authentication, secure communication protocols, and integrity checks, is essential for ensuring the resilience and safety of IoT ecosystems.

API security is paramount in the context of third-party integrations and partnerships. Many applications leverage third-party APIs to extend functionality, integrate with external services, or enhance user experience. However, integrating external APIs introduces potential risks, as organizations may have limited control over the security practices of third-party providers. Verifying the security posture of third-party APIs, enforcing strict access controls, and implementing measures such as rate limiting and data validation become critical to prevent security vulnerabilities arising from external integrations.

The importance of securing APIs in the context of business ecosystems cannot be overstated. APIs serve as the foundation for digital business strategies, enabling organizations to collaborate, share data, and create innovative services. However, this interconnectivity introduces the risk of supply chain attacks, where a compromise in one part of the ecosystem can propagate across interconnected APIs. Implementing secure coding practices, conducting thorough security assessments, and fostering a culture of shared responsibility among ecosystem participants are essential to mitigate the potential impact of supply chain vulnerabilities.

The financial implications of API security breaches accentuate the need for organizations to prioritize API security measures. A security incident involving APIs can result in significant financial losses, including the costs associated with incident response, remediation, legal consequences, and reputational damage. The loss of customer trust and confidence can have far-reaching consequences, impacting customer retention, market share, and overall business viability. Investing in robust API security measures becomes not only a security imperative but also a prudent financial decision to safeguard organizational assets and maintain stakeholder trust.

Securing APIs aligns with broader regulatory requirements and compliance standards governing data protection and privacy. As governments and regulatory bodies enact stringent laws such as the General Data Protection Regulation (GDPR), the California Consumer Privacy Act (CCPA), and others, organizations must ensure that their APIs adhere to the specified data protection principles. API security measures, including data encryption, user consent mechanisms, and audit trails, play a crucial role in demonstrating compliance with these regulations. Failure to secure APIs may result in legal repercussions, fines, and damage to an organization's reputation.

The growing sophistication of cyber threats and the evolving tactics employed by attackers underscore the dynamic nature of the cybersecurity landscape. Securing APIs requires organizations to adopt a proactive stance, staying ahead of emerging threats through continuous monitoring, threat intelligence integration, and timely security updates. The importance of incorporating security into the development lifecycle of APIs, from design to deployment and maintenance, cannot be overstated. Regular security assessments, penetration testing, and adherence to industry best practices contribute to building resilient APIs that can withstand the evolving threat landscape.

In conclusion, securing Application Programming Interfaces (APIs) is of paramount importance in the contemporary digital landscape, where interconnectedness and data sharing drive innovation but also introduce significant security challenges. APIs serve as the linchpin of modern software development, enabling the seamless integration of applications, services, and systems. The importance of securing APIs lies in safeguarding sensitive data, protecting against cyber threats, ensuring compliance with regulations, and preserving user trust. By implementing robust authentication, authorization, encryption, and monitoring measures, organizations can fortify their APIs against potential vulnerabilities and contribute to a secure and resilient digital ecosystem.

Explore the security challenges associated with containerized applications.

The adoption of containerized applications, facilitated by technologies like Docker and Kubernetes, has revolutionized software development and deployment, offering scalability, portability, and efficiency. However, this paradigm shift towards containerization also introduces a myriad of security challenges that organizations must address to ensure the robust protection of their applications and data.

One of the primary security challenges associated with containerized applications lies in the shared kernel architecture. Containers within the same host share the underlying kernel, which can potentially lead to security vulnerabilities if not adequately isolated. A compromised container may exploit shared resources to compromise other containers or the host itself. Implementing strong isolation mechanisms, such as container runtimes with enhanced security features and leveraging technologies like SELinux or AppArmor, becomes crucial to mitigate the risks associated with shared kernel vulnerabilities.

The dynamic and ephemeral nature of containers poses challenges in maintaining visibility and control over containerized environments. Containers can be rapidly instantiated, moved, and terminated, making it challenging for traditional security tools to provide comprehensive monitoring and threat detection. This lack of visibility may result in delayed detection of security incidents or unauthorized activities within containerized environments. Adopting container-aware security solutions, integrating logging and monitoring tools designed for containerized applications, and implementing continuous monitoring practices are essential to overcome these challenges and enhance the security posture of containerized environments.

Container images, the building blocks of containerized applications, introduce security challenges related to their composition and provenance. Using insecure or untrusted base images, neglecting image scanning for vulnerabilities, or including unnecessary components in images can expose applications to various risks. Ensuring the integrity and security of container images requires implementing secure image-building practices, regularly scanning images for vulnerabilities, and establishing policies for image verification and signing. By addressing these challenges, organizations can minimize the risk of deploying containerized applications with compromised or vulnerable components.

Container orchestration platforms, such as Kubernetes, introduce their own set of security challenges. Misconfigurations in Kubernetes clusters can lead to unauthorized access, privilege escalation, or exposure of sensitive data. The complexity of Kubernetes configurations and the lack of proper access controls may result in security gaps that attackers can exploit. Organizations need to adopt security best practices for Kubernetes, conduct regular audits of cluster configurations, and enforce strong access controls to mitigate the security risks associated with container orchestration.

Network security within containerized environments poses unique challenges due to the highly dynamic and interconnected nature of containers. Traditional network security measures may struggle to adapt to the rapid creation and deletion of containers, leading to challenges in enforcing network segmentation and isolation. Implementing container-native network security solutions, utilizing network policies to control traffic between containers, and leveraging technologies like container firewalls help organizations address the challenges associated with securing the network within containerized environments.

The use of microservices architecture, often coupled with containerization, introduces challenges related to inter-service communication security. Microservices rely on APIs and network communication to interact with each other, making it essential to secure these communication channels. Inadequate authentication, lack of encryption, or insufficient access controls in microservices communication can expose sensitive data to interception or manipulation. Implementing strong authentication mechanisms, encrypting inter-service communication, and enforcing proper access controls contribute to securing the communication pathways within microservices-based containerized applications.

Container runtime security is a critical aspect of securing containerized applications, as it involves protecting the runtime environment where containers execute. Runtime security challenges include the potential for privilege escalation within containers, unauthorized access to host resources, and exploitation of runtime vulnerabilities. Employing container runtimes with security features like user namespaces, seccomp, and secure computing modes helps mitigate the risks associated with container runtime security. Regularly updating container runtimes, monitoring for runtime anomalies, and leveraging runtime security solutions contribute to maintaining a secure runtime environment for containerized applications.

The management of secrets and sensitive data within containers poses significant security challenges. Containers often require access to credentials, API keys, or other sensitive information to interact with external services or databases. Storing and managing these secrets securely is crucial to prevent unauthorized access or misuse. Adopting secure container orchestration platforms that provide robust secret management capabilities, utilizing external secret management tools, and implementing encryption mechanisms for sensitive data within containers help organizations address the challenges associated with securing secrets in containerized environments.

The integration of security into the continuous integration and continuous deployment (CI/CD) pipeline for containerized applications is essential but comes with its own set of challenges. Automated workflows may introduce vulnerabilities if not properly configured, and the rapid pace of deployment in CI/CD pipelines may result in security oversights. Implementing security checks at each stage of the CI/CD pipeline, incorporating vulnerability scanning into the build process, and automating security testing help organizations address the challenges associated with integrating security seamlessly into the containerized application development lifecycle.

The presence of container escape vulnerabilities, where an attacker gains unauthorized access to the host system from within a container, poses a severe risk to containerized environments. Exploiting such vulnerabilities allows attackers to compromise the entire host and potentially other containers running on the same system. Employing host OS hardening measures, keeping the host system updated, and leveraging container runtime security features contribute to preventing and mitigating the risks associated with container escape vulnerabilities.

The lack of proper identity and access management for containers can lead to security challenges related to unauthorized access and privilege escalation. Containers often run with elevated privileges, and misconfigurations may expose unnecessary permissions. Implementing strong identity management practices, enforcing the principle of least privilege, and leveraging technologies like role-based access control (RBAC) contribute to addressing the challenges associated with identity and access management in containerized environments.

Compliance with regulatory requirements and industry standards poses challenges in the context of containerized applications. Meeting compliance standards such as the Payment Card Industry Data Security Standard (PCI DSS), Health Insurance Portability and Accountability Act (HIPAA), or General Data Protection Regulation (GDPR) requires organizations to ensure that their containerized environments adhere to specific security and privacy controls. Adopting container security solutions that provide compliance checks, conducting regular audits, and documenting security controls contribute to addressing the challenges associated with achieving and maintaining compliance in containerized environments.

The complexity of orchestrating and managing a large number of containers in production introduces challenges related to scaling security measures effectively. Traditional security practices may struggle to keep pace with the dynamic nature of containerized environments, resulting in difficulties in maintaining consistent security policies across a large number of containers. Leveraging automation for security policy enforcement, utilizing container security platforms that offer centralized management, and implementing declarative security policies contribute to overcoming the challenges associated with scaling security in containerized environments.

In conclusion, while containerization offers numerous benefits in terms of agility, scalability, and efficiency, it also introduces a complex array of security challenges that organizations must navigate. From shared kernel vulnerabilities to container runtime security, network security, and compliance considerations, addressing these challenges requires a holistic and proactive approach to container security. By adopting best practices, leveraging container-native security solutions, and integrating security seamlessly into the containerized application development lifecycle, organizations can build a resilient security posture that aligns with the dynamic nature of modern containerized environments.

Discuss the security implications of serverless computing.

Serverless computing, a paradigm that abstracts server management and allows developers to focus on writing code without the need to provision or manage servers, introduces a unique set of security implications and considerations that organizations must address to ensure the robust protection of their applications and data. While serverless computing offers advantages in terms of scalability, cost efficiency, and rapid deployment, understanding and mitigating the associated security risks is imperative for organizations embracing this paradigm.

One fundamental security consideration in serverless computing is the shared responsibility model inherent in cloud environments. While cloud service providers (CSPs) manage the underlying infrastructure, security responsibilities shift to the application layer for serverless applications. This shared responsibility model necessitates a clear understanding of the security measures provided by the CSP and the developer's obligations in terms of securing the application code, dependencies, and configurations. Organizations need to implement secure coding practices, conduct regular security assessments, and stay informed about the security features and updates provided by the chosen serverless platform.

The ephemeral nature of serverless functions, which are short-lived and stateless, poses challenges in terms of maintaining persistent security controls. Traditional security measures designed for long-running servers may not seamlessly adapt to the serverless model. Ensuring the continuity of security controls, such as encryption, access controls, and logging, requires thoughtful design and implementation within the serverless architecture. Organizations need to integrate security into the development lifecycle, leveraging automation for consistent security policy enforcement and ensuring that security controls persist across transient serverless instances.

Authentication and authorization are critical security considerations in serverless computing, particularly given the event-driven nature of serverless applications. Functions triggered by events must have proper authentication mechanisms in place to ensure that only authorized entities can invoke them. Additionally, fine-grained access controls are essential to prevent unauthorized access to sensitive data or functions within the serverless environment. Implementing robust identity and access management (IAM) policies, leveraging federated identities, and incorporating strong authentication mechanisms contribute to mitigating the security risks associated with unauthorized access to serverless functions.

The secure deployment and management of dependencies in serverless computing present distinct challenges. Serverless applications often rely on external dependencies, such as libraries or third-party services, which may introduce security vulnerabilities or pose risks if not carefully managed. Organizations need to conduct thorough security assessments of dependencies, prioritize the use of trusted and well-maintained libraries, and monitor for security updates or vulnerabilities in external services. Implementing containerization or serverless container platforms, when applicable, can offer additional control over dependencies and enhance the security posture of serverless applications.

Serverless applications may leverage cloud-native storage solutions, introducing security considerations related to data protection and privacy. Organizations must implement robust encryption mechanisms to protect sensitive data both in transit and at rest. Additionally, access controls and proper configuration of storage services are crucial to prevent unauthorized access or data exposure. Compliance with data protection regulations, such as the General Data Protection Regulation (GDPR) or the Health Insurance Portability and Accountability Act (HIPAA), requires organizations to adopt a comprehensive approach to data security within the serverless paradigm.

The inherent multitenancy of serverless computing introduces challenges related to isolation and potential security risks arising from shared resources. Serverless functions may share the same underlying infrastructure, and vulnerabilities in one function could potentially impact others. Implementing strong isolation mechanisms, leveraging containerization or function-level security controls, and staying informed about the security practices of the chosen serverless provider contribute to mitigating the risks associated with multitenancy in serverless computing.

The monitoring and logging capabilities in serverless computing are vital for detecting and responding to security incidents. Given the event-driven nature of serverless applications, organizations must implement comprehensive logging practices, capturing relevant information about function invocations, errors, and potential security events. Integrating serverless-compatible monitoring and logging tools, utilizing cloud-native logging services, and establishing alerting mechanisms contribute to building effective incident response capabilities within serverless environments.

Serverless computing introduces the challenge of securing the deployment pipeline, especially in continuous integration and continuous deployment (CI/CD) workflows. The automation and rapid deployment inherent in serverless architectures require organizations to implement security checks at each stage of the CI/CD pipeline. Integrating security testing tools, conducting vulnerability assessments, and enforcing security policies in the automated deployment process help organizations identify and remediate security issues before they reach production. The principles of DevSecOps, where security is integrated into the development and deployment lifecycle, are particularly relevant in serverless computing to ensure a proactive approach to security.

Another security consideration in serverless computing is the potential for function sprawl, where a large number of functions may be deployed without proper oversight or management. Each function represents a potential attack surface, and an excessive number of functions may increase the attack vector. Organizations need to establish clear policies for function deployment, conduct regular reviews to identify and decommission unnecessary functions, and enforce naming conventions and tagging for better management and visibility. Controlling function sprawl contributes to a more manageable and secure serverless environment.

The cold start problem in serverless computing, where there may be a delay in the initial invocation of a function, poses security challenges related to performance and resource allocation. Cold starts may affect the responsiveness of security measures, such as authentication or access controls, during the initial execution of a function. Organizations must consider the implications of cold starts on security and implement measures to mitigate potential delays in the enforcement of security controls. This may include optimizing function initialization times, pre-warming functions in anticipation of traffic spikes, or implementing strategies to ensure security measures are effective even during cold starts.

Serverless applications may rely on third-party services or APIs, introducing security considerations related to the integration and communication with external entities. Organizations need to ensure the secure configuration of API connections, validate the security practices of third-party services, and implement proper authentication and authorization mechanisms for external integrations. The compromise of external services or APIs could impact the security of the entire serverless application, making it essential for organizations to conduct due diligence on the security practices of external dependencies.

Compliance with regulatory requirements remains a significant consideration in serverless computing, especially for organizations operating in regulated industries. Ensuring that serverless applications adhere to industry-specific regulations and standards requires a thorough understanding of the security controls and practices necessary for compliance. Organizations need to conduct regular audits, implement controls for data protection and privacy, and document security measures to demonstrate compliance with applicable regulations.

In conclusion, while serverless computing offers numerous benefits in terms of efficiency, scalability, and cost-effectiveness, organizations must navigate a complex landscape of security considerations to ensure the robust protection of their applications and data. From shared responsibility models to ephemeral function instances, authentication, data protection, and compliance considerations, addressing these security implications demands a holistic and proactive approach. By integrating security into the development lifecycle, adopting serverless-compatible security tools, and staying informed about best practices, organizations can harness the advantages of serverless computing while effectively mitigating the associated security risks.

Explain the role of WAF in protecting web applications from common vulnerabilities.

Web Application Firewalls (WAFs) play a crucial role in safeguarding web applications by acting as a protective barrier between the applications and potential cyber threats. In the ever-evolving landscape of cybersecurity, web applications are prime targets for various malicious activities, and WAFs serve as a frontline defense mechanism, mitigating the risks associated with common vulnerabilities. Understanding the role of WAFs involves delving into the nature of web application vulnerabilities and how these firewalls employ sophisticated techniques to detect, prevent, and respond to potential threats.

One of the primary functions of a WAF is to address injection attacks, a prevalent category of web application vulnerabilities. Injection attacks, such as SQL injection and Cross-Site Scripting (XSS), involve malicious actors injecting malicious code into user inputs or data fields, aiming to manipulate the behavior of the application. WAFs employ signature-based detection, anomaly detection, and heuristic analysis to scrutinize incoming requests and responses for patterns indicative of injection attacks. By meticulously examining the traffic between users and web applications, WAFs can identify and block malicious payloads, preventing unauthorized access and potential data breaches.

Cross-Site Scripting (XSS) represents a significant threat to web applications, allowing attackers to inject malicious scripts into web pages viewed by other users. WAFs contribute to XSS prevention by scrutinizing the content of web requests and responses, identifying and blocking scripts that could compromise the integrity of the application or steal sensitive user information. Additionally, WAFs can enforce strict content security policies, such as the use of secure headers, to mitigate the risk of XSS attacks. Through real-time analysis of web traffic, WAFs act as a shield against the exploitation of XSS vulnerabilities.

SQL injection attacks pose a severe risk to web applications by exploiting vulnerabilities in database queries. WAFs play a pivotal role in mitigating SQL injection threats by inspecting user inputs for malicious SQL code patterns. Through signature-based detection and pattern matching, WAFs can identify and block attempts to manipulate SQL queries, safeguarding databases from unauthorized access or data manipulation. By scrutinizing both inbound and outbound traffic, WAFs act as a gatekeeper, preventing SQL injection attacks from compromising the confidentiality and integrity of sensitive information.

Another critical aspect of web application security addressed by WAFs is the prevention of Cross-Site Request Forgery (CSRF) attacks. CSRF attacks involve tricking users into performing unintended actions without their consent, potentially leading to unauthorized transactions or changes in their account settings. WAFs employ token-based protection mechanisms to validate the authenticity of requests, ensuring that only legitimate and authorized requests are processed. By embedding unique tokens within web forms and validating them during subsequent requests, WAFs mitigate the risk of CSRF attacks, providing an additional layer of defense against unauthorized actions.

Authentication and session management vulnerabilities represent common targets for attackers seeking unauthorized access to web applications. WAFs play a role in protecting against such threats by scrutinizing login attempts, enforcing strong authentication mechanisms, and detecting suspicious or anomalous behavior related to session management. Through the analysis of user sessions, login patterns, and access behaviors, WAFs can identify and block attempts to compromise user credentials, helping prevent unauthorized access and maintaining the confidentiality of user accounts.

WAFs contribute significantly to the protection against security misconfigurations, a prevalent issue in web application development that can lead to vulnerabilities if not addressed properly. Security misconfigurations may result from improper server configurations, default settings, or overlooked access controls. WAFs can detect and mitigate security misconfigurations by actively inspecting application traffic for signs of anomalies or deviations from secure configurations. By continuously monitoring and analyzing web requests and responses, WAFs act as a proactive defense mechanism, identifying and blocking potential security misconfigurations before they can be exploited by attackers.

Web applications often rely on third-party components, libraries, and frameworks, introducing the risk of vulnerabilities in these dependencies. WAFs address this risk by scrutinizing the usage of external components and identifying potential security weaknesses. Through regular monitoring of application dependencies and automated scanning for known vulnerabilities, WAFs contribute to the early detection and prevention of security issues stemming from third-party components. By leveraging threat intelligence feeds and maintaining an up-to-date knowledge base of known vulnerabilities, WAFs help organizations maintain a secure and resilient web application environment.

WAFs excel in safeguarding web applications against Distributed Denial of Service (DDoS) attacks, a threat that aims to disrupt the availability of web services by overwhelming servers with a massive volume of traffic. WAFs act as a traffic filter, distinguishing between legitimate user requests and malicious traffic associated with DDoS attacks. By implementing rate limiting, traffic analysis, and behavioral heuristics, WAFs can identify and mitigate DDoS attacks in real-time, ensuring the uninterrupted availability of web applications even in the face of orchestrated and volumetric attacks.

The role of WAFs extends to protecting sensitive data transmitted between users and web applications. Encryption is a fundamental aspect of data protection, and WAFs facilitate secure communication by enforcing the use of secure protocols such as HTTPS. By inspecting and validating SSL/TLS certificates, WAFs ensure the integrity of encrypted connections, preventing man-in-the-middle attacks and eavesdropping attempts. Additionally, WAFs can identify and block attempts to exfiltrate sensitive data through encrypted channels, offering comprehensive protection for data in transit.

Web applications often face the challenge of maintaining compliance with industry-specific regulations and standards governing data protection and privacy. WAFs play a crucial role in supporting compliance efforts by enforcing security controls, such as access controls, encryption, and logging, that align with regulatory requirements. By providing audit logs, reports, and compliance checks, WAFs assist organizations in demonstrating adherence to standards like the Payment Card Industry Data Security Standard (PCI DSS), the Health Insurance Portability and Accountability Act (HIPAA), and others.

WAFs contribute to threat intelligence-driven security by leveraging information about emerging threats, attack patterns, and malicious IP addresses. Through integration with threat intelligence feeds, WAFs can proactively identify and block traffic associated with known malicious entities. This dynamic approach to security enhances the ability of WAFs to defend against evolving threats, ensuring that web applications remain protected against the latest attack vectors. Regular updates to threat intelligence databases enable WAFs to adapt to the ever-changing threat landscape, providing organizations with a proactive defense mechanism against emerging cyber threats.

WAFs play a crucial role in incident response for web applications by providing real-time monitoring, alerting, and reporting capabilities. In the event of a security incident, WAFs can generate alerts based on predefined security policies, enabling rapid response to potential threats. By logging relevant information about detected incidents, WAFs facilitate post-incident analysis and forensic investigations. The ability to generate detailed reports and insights into security events empowers organizations to assess the impact of incidents, identify the root causes, and implement remediation measures effectively.

In conclusion, Web Application Firewalls (WAFs) serve as indispensable guardians of web applications, offering a comprehensive defense against common vulnerabilities and emerging cyber threats. From injection attacks to authentication vulnerabilities, security misconfigurations, and DDoS attacks, WAFs play a multifaceted role in safeguarding the confidentiality, integrity, and availability of web applications. By employing a combination of signature-based detection, anomaly analysis, threat intelligence integration, and proactive security measures, WAFs provide organizations with a robust defense mechanism that adapts to the dynamic nature of the cybersecurity landscape. As organizations continue to rely on web applications for critical functions, the role of WAFs remains pivotal in ensuring a secure and resilient digital environment.

Discuss strategies for protecting sensitive data within cloud applications.

Protecting sensitive data within cloud applications is a multifaceted challenge that demands a comprehensive and layered approach to security. As organizations increasingly leverage cloud services to store, process, and transmit sensitive information, strategies must encompass encryption, access controls, identity management, monitoring, and compliance measures to ensure robust protection against potential threats and unauthorized access.

One fundamental strategy for safeguarding sensitive data in cloud applications is the implementation of strong encryption mechanisms. Data encryption serves as a critical line of defense, ensuring that even if unauthorized access occurs, the data remains unintelligible without the appropriate decryption keys. Adopting end-to-end encryption, where data is encrypted throughout its entire lifecycle—from storage to transit and processing—is essential. Utilizing industry-standard encryption algorithms and regularly updating encryption keys enhances the security posture, mitigating risks associated with data breaches or unauthorized data access within the cloud environment.

Effective access controls play a pivotal role in limiting and managing permissions to sensitive data within cloud applications. Role-Based Access Control (RBAC) and Attribute-Based Access Control (ABAC) models enable organizations to define granular access policies based on user roles, responsibilities, and attributes. By enforcing the principle of least privilege, organizations can restrict access to sensitive data to only those individuals or systems that require it for legitimate purposes. Cloud Identity and Access Management (IAM) solutions facilitate the centralized management of access controls, ensuring that changes in user roles or responsibilities are promptly reflected across cloud applications.

Authentication mechanisms are integral components of strategies for protecting sensitive data in the cloud. Implementing multi-factor authentication (MFA) adds an additional layer of security by requiring users to provide multiple forms of identification before gaining access to sensitive data. Strong password policies, periodic password rotations, and the use of secure authentication protocols further bolster the authentication process. Integration with Single Sign-On (SSO) solutions streamlines access management, providing a centralized point for user authentication and reducing the risk of unauthorized access to sensitive information.

Monitoring and logging mechanisms are essential for detecting and responding to potential security incidents within cloud applications. Continuous monitoring of user activities, data access patterns, and system behavior enables the timely identification of suspicious or anomalous events. Cloud Security Information and Event Management (SIEM) solutions aggregate and analyze log data from various cloud services, providing organizations with insights into potential security threats. Real-time alerts and automated response mechanisms contribute to a proactive security posture, allowing organizations to mitigate risks promptly and enhance their ability to protect sensitive data.

Data Loss Prevention (DLP) solutions play a critical role in preventing the unauthorized disclosure or leakage of sensitive information within cloud applications. DLP policies define rules and conditions for identifying and blocking the transmission of sensitive data based on predefined criteria such as content, context, and user behavior. Integrating DLP solutions with cloud services enables organizations to enforce consistent data protection policies across diverse data repositories, ensuring that sensitive information is not inadvertently shared or exposed. Regularly updating and fine-tuning DLP policies to align with evolving business requirements and compliance standards enhances the effectiveness of data protection measures.

Cloud providers offer a range of security services and features that organizations can leverage to enhance the protection of sensitive data. Utilizing encryption services provided by cloud platforms, such as AWS Key Management Service (KMS) or Azure Key Vault, simplifies the management of encryption keys and ensures the integrity of data at rest. Cloud Access Security Brokers (CASBs) act as intermediaries between users and cloud services, providing additional visibility, control, and security for data in transit and at rest. By adopting cloud-native security services, organizations can capitalize on the expertise and infrastructure provided by cloud providers to reinforce their data protection strategies.

Regular security assessments and audits are integral components of strategies for protecting sensitive data within cloud applications. Conducting vulnerability assessments, penetration testing, and security audits help organizations identify and remediate potential weaknesses or misconfigurations in cloud environments. Regularly reviewing and validating security controls, configurations, and access permissions contribute to maintaining a resilient security posture. Compliance audits, aligned with industry-specific regulations and standards, validate that cloud applications adhere to data protection and privacy requirements, ensuring that sensitive information is handled in accordance with legal and regulatory frameworks.

Data classification is a foundational strategy for identifying and prioritizing sensitive information within cloud applications. Categorizing data based on its sensitivity, confidentiality, and regulatory implications enables organizations to apply tailored security controls and protection measures. Automated classification tools can assist in tagging and labeling data, facilitating consistent application of security policies across diverse datasets. Data classification forms the basis for implementing differentiated access controls, encryption strategies, and data protection measures, ensuring that sensitive information receives heightened security attention within the cloud environment.

Implementing a robust incident response plan is essential for organizations to effectively address and mitigate the impact of security incidents related to sensitive data in the cloud. Clearly defined incident response procedures, communication protocols, and escalation pathways enable organizations to respond promptly to security breaches or unauthorized access. Regularly conducting tabletop exercises and simulations ensures that incident response teams are well-prepared to handle various scenarios. Post-incident analysis and documentation contribute to continuous improvement, enabling organizations to learn from security incidents and refine their data protection strategies.

Integration with threat intelligence feeds and information-sharing platforms enhances the proactive capabilities of strategies for protecting sensitive data in the cloud. Leveraging threat intelligence enables organizations to stay informed about emerging threats, malicious actors, and evolving attack vectors. Integrating threat intelligence into security controls, such as access policies and anomaly detection mechanisms, enhances the ability to detect and respond to sophisticated threats. Collaboration within threat intelligence communities and information-sharing forums provides organizations with insights into the broader threat landscape, empowering them to anticipate and mitigate potential risks to sensitive data.

Compliance with data protection regulations and privacy standards is a foundational element of strategies for safeguarding sensitive data within cloud applications. Organizations must understand and adhere to applicable regulations, such as the General Data Protection Regulation (GDPR), the Health Insurance Portability and Accountability Act (HIPAA), or industry-specific standards like the Payment Card Industry Data Security Standard (PCI DSS). Aligning data protection measures with regulatory requirements involves implementing specific controls, documenting compliance efforts, and engaging with legal and compliance teams to ensure that cloud applications meet the necessary standards for handling sensitive information.

Educating and raising awareness among users and stakeholders is a crucial component of strategies for protecting sensitive data within cloud applications. Security awareness training programs inform users about the risks associated with handling sensitive information, the importance of following security best practices, and recognizing social engineering attempts. Promoting a culture of security consciousness encourages users to be vigilant, report suspicious activities, and adhere to data protection policies. Informed and empowered users contribute to the overall effectiveness of security measures and act as additional layers of defense against potential insider threats or unintentional data exposures.

In conclusion, safeguarding sensitive data within cloud applications requires a holistic and adaptive approach that integrates encryption, access controls, identity management, monitoring, and compliance measures. The evolving nature of cyber threats and the dynamic landscape of cloud services demand continuous efforts to enhance security postures and adapt strategies to emerging challenges. By adopting a layered defense approach, leveraging cloud-native security services, and aligning data protection efforts with regulatory requirements, organizations can build a resilient framework for protecting sensitive information within the cloud environment.

Highlight the importance of continuous monitoring for identifying and addressing application vulnerabilities.

Continuous monitoring plays a pivotal role in the proactive identification and timely addressing of application vulnerabilities, offering organizations a dynamic and adaptive approach to cybersecurity that aligns with the evolving threat landscape. As modern applications become more complex and interconnected, with frequent updates and releases, the traditional, periodic vulnerability assessments are no longer sufficient to ensure robust security. Continuous monitoring, on the other hand, provides a real-time and comprehensive view of the application's security posture, allowing organizations to detect and respond to vulnerabilities promptly, minimizing the window of exposure and mitigating potential risks.

One of the primary advantages of continuous monitoring in identifying application vulnerabilities lies in its ability to provide a persistent and up-to-date assessment of the security landscape. Traditional, point-in-time vulnerability assessments may miss emerging threats or vulnerabilities introduced after the assessment was conducted. Continuous monitoring, however, operates in real-time, enabling organizations to stay abreast of the latest vulnerabilities, exploit techniques, and security best practices. This ensures that the security posture remains current and adaptive, addressing both known vulnerabilities and emerging threats as they evolve.

The dynamic nature of modern application development, often driven by agile and DevOps practices, underscores the need for continuous monitoring. In an environment where code changes are frequent and releases are rapid, vulnerabilities can be introduced inadvertently. Continuous monitoring allows organizations to track these changes, assess the security implications, and identify vulnerabilities early in the development lifecycle. By integrating security into the continuous integration and continuous deployment (CI/CD) pipeline, organizations can automate security checks, leveraging continuous monitoring to identify vulnerabilities as code changes progress through the development stages.

Continuous monitoring plays a crucial role in addressing the persistence of vulnerabilities, ensuring that organizations maintain visibility into their security posture over time. Traditional assessments, conducted sporadically, may provide a momentary snapshot of vulnerabilities but fail to account for changes in the threat landscape or the introduction of new vulnerabilities. Continuous monitoring, with its ongoing and automated nature, allows organizations to track the status of vulnerabilities persistently. This persistence is crucial for addressing vulnerabilities that may not be immediately remediated, providing organizations with the awareness needed to prioritize and remediate vulnerabilities based on risk.

The correlation of data from diverse sources is a key strength of continuous monitoring in identifying application vulnerabilities. Instead of relying solely on vulnerability scans, continuous monitoring incorporates data from various security sources, including logs, network traffic, user behavior, and threat intelligence feeds. This holistic approach enables organizations to detect vulnerabilities that may not be apparent through traditional scanning methods. For instance, anomalous patterns in user behavior or unexpected network activity may indicate a potential exploit or compromise that traditional assessments might overlook. Continuous monitoring enhances the depth and breadth of vulnerability detection by correlating multiple data points, providing a more comprehensive understanding of the security landscape.

Automated vulnerability scanning is an integral component of continuous monitoring, offering organizations the ability to scan for vulnerabilities consistently and efficiently. Automated scans can be scheduled to run at predefined intervals, ensuring that the application's security posture is continuously assessed without manual intervention. This not only saves time and resources but also allows organizations to identify vulnerabilities promptly. Automated scanning tools can cover a wide range of vulnerabilities, including known software vulnerabilities, misconfigurations, and compliance issues. The ability to conduct automated scans at scale is particularly valuable in large and complex application environments where manual assessments may be impractical.

Continuous monitoring enhances the speed and efficiency of vulnerability identification, aligning with the principles of DevSecOps. By integrating security checks into the development pipeline, organizations can identify and address vulnerabilities in near real-time as code changes progress through various stages. This integration ensures that security is not a separate and isolated phase but an integral part of the development lifecycle. The collaboration between development, operations, and security teams is facilitated by continuous monitoring, fostering a culture of shared responsibility for security. DevSecOps practices emphasize the importance of addressing vulnerabilities early in the development process, and continuous monitoring is a key enabler of this shift-left approach to security.

The importance of continuous monitoring becomes evident in its role in detecting and responding to zero-day vulnerabilities. Traditional vulnerability assessments may not be effective in identifying vulnerabilities for which no patch or signature exists. Zero-day vulnerabilities, by their nature, are unknown to the organization and security vendors until they are actively exploited. Continuous monitoring, with its focus on real-time data analysis and anomaly detection, provides a better chance of detecting indicators of compromise associated with zero-day attacks. This early detection allows organizations to respond promptly, implement mitigations, and reduce the potential impact of zero-day vulnerabilities on their applications.

Continuous monitoring contributes to the effectiveness of risk management by providing organizations with a dynamic risk profile based on the current threat landscape and the status of vulnerabilities. By continuously assessing vulnerabilities, organizations can prioritize remediation efforts based on the severity of vulnerabilities, potential exploitability, and the overall risk to the business. This risk-based approach ensures that resources are allocated efficiently, focusing on addressing the most critical vulnerabilities that pose the highest risk to the organization. Continuous monitoring helps organizations move away from a reactive, checkbox compliance mindset and towards a proactive, risk-driven security posture.

The feedback loop created by continuous monitoring is instrumental in the iterative improvement of security measures. The insights gained from monitoring vulnerabilities, incidents, and responses contribute to refining security policies, adjusting risk assessments, and enhancing security controls. Continuous monitoring allows organizations to learn from security incidents, understand the tactics and techniques employed by adversaries, and implement measures to prevent similar incidents in the future. This iterative and adaptive approach is essential in the constantly evolving landscape of cyber threats, enabling organizations to continually enhance their security postures based on real-world experiences.

Compliance requirements, whether industry-specific regulations or internal policies, often necessitate ongoing monitoring and documentation of the security posture. Continuous monitoring supports compliance efforts by providing a consistent and updated view of vulnerabilities, security controls, and risk mitigations. Automated reporting tools within continuous monitoring solutions facilitate the generation of compliance reports, helping organizations demonstrate adherence to regulatory standards during audits. The persistent and real-time nature of continuous monitoring ensures that compliance documentation reflects the current state of the organization's security controls and the measures taken to address vulnerabilities.

The ability of continuous monitoring to provide insights into user behavior and access patterns is invaluable for identifying and addressing vulnerabilities related to insider threats. By monitoring user activities, organizations can detect unusual or suspicious behavior that may indicate an insider attempting unauthorized access or data exfiltration. Continuous monitoring solutions can establish baseline behavior for users and systems, flagging deviations from normal patterns. This behavioral analysis enhances the organization's ability to detect not only external threats but also insider threats, contributing to a more comprehensive approach to vulnerability identification and response.

The importance of continuous monitoring extends to the identification of vulnerabilities in third-party components and services. Modern applications often rely on a multitude of third-party libraries, frameworks, and services, introducing potential vulnerabilities that may not be directly visible in the organization's code. Continuous monitoring enables organizations to track and assess vulnerabilities in third-party components, ensuring that any associated risks are promptly addressed. Regularly updating and patching third-party dependencies based on continuous monitoring findings is crucial for maintaining the overall security of the application ecosystem.

In conclusion, continuous monitoring is an indispensable strategy for identifying and addressing application vulnerabilities in the dynamic and interconnected landscape of modern cybersecurity. Its real-time, automated, and comprehensive nature aligns with the principles of agile development, DevOps, and risk management, providing organizations with the ability to detect vulnerabilities promptly, respond proactively, and adapt to the evolving threat landscape. By integrating continuous monitoring into the development lifecycle, organizations can move towards a more secure and resilient posture, mitigating risks, and enhancing their ability to protect critical assets and sensitive information from potential exploits.

Outline a framework for incident response specific to cloud-based applications.

Establishing a robust incident response framework tailored to the unique challenges and characteristics of cloud-based applications is imperative for organizations relying on cloud services. Cloud environments introduce new complexities related to shared responsibility models, dynamic resource allocation, and distributed architecture. A comprehensive incident response framework for cloud-based applications should encompass preparation, identification, containment, eradication, recovery, and lessons learned phases, aligning with established best practices for incident response.

The preparation phase of the incident response framework for cloud-based applications is foundational for effective incident handling. Organizations need to define clear incident response policies and procedures specifically tailored to the cloud environment. This involves understanding the shared responsibility model between the cloud service provider (CSP) and the organization, delineating the roles and responsibilities for incident response. Establishing communication and collaboration channels with the CSP, incident response teams, and relevant stakeholders ensures a coordinated and effective response when incidents occur. Additionally, conducting regular training and simulations helps personnel familiarize themselves with the incident response plan, ensuring a swift and coordinated response in the event of an incident.

The identification phase involves the continuous monitoring and detection of security incidents within cloud-based applications. Leveraging cloud-native monitoring tools, log analysis, and anomaly detection mechanisms enable organizations to identify unusual activities or potential security breaches. Real-time visibility into cloud resources, network traffic, and user activities is essential for promptly detecting unauthorized access, data breaches, or other security incidents. Integrating threat intelligence feeds and leveraging security information and event management (SIEM) solutions enhance the organization's ability to correlate data and detect patterns indicative of malicious behavior. Automated alerts and notifications further expedite the identification of potential incidents.

Once an incident is identified, the containment phase becomes crucial in preventing further damage and limiting the impact on cloud-based applications. Cloud environments offer unique challenges in terms of isolating affected resources, given their dynamic and distributed nature. Implementing network segmentation, access controls, and automated response mechanisms enables organizations to contain incidents effectively. Cloud-specific tools such as security groups, network ACLs, and cloud access security brokers (CASBs) contribute to controlling lateral movement and isolating compromised resources. Rapid and precise containment measures are essential to prevent the escalation of incidents within the cloud infrastructure.

The eradication phase focuses on eliminating the root cause of the incident and remediating vulnerabilities in cloud-based applications. Organizations need to conduct a thorough analysis of the incident, identifying the vulnerabilities or misconfigurations that led to the security breach. Automated scanning tools specific to cloud environments can assist in identifying and remediating vulnerabilities in a scalable manner. The eradication process should include patching or updating affected resources, revising configurations, and implementing security best practices to prevent similar incidents in the future. Continuous monitoring during the eradication phase is essential to ensure the effectiveness of remediation efforts and to detect any residual threats.

The recovery phase involves restoring cloud-based applications and services to normal operation after an incident. Organizations must have a well-defined recovery plan that outlines the steps to restore affected resources, validate their integrity, and resume normal operations. Utilizing backups, snapshots, and replication mechanisms specific to cloud environments ensures data integrity and minimizes downtime. Organizations should also communicate transparently with users and stakeholders about the incident, its resolution, and any potential impacts on services. Conducting post-incident testing and validation is crucial to ensure that the recovery process aligns with business continuity objectives and that the cloud-based applications are fully operational.

The lessons learned phase is integral to the continuous improvement of the incident response framework for cloud-based applications. After the incident has been resolved, organizations should conduct a comprehensive post-mortem analysis. This involves evaluating the effectiveness of incident response processes, identifying areas for improvement, and refining the incident response plan accordingly. Capturing lessons learned from each incident contributes to a more resilient security posture, enabling organizations to adapt and enhance their incident response capabilities over time. The feedback loop established through the lessons learned phase ensures that the incident response framework remains adaptive and responsive to emerging threats and evolving cloud environments.

Cloud-based applications often rely on external service providers and third-party integrations, adding complexity to incident response. Therefore, organizations should establish clear communication and collaboration channels with external parties, including

CSPs, vendors, and relevant authorities. Understanding the contractual obligations and support mechanisms provided by CSPs is critical for effective incident response in the cloud. Organizations should also engage with external incident response teams, regulatory bodies, and law enforcement when necessary. Collaborative efforts contribute to a more holistic and coordinated response, ensuring that incidents are addressed comprehensively and in compliance with legal and regulatory requirements.

Integration with threat intelligence feeds and sharing information with the broader security community enhance the incident response framework for cloud-based applications. By staying informed about emerging threats, new attack vectors, and evolving tactics, organizations can proactively enhance their detection and response capabilities. Cloud-specific threat intelligence helps organizations anticipate potential risks to their cloud environments and tailor their incident response strategies accordingly. Regularly participating in information-sharing forums, industry groups, and threat intelligence communities fosters a collective defense approach, enabling organizations to benefit from shared insights and lessons learned from the wider security community.

The incident response framework for cloud-based applications should prioritize the preservation of forensic evidence for investigative purposes. Cloud environments introduce challenges related to the ephemeral nature of resources and the dynamic allocation of computing resources. Implementing logging and auditing mechanisms specific to cloud services ensures the capture of relevant forensic data. Organizations should define procedures for preserving and analyzing logs, artifacts, and metadata to understand the timeline and impact of security incidents. Leveraging cloud-native logging and monitoring solutions contributes to the retention of valuable forensic evidence for incident investigations and legal proceedings.

Continuous improvement and adaptation are central tenets of an effective incident response framework for cloud-based applications. Organizations should regularly review and update their incident response plans to align with changes in cloud architecture, business processes, and emerging threat landscapes. Conducting regular tabletop exercises and simulations ensures that incident response teams remain well-prepared and can practice their roles and responsibilities in a controlled environment. Engaging in red teaming exercises, where simulated attacks are conducted to test the effectiveness of the incident response framework, provides valuable insights into potential vulnerabilities and areas for improvement.

In conclusion, a robust incident response framework tailored to the specific nuances of cloud-based applications is essential for organizations navigating the dynamic and interconnected landscape of cloud security. By encompassing preparation, identification, containment, eradication, recovery, and lessons learned phases, this framework provides a structured and adaptive approach to incident response. Leveraging cloud-specific tools, continuous monitoring, collaboration with external parties, and the preservation of forensic evidence contribute to the effectiveness of incident response in cloud environments. As organizations increasingly rely on cloud-based applications, an agile and well-defined incident response framework becomes a cornerstone of their overall cybersecurity strategy.

Emphasize the role of education in empowering developers to build secure applications.

Education plays a pivotal role in empowering developers to build secure applications, fostering a culture of security awareness and best practices that are fundamental to the increasingly interconnected and complex digital landscape. As the architects of software solutions, developers wield significant influence over the security posture of applications, making their knowledge and skills in secure coding practices paramount. A comprehensive educational approach begins with instilling a foundational understanding of cybersecurity principles, including threat landscapes, attack vectors, and the potential consequences of insecure coding. This foundational knowledge forms the basis upon which developers can build a security-first mindset, recognizing the importance of integrating security considerations throughout the entire software development lifecycle.

One key aspect of developer education in building secure applications involves imparting knowledge about common vulnerabilities and exploits. Developers need to be familiar with prevalent security risks such as injection attacks, cross-site scripting (XSS), and insecure deserialization, among others. Understanding the mechanics of these vulnerabilities equips developers with the ability to proactively identify and mitigate such risks during the coding phase. By delving into real-world examples and case studies, educational programs can illustrate the impact of security vulnerabilities on applications and their users, emphasizing the tangible consequences of inadequate security measures.

Secure coding practices, encompassing techniques to prevent and mitigate vulnerabilities, form the core of developer education initiatives. Educating developers on secure coding involves elucidating principles such as input validation, proper authentication and authorization mechanisms, secure data storage, and secure communication protocols. Through hands-on exercises, workshops, and practical examples, developers can gain proficiency in implementing these practices within their codebase. By weaving secure coding principles into the fabric of development education, organizations cultivate a generation of developers capable of producing resilient and robust applications that stand up to evolving cybersecurity threats.

Education in secure application development extends beyond theoretical knowledge to practical skills in using security tools and frameworks. Developers should be adept at leveraging static analysis tools, dynamic analysis tools, and interactive application security testing (IAST) solutions to identify vulnerabilities and weaknesses in their code. Education should focus on integrating these tools seamlessly into the development workflow, enabling developers to conduct continuous security assessments throughout the software development lifecycle. By demystifying the use of security tools and fostering a hands-on approach, educational programs empower developers to proactively identify and address security issues before they manifest into critical vulnerabilities.

The role of education in building secure applications is closely tied to the concept of threat modeling, which involves identifying potential security threats and vulnerabilities specific to an application or system. Developers should be trained to conduct threat modeling exercises that analyze the application's architecture, data flow, and interactions to anticipate potential security risks. This proactive approach, integrated into the development process, enables developers to design and implement security controls that align with the identified threats. Education in threat modeling instills a mindset of anticipating and mitigating security risks at the design phase, contributing to the creation of inherently secure applications.

Secure coding education also emphasizes the importance of staying abreast of evolving security standards and best practices. Developers should be encouraged to participate in industry-recognized training programs, certifications, and conferences that focus on the latest advancements in secure coding methodologies. This ongoing commitment to professional development ensures that developers remain informed about emerging security threats, new vulnerabilities, and evolving best practices. By fostering a culture of continuous learning, organizations empower developers to adapt their skills to the dynamic landscape of cybersecurity, enabling them to contribute to the creation of resilient applications in the face of emerging threats.

A critical component of developer education in building secure applications is the awareness of the unique security considerations associated with different development environments and platforms. Cloud-native development, for example, introduces specific challenges and security considerations related to shared responsibility models, serverless architectures, and containerized deployments. Educational programs should provide developers with insights into securing cloud-based applications, including secure configuration management, data encryption, and identity and access management in cloud environments. Similarly, awareness of security practices in mobile application development, web applications, and Internet of Things (IoT) devices equips developers with platform-specific knowledge to address potential vulnerabilities effectively.

Beyond technical skills, education in secure application development should instill a sense of ethical responsibility among developers. Developers are custodians of user data and privacy, and understanding the ethical implications of their coding decisions is crucial. Education programs should emphasize the importance of respecting user privacy, adhering to data protection regulations, and implementing secure data handling practices. By instilling ethical considerations into the fabric of developer education, organizations can cultivate a sense of responsibility that transcends the technical realm, fostering a commitment to building applications that prioritize user trust and data security.

Collaboration and communication skills are integral facets of secure application development that should be emphasized in developer education. Security is a collaborative effort that involves cross-functional teams, including developers, security professionals, and operations teams. Educational programs should promote a collaborative mindset, encouraging developers to actively engage with security teams, participate in code reviews with a security focus, and communicate effectively about potential security risks. By fostering a culture of collaboration, education empowers developers to leverage the collective expertise of diverse teams, enhancing the overall security posture of applications.

Education in secure application development should encompass the principles of secure DevOps, integrating security practices seamlessly into the DevOps pipeline. Developers should be educated on the concepts of DevSecOps, which emphasize the collaboration and integration of security practices throughout the entire development and operations lifecycle. Educational programs should guide developers on incorporating security into continuous integration and continuous deployment (CI/CD) processes, enabling automated security testing, code analysis, and vulnerability scanning. By aligning education with DevSecOps principles, organizations can bridge the gap between development and security teams, fostering a unified approach to building and maintaining secure applications.

In conclusion, education plays a central and transformative role in empowering developers to build secure applications. By cultivating a comprehensive understanding of cybersecurity principles, instilling secure coding practices, and providing hands-on experience with security tools, education forms the bedrock of a security-first mindset among developers. The integration of threat modeling, continuous learning, and platform-specific security considerations further enhances the developer's ability to contribute to the creation of resilient and secure applications. As developers become ethical custodians of user data and collaborate effectively with cross-functional teams, education becomes the linchpin in fostering a culture where secure application development is not just a skill but a guiding principle.

Chapter 6: Compliance and Governance in Cloud Security

Define the concept of compliance and its relevance in cloud security.

Compliance, in the realm of cloud security, refers to the adherence of an organization's cloud practices to a set of predefined standards, regulations, and industry-specific requirements aimed at ensuring the confidentiality, integrity, and availability of data and systems. As businesses increasingly leverage cloud services for data storage, processing, and application deployment, the need for a structured framework to address security concerns and regulatory obligations becomes paramount. Compliance in cloud security encompasses a multifaceted approach, addressing legal, industry, and organizational requirements that vary based on the nature of the business, the geographical location of operations, and the sensitivity of the data being handled.

The relevance of compliance in cloud security is underscored by the dynamic and complex nature of cloud environments, where data traverses virtualized infrastructures, shared resources, and geographically dispersed servers. Cloud service providers (CSPs) operate under a shared responsibility model, wherein the provider assumes responsibility for the security of the cloud infrastructure, while customers retain responsibility for securing their data, applications, and user access. Compliance frameworks serve as benchmarks, guiding organizations in establishing robust security controls, policies, and procedures to align with legal requirements and industry standards.

One of the primary drivers for compliance in cloud security is the need to meet regulatory obligations imposed by governmental bodies and industry regulators. Regulations such as the General Data Protection Regulation (GDPR), the Health Insurance Portability and Accountability Act (HIPAA), and the Payment Card Industry Data Security Standard (PCI DSS) impose stringent requirements on how organizations handle and protect sensitive information. Cloud users must ensure that their cloud configurations, data handling practices, and security measures align with the specific stipulations of these regulations. Failure to comply not only risks financial penalties but also damages the organization's reputation and erodes the trust of customers and stakeholders.

In the context of compliance in cloud security, organizations often contend with the challenge of navigating a global regulatory landscape. Different countries and regions have varying data protection laws and privacy requirements. Transborder data flows, a common occurrence in cloud computing, necessitate careful consideration of international regulations. Compliance efforts in cloud security, therefore, must encompass a comprehensive understanding of regional and global legal frameworks to ensure that data is handled in accordance with the applicable laws. This involves assessing data residency requirements, cross-border data transfer mechanisms, and the impact of jurisdictional variations on cloud operations.

Beyond legal and regulatory aspects, compliance in cloud security extends to industry-specific standards and best practices. Different sectors, such as finance, healthcare, and government, often have specific compliance frameworks that mandate additional security controls tailored to the unique challenges of their respective domains. For instance, the financial sector adheres to regulations such as the Sarbanes-Oxley Act (SOX) and the Federal Financial Institutions Examination Council (FFIEC) guidelines, while the healthcare industry follows HIPAA standards. Cloud users in these sectors must integrate these industry-specific compliance requirements into their cloud security strategies to mitigate risks and ensure the protection of sensitive information.

The shared responsibility model inherent in cloud computing amplifies the importance of compliance as organizations grapple with delineating responsibilities between themselves and their CSPs. While CSPs manage the security of the underlying cloud infrastructure, customers are accountable for securing their data, configuring access controls, and implementing additional security measures. Compliance frameworks provide a structured approach for customers to assess and enhance their adherence to security best practices within the shared responsibility model. This collaborative effort between cloud providers and customers is critical for establishing a cohesive security posture that comprehensively addresses potential threats and vulnerabilities.

The advent of cloud-native services and technologies introduces new dimensions to compliance in cloud security. Organizations leveraging Infrastructure as a Service (IaaS), Platform as a Service (PaaS), and Software as a Service (SaaS) models need to adapt their compliance strategies to the specific characteristics of these services. For instance, securing serverless architectures and containerized applications requires tailored security measures aligned with the ephemeral nature of these technologies. Compliance frameworks must evolve to encompass the nuances of cloud-native security, accounting for factors such as microservices, API security, and the dynamic scalability inherent in cloud environments.

Compliance in cloud security serves as a strategic enabler for building and maintaining trust among stakeholders. Customers, partners, and investors increasingly demand transparency and assurance regarding the security practices of organizations, especially when it comes to the handling of sensitive data in the cloud. Achieving and demonstrating compliance with recognized frameworks becomes a means of establishing credibility and demonstrating a commitment to maintaining a robust security posture. Cloud providers often undergo third-party audits and certifications to validate their adherence to industry standards, providing customers with assurance that their cloud services meet stringent security criteria.

Effective compliance in cloud security requires a holistic approach that spans people, processes, and technology. Education and awareness programs are essential components, ensuring that personnel across the organization understand the significance of compliance, their roles in maintaining it, and the potential consequences of non-compliance. Establishing documented policies and procedures aligns operational practices with compliance requirements, guiding employees in their day-to-day activities related to cloud security. Technology solutions, including encryption, access controls, and monitoring tools, play a pivotal role in enforcing and maintaining compliance, providing the technical underpinnings necessary to meet regulatory and industry-specific mandates.

Continuous monitoring and auditing are integral to maintaining compliance in dynamic cloud environments. Regular assessments of security controls, configurations, and access permissions help organizations identify and rectify deviations from compliance requirements promptly. Automated tools that provide real-time visibility into the cloud environment contribute to ongoing compliance management, enabling organizations to respond rapidly to changes, incidents, and emerging threats. Compliance, therefore, is not a one-time achievement but an ongoing commitment that necessitates continuous monitoring, assessment, and improvement to adapt to evolving security landscapes.

In conclusion, compliance in cloud security is a cornerstone of a resilient and trustworthy cloud computing ecosystem. It encompasses legal obligations, industry standards, and organizational best practices, guiding organizations in securing their data and applications in the cloud. The shared responsibility model, global regulatory variations, and the evolution of cloud-native technologies amplify the complexity of compliance in cloud security. However, by embracing compliance frameworks, fostering a culture of security awareness, and leveraging advanced security technologies, organizations can navigate the intricate landscape of cloud security, instill trust among stakeholders, and build a foundation for secure and compliant cloud operations.

Explore established frameworks for cloud security compliance.

Several established frameworks for cloud security compliance serve as essential guides for organizations striving to meet stringent security standards in their cloud environments. These frameworks provide a structured approach to assessing, implementing, and maintaining security controls, aligning with industry regulations, international standards, and best practices. Among these frameworks, the Health Insurance Portability and Accountability Act (HIPAA) stands out as a critical compliance standard in the healthcare sector. HIPAA establishes requirements for protecting the privacy and security of patients' sensitive health information. In the context of cloud computing, organizations handling health data must adhere to HIPAA's Security Rule, which outlines specific safeguards for electronic protected health information (ePHI). Compliance with HIPAA requires implementing measures such as access controls, encryption, and audit trails to safeguard ePHI in cloud environments.

Another prominent framework is the Payment Card Industry Data Security Standard (PCI DSS), which is essential for organizations handling payment card information. PCI DSS outlines security requirements to protect cardholder data and secure payment card transactions. Cloud service providers and organizations utilizing cloud services for payment processing must ensure that their environments comply with PCI DSS. This involves implementing secure network configurations, encrypting cardholder data, and conducting regular security assessments. The challenge in cloud environments lies in navigating the shared responsibility model and ensuring that both the organization and the cloud provider meet PCI DSS requirements.

For a comprehensive and globally recognized framework, the International Organization for Standardization (ISO) offers ISO/IEC 27001 and ISO/IEC 27002. ISO/IEC 27001 provides a systematic approach to information security management systems (ISMS), offering a risk-based framework for establishing, implementing, maintaining, and continually improving security controls. ISO/IEC 27002, on the other hand, provides a set of best practices and guidelines for implementing specific security controls. Organizations seeking ISO certification for cloud security compliance can use these standards to structure their security programs, assess risks, and establish a robust ISMS. Achieving ISO/IEC 27001 certification demonstrates a commitment to a high level of information security, bolstering trust with customers, partners, and regulators.

The National Institute of Standards and Technology (NIST) has also contributed significantly to cloud security with its Special Publication 800-53 and Special Publication 800-37. NIST SP 800-53 offers a comprehensive catalog of security controls for federal information systems, providing a foundation for cloud security frameworks. Organizations in both the public and private sectors can leverage this framework to define and implement security controls tailored to their specific requirements. NIST SP 800-37, known as the Risk Management Framework (RMF), provides guidance on integrating risk management into the system development lifecycle. By applying the RMF, organizations can systematically manage risks associated with cloud-based systems, ensuring a proactive and adaptive approach to security.

The Cloud Security Alliance (CSA) has played a pivotal role in shaping cloud security best practices through its Cloud Controls Matrix (CCM) and the Consensus Assessments Initiative Questionnaire (CAIQ). The CCM provides a set of security controls mapped to leading compliance frameworks, helping organizations assess the security posture of cloud providers. It serves as a valuable tool for evaluating and comparing the security capabilities of different cloud services. The CAIQ, aligned with the CCM, offers a standardized set of questions for cloud consumers and auditors to assess the security capabilities of cloud providers. Both the CCM and CAIQ contribute to transparency and shared understanding between cloud providers and consumers.

In the realm of European data protection, the General Data Protection Regulation (GDPR) stands as a landmark framework with global implications. GDPR mandates strict requirements for the protection of personal data and grants individuals greater control over their data. Cloud providers and organizations leveraging cloud services must navigate GDPR's intricate provisions related to data processing, consent, and the rights of data subjects. Ensuring GDPR compliance in the cloud involves implementing robust data protection measures, conducting data impact assessments, and establishing mechanisms for data subjects to exercise their rights. GDPR's extraterritorial reach makes it a crucial consideration for any organization operating in the global digital landscape.

The Federal Risk and Authorization Management Program (FedRAMP) is a U.S. government initiative that standardizes the security assessment and authorization process for cloud services. FedRAMP establishes a baseline of security controls and requires cloud service providers to undergo rigorous assessments to demonstrate compliance. Government agencies can leverage FedRAMP-compliant cloud services, streamlining the procurement of secure cloud solutions. FedRAMP's impact extends beyond the federal government, influencing the broader cloud industry by setting a high bar for security standards and transparency.

The Center for Internet Security (CIS) provides a set of critical security controls known as the CIS Controls. These controls offer a prioritized and prescriptive framework for safeguarding information systems and data. Organizations can adopt the CIS Controls to enhance their security posture, aligning with best practices for risk management, incident response, and secure configuration. The CIS Controls are particularly valuable in the context of cloud security, offering a pragmatic and actionable approach to addressing common threats and vulnerabilities in cloud environments.

The International Electrotechnical Commission (IEC) has developed the IEC 62443 series of standards, specifically tailored for industrial automation and control systems (IACS). These standards address the unique security challenges associated with industrial systems, including those deployed in the cloud. IEC 62443 provides a systematic framework for implementing security measures in industrial environments, covering aspects such as network security, access control, and incident response. As industries increasingly adopt cloud-based solutions for their operational technology, compliance with IEC 62443 becomes crucial to ensure the resilience and security of critical infrastructure.

The European Union Agency for Cybersecurity (ENISA) contributes to the cloud security landscape through its Cloud Certification Schemes and the "EU Cybersecurity Act." ENISA's certification schemes provide a harmonized framework for assessing and certifying the security of cloud services across the European Union. The "EU Cybersecurity Act" establishes a European cybersecurity certification framework, enabling organizations to obtain a certification that is recognized across EU member states. These initiatives aim to create a unified approach to cloud security certification within the

EU, fostering trust and facilitating the cross-border provision of secure cloud services.

In the context of risk management, the Factor Analysis of Information Risk (FAIR) framework provides a quantitative approach to assessing and managing information security risk. While not specific to cloud security, FAIR offers a valuable methodology for organizations to evaluate the financial impact of security incidents and make informed risk-based decisions. This framework enhances the risk management capabilities of organizations operating in the cloud, allowing them to prioritize security investments based on a quantifiable understanding of potential risks.

In conclusion, the landscape of cloud security compliance is rich with established frameworks that cater to diverse industries, regulatory environments, and risk management approaches. These frameworks provide organizations with a structured roadmap to fortify their cloud security postures, navigate shared responsibility models, and meet the evolving demands of a dynamic threat landscape. Whether it's healthcare, finance, government, or industry-specific standards, adherence to these frameworks not only ensures regulatory compliance but also fosters a culture of security and trust among stakeholders. As organizations continue to embrace cloud technologies, the strategic adoption of these frameworks becomes instrumental in achieving and maintaining robust security practices in the cloud.

Discuss the impact of data privacy regulations on cloud security.

Data privacy regulations wield a profound impact on cloud security, reshaping the landscape in which organizations operate, manage, and safeguard sensitive information. One of the most influential regulations globally is the General Data Protection Regulation (GDPR), enacted by the European Union. GDPR sets stringent standards for the protection of personal data and grants individuals greater control over their information. The extraterritorial reach of GDPR means that any organization, irrespective of its physical location, processing the personal data of EU residents must comply with its provisions. This has far-reaching implications for cloud service providers (CSPs) and cloud users alike, as the regulation mandates robust measures to ensure the confidentiality, integrity, and availability of personal data in the cloud.

Organizations leveraging cloud services often find themselves navigating the intricate provisions of GDPR related to data processing, consent, and the rights of data subjects. Cloud users must establish clear agreements with their CSPs, ensuring that the processing of personal data adheres to GDPR requirements. This involves implementing strong contractual safeguards, conducting due diligence on the security practices of the chosen cloud provider, and having mechanisms in place to respond to data subject requests promptly. The shared responsibility model inherent in cloud computing requires organizations to carefully delineate responsibilities with their CSPs to ensure GDPR compliance at all levels of data processing.

Beyond GDPR, other data privacy regulations, such as the California Consumer Privacy Act (CCPA) and Brazil's Lei Geral de Proteção de Dados (LGPD), introduce additional complexities for organizations operating in the cloud. The CCPA, applicable to businesses that process the personal information of California residents, grants consumers the right to know what personal information is collected and how it is used, as well as the right to opt-out of the sale of their information. The LGPD, similar to GDPR, outlines principles for the processing of personal data, requiring organizations to implement measures to protect the privacy of Brazilian citizens. Cloud users must align their cloud security practices with the specific requirements of these regulations, incorporating mechanisms for data subject rights and robust consent management.

The impact of data privacy regulations on cloud security extends to the way organizations handle data breaches and security incidents. Many regulations, including GDPR, mandate the notification of data breaches to supervisory authorities and affected individuals within a specific timeframe. In the context of cloud security, organizations must have incident response plans that seamlessly integrate with the requirements of data privacy regulations. This involves conducting regular assessments of the cloud environment's security posture, implementing detection and response mechanisms, and having clear procedures for investigating and reporting incidents. The shared nature of cloud environments requires organizations to collaborate closely with their CSPs during incident response, ensuring a coordinated and timely notification process in the event of a security incident.

Compliance with data privacy regulations necessitates a comprehensive approach to data governance within cloud environments. Organizations must have a clear understanding of the types of data they process, where it resides in the cloud, and how it flows across different services. Data classification becomes a critical component, as organizations must identify and categorize sensitive data to apply appropriate security controls. Encryption, access controls, and data residency considerations become integral elements of cloud security strategies in compliance with data privacy regulations. Cloud users need to implement robust data protection measures to prevent unauthorized access, disclosure, or alteration of personal data, aligning with the principles of confidentiality and privacy.

The impact of data privacy regulations on cloud security is particularly evident in the realm of cross-border data transfers. Many regulations, including GDPR, impose restrictions on the transfer of personal data outside the geographic regions covered by the respective regulations. Cloud users engaging with global CSPs must ensure that data transfers comply with these regulations, leveraging mechanisms such as Standard Contractual Clauses (SCCs) or Binding Corporate Rules (BCRs) to establish a legal basis for international data transfers. Cloud providers, in turn, play a crucial role in providing transparent data transfer mechanisms, offering data processing agreements that align with the requirements of data privacy regulations.

Data privacy regulations amplify the importance of transparency and accountability in cloud security practices. Organizations must be able to demonstrate their compliance with regulations through documentation, audits, and assessments. This includes maintaining records of data processing activities, conducting privacy impact assessments, and engaging in regular audits of the cloud environment's security controls. CSPs, in response to the heightened scrutiny brought about by data privacy regulations, often undergo third-party assessments and certifications to validate their security practices. These certifications, such as the ISO/IEC 27001, demonstrate a commitment to industry-recognized security standards, providing cloud users with assurance regarding the security and privacy of their data.

The evolving landscape of data privacy regulations introduces a dynamic element to cloud security, necessitating adaptability and continuous improvement. Regulatory frameworks are subject to updates, amendments, and the introduction of new legislation. Cloud users and CSPs must remain vigilant to changes in data privacy regulations, ensuring that their security practices evolve to align with the evolving legal landscape. This requires active engagement with legal counsel, regulatory bodies, and industry associations to stay informed about emerging requirements. The ability to adapt cloud security measures in response to regulatory changes is crucial for organizations seeking to maintain compliance and mitigate risks associated with non-compliance.

The impact of data privacy regulations on cloud security extends beyond legal and technical considerations to encompass organizational culture and awareness. Data privacy is not solely a responsibility of the legal and IT departments; it is a shared responsibility that permeates all levels of an organization. Education and awareness programs play a crucial role in fostering a culture of privacy and security among employees. Cloud users must ensure that their workforce understands the implications of data privacy regulations, the importance of protecting personal information, and their roles in maintaining compliance. This includes training on secure cloud usage, recognizing and reporting potential privacy incidents, and adhering to privacy-by-design principles in the development and deployment of cloud-based applications.

The interplay between data privacy regulations and cloud security is evident in the burgeoning field of privacy-enhancing technologies (PETs). As organizations seek innovative solutions to protect personal data while harnessing the capabilities of cloud computing, PETs become instrumental. Technologies such as homomorphic encryption, differential privacy, and secure multi-party computation enable organizations to perform computations on encrypted data, share insights without exposing sensitive information, and collaborate securely in the cloud. The integration of PETs into cloud security strategies reflects a proactive approach to privacy, aligning with the principles of data minimization and user-centric control advocated by data privacy regulations.

In conclusion, the impact of data privacy regulations on cloud security is transformative, reshaping the way organizations approach the protection of sensitive information in cloud environments. GDPR, CCPA, LGPD, and other regulations compel organizations to elevate their cloud security practices, emphasizing transparency, accountability, and adaptability. The shared responsibility model inherent in cloud computing necessitates close collaboration between cloud users and CSPs to ensure compliance with data privacy regulations at every layer of the cloud stack. As the regulatory landscape evolves, organizations must embrace a holistic approach to cloud security that encompasses legal, technical, organizational, and cultural dimensions, establishing a foundation for trust and privacy in the digital age.

Explain the role of risk assessment in achieving and maintaining compliance.

The role of risk assessment in achieving and maintaining compliance is foundational to a robust and effective governance framework. Compliance, whether with regulatory standards, industry-specific requirements, or internal policies, involves navigating a complex landscape of potential risks and threats. A risk assessment serves as a systematic and structured approach to identifying, evaluating, and prioritizing these risks, providing organizations with insights into the potential impact and likelihood of non-compliance. By integrating risk assessment into the compliance process, organizations can proactively address vulnerabilities, allocate resources strategically, and establish a resilient foundation for meeting and sustaining regulatory obligations.

Risk assessment plays a pivotal role in the initial stages of compliance efforts, serving as a diagnostic tool to understand the unique challenges and exposures faced by an organization. This process often begins with the identification of relevant regulations and standards applicable to the industry and geographical location in which the organization operates. Once these are identified, the risk assessment process delves into the intricacies of the organization's operations, data handling practices, and IT infrastructure to pinpoint areas where compliance vulnerabilities may exist. This holistic understanding is crucial for tailoring compliance strategies to the specific risk profile of the organization, ensuring that efforts are focused on the areas of highest impact.

In the realm of risk assessment for compliance, a key consideration is the dynamic nature of the regulatory landscape. Regulations evolve, new standards emerge, and the business environment undergoes constant changes. Risk assessment acts as a continuous monitoring mechanism, allowing organizations to adapt to evolving compliance requirements. Regular and ongoing risk assessments ensure that compliance efforts remain aligned with the latest regulatory developments, enabling organizations to stay ahead of the curve and preemptively address emerging challenges. This adaptability is particularly critical in industries with rapidly changing regulatory frameworks, such as financial services and healthcare.

One of the core aspects of risk assessment in compliance is the evaluation of the potential impact and consequences of non-compliance. Risks are assessed not only in terms of their likelihood but also in terms of the magnitude of harm they can inflict on the organization. This multifaceted evaluation aids in prioritizing risk mitigation efforts, directing resources toward addressing the most significant compliance threats. The impact assessment considers not only financial repercussions but also the potential damage to the organization's reputation, legal consequences, and the overall stability of business operations. By quantifying and qualifying these impacts, risk assessment guides organizations in making informed decisions about resource allocation and risk mitigation strategies.

Risk assessment also plays a crucial role in the development and implementation of controls designed to mitigate compliance risks. Once potential risks are identified and evaluated, organizations can design and implement control measures to manage and reduce these risks to an acceptable level. Controls may include policy and procedural changes, technological safeguards, training programs, and other measures aimed at fortifying the organization's compliance posture. The effectiveness of these controls is continually assessed through ongoing risk monitoring and periodic reassessments, ensuring that they remain relevant and capable of addressing the evolving landscape of compliance risks.

In the context of risk assessment for compliance, the concept of the risk appetite and tolerance of an organization becomes instrumental. Risk appetite defines the level of risk an organization is willing to accept in pursuit of its objectives, while risk tolerance specifies the acceptable variation from this risk appetite. Establishing and understanding these parameters is a fundamental aspect of risk assessment, guiding decision-makers in determining the acceptable level of compliance risk. This not only informs the design of control measures but also shapes the organization's overall risk management strategy, ensuring a balanced approach that aligns with business objectives while maintaining compliance integrity.

Risk assessment in compliance is intricately linked to the concept of the risk register or risk inventory. This is a comprehensive database that catalogues identified risks, their corresponding assessments, and the control measures in place. The risk register serves as a central repository of information, providing a holistic view of the compliance risk landscape. It becomes an invaluable tool for decision-makers, allowing them to prioritize risks, track the effectiveness of controls, and communicate risk-related information across different levels of the organization. A well-maintained risk register fosters transparency and accountability, essential elements in the pursuit of compliance excellence.

The role of risk assessment extends beyond mere identification and mitigation; it serves as a mechanism for strategic decision-making in the context of compliance. As organizations navigate complex regulatory requirements, they often encounter situations where choices must be made regarding resource allocation, process optimization, and strategic direction. Risk assessment provides the data and insights necessary for informed decision-making, aligning compliance efforts with broader organizational goals. This strategic alignment ensures that compliance is not viewed in isolation but as an integral component of organizational resilience and sustainable growth.

In the pursuit of compliance, organizations are often confronted with resource constraints, necessitating a pragmatic approach to risk management. Risk assessment aids in prioritizing efforts, allowing organizations to focus on high-impact compliance risks while acknowledging and managing lower-priority risks within acceptable parameters. This prioritization is vital for optimizing resource utilization, ensuring that compliance efforts are directed where they can deliver the greatest value. Moreover, by aligning risk assessments with business objectives, organizations can make strategic decisions that not only enhance compliance but also contribute to overall operational efficiency and effectiveness.

The integration of risk assessment into compliance strategies also facilitates a proactive rather than reactive approach to risk management. By identifying potential compliance risks before they materialize into issues, organizations can take preemptive measures to address vulnerabilities and prevent non-compliance. This proactive stance minimizes the likelihood of regulatory violations, reducing the associated costs and disruptions. It transforms risk management from a reactive firefighting activity to a strategic capability that enhances the organization's resilience and adaptability in the face of regulatory challenges.

Collaboration and communication are integral aspects of risk assessment in the context of compliance. The insights derived from risk assessments need to be effectively communicated across different levels of the organization, from executives to front-line employees. This ensures a shared understanding of compliance risks, responsibilities, and the broader risk management strategy. Regular communication fosters a culture of risk awareness and accountability, empowering employees to contribute actively to compliance efforts. Additionally, collaboration with external stakeholders, such as regulatory bodies, industry associations, and auditors, enhances the organization's ability to stay attuned to the latest regulatory developments and align risk assessments with external expectations.

Continuous improvement is a central tenet of risk assessment in compliance. Organizations must view risk assessment not as a one-time activity but as an ongoing and iterative process. Regular reassessment of compliance risks allows organizations to adapt to changes in the regulatory environment, emerging threats, and evolving business conditions. Feedback loops, derived from monitoring and assessment activities, contribute to the refinement of risk management strategies and the optimization of control measures. This iterative approach positions organizations to not only achieve compliance but to sustain it over time, fostering a culture of continuous improvement that aligns with the dynamic nature of regulatory requirements.

In conclusion, the role of risk assessment in achieving and maintaining compliance is multifaceted and integral to a comprehensive governance framework. From the identification and evaluation of compliance risks to the design and implementation of controls, risk assessment guides organizations in navigating the complex regulatory landscape. Its strategic impact extends to resource allocation, decision-making, and proactive risk management, ensuring that compliance efforts are aligned with business objectives. As organizations recognize the interconnectedness of compliance and risk management, risk assessment becomes a cornerstone for building resilience, adaptability, and sustainable compliance practices in an ever-evolving regulatory environment.

Discuss the importance of regular auditing for assessing compliance.

Regular auditing plays a pivotal role in assessing compliance across various sectors and industries, serving as a robust mechanism to ensure that organizations adhere to established standards, regulations, and internal policies. The importance of auditing in this context cannot be overstated, as it not only safeguards the integrity of operations but also fosters transparency, accountability, and trust among stakeholders.

One of the primary functions of regular auditing is to verify and validate adherence to legal and regulatory frameworks. In a rapidly evolving global landscape, where laws and regulations are subject to constant updates, audits serve as a crucial tool to evaluate whether organizations remain compliant with the latest statutory requirements. This ensures that entities operate within the boundaries set by governing bodies, mitigating the risk of legal repercussions and fostering a culture of legal and ethical responsibility.

Moreover, auditing provides a comprehensive assessment of internal policies and procedures, which are often tailored to industry-specific standards or best practices. Through meticulous examination, auditors can identify gaps or inefficiencies in these internal mechanisms, offering organizations an opportunity to refine and enhance their operational frameworks. This proactive approach not only minimizes the likelihood of compliance breaches but also optimizes organizational efficiency, ultimately contributing to sustained growth and competitiveness.

In the realm of financial compliance, auditing plays a critical role in verifying the accuracy and reliability of financial statements. Financial audits are instrumental in assessing whether an organization's financial records faithfully represent its economic transactions and financial position. This is of paramount importance for investors, creditors, and other stakeholders who rely on transparent and accurate financial information to make informed decisions. Regular financial audits instill confidence in the financial markets and contribute to the stability of the economic ecosystem.

Auditing also serves as a powerful tool for risk management. By systematically evaluating processes and controls, auditors can identify potential risks and vulnerabilities that may expose an organization to financial, operational, or reputational harm. This risk-centric approach allows organizations to implement preventive measures and develop contingency plans, fortifying their resilience in the face of unforeseen challenges. In essence, auditing provides a proactive means of risk identification and mitigation, aligning organizational strategies with the goal of long-term sustainability.

Furthermore, auditing plays a crucial role in ensuring the effectiveness of internal controls. Internal controls are the checks and balances within an organization designed to safeguard assets, maintain accurate financial records, and promote operational efficiency. Regular audits help organizations assess the adequacy and functionality of these internal controls. This not only deters fraudulent activities but also ensures that resources are utilized judiciously, fostering an environment of trust and accountability among employees.

In the context of information technology and data security, auditing becomes indispensable in an era where digital transformation is pervasive. Audits of IT systems and data protection protocols are essential to verify compliance with data privacy laws, safeguard sensitive information, and prevent cyber threats. As organizations increasingly rely on technology for their day-to-day operations, regular IT audits become instrumental in identifying vulnerabilities, ensuring data integrity, and fortifying cybersecurity measures.

Beyond the realm of regulatory and financial compliance, auditing also contributes significantly to ethical and corporate social responsibility (CSR) compliance. Auditors assess whether organizations uphold ethical standards in their business practices, treat their employees fairly, and contribute positively to the communities in which they operate. This holistic approach to compliance ensures that organizations not only meet legal requirements but also fulfill their ethical and societal obligations, enhancing their reputation and fostering long-term stakeholder relationships.

Regular auditing, therefore, acts as a cornerstone for building and sustaining trust among stakeholders. Whether it be shareholders, customers, employees, or regulatory bodies, the assurance provided by audited compliance instills confidence in an organization's ability to operate responsibly and ethically. This trust, once established, becomes a valuable intangible asset that can significantly impact an organization's reputation and brand equity.

In conclusion, the importance of regular auditing for assessing compliance cannot be overstated. It is a multifaceted tool that not only ensures adherence to legal and regulatory frameworks but also promotes operational efficiency, risk management, financial transparency, and ethical business practices. As organizations navigate an increasingly complex and dynamic business environment, the role of auditing becomes even more critical in safeguarding their integrity, reputation, and long-term viability. Embracing a culture of regular and comprehensive auditing is, therefore, a strategic imperative for organizations seeking to thrive in an era defined by accountability, transparency, and responsible business conduct.

Address legal aspects related to cloud security, including contractual agreements.

The legal landscape surrounding cloud security is a complex and evolving domain that necessitates a thorough understanding of contractual agreements to ensure the protection of sensitive data and adherence to regulatory frameworks. Cloud computing, with its inherent advantages of scalability and accessibility, introduces a myriad of legal considerations that organizations must navigate to safeguard their interests and those of their clients.

Contractual agreements form the bedrock of cloud security arrangements, defining the terms and conditions governing the relationship between cloud service providers (CSPs) and their clients.

These agreements, often encapsulated in Service Level Agreements (SLAs) and Terms of Service (ToS), outline the responsibilities and obligations of both parties. They detail the security measures implemented by the CSPs and the corresponding expectations of the clients regarding the protection of their data.

One of the paramount legal considerations in cloud security is data protection and privacy. With the rise of stringent data protection laws such as the General Data Protection Regulation (GDPR) and various regional equivalents, organizations entrusting their data to the cloud must ensure that contractual agreements explicitly address compliance with these regulations. Clauses pertaining to data ownership, processing, and transfer must be meticulously drafted to align with the legal requirements of the jurisdictions involved, ensuring that both the CSP and the client adhere to applicable data protection laws.

Moreover, the contractual framework must incorporate provisions related to data breach notification and incident response. As data breaches have become a prevalent threat, both parties need to establish clear protocols for promptly notifying each other in the event of a security incident. This not only facilitates a swift and coordinated response but also ensures compliance with legal obligations that may mandate timely reporting to regulatory authorities and affected individuals.

The issue of jurisdiction and applicable law is another critical facet of cloud security contractual agreements. As data traverses borders in the cloud environment, determining the legal jurisdiction governing potential disputes becomes a complex undertaking. Cloud service contracts should delineate the applicable laws and the venue for dispute resolution, providing clarity to both parties and minimizing legal ambiguities that could arise in cross-border scenarios.

Furthermore, compliance with industry-specific regulations adds another layer of complexity to cloud security contracts. Depending on the nature of the data and the industry in which the client operates, there may be sector-specific regulations governing the storage and processing of information. Healthcare, finance, and government sectors, for example, often have stringent compliance requirements that must be explicitly addressed in contractual agreements to avoid legal repercussions.

In the contractual realm, the concept of liability and indemnification assumes paramount importance. Cloud security agreements must establish the extent of liability each party assumes in the event of a security incident, data loss, or service interruption. Indemnification clauses should be carefully crafted to allocate responsibilities and potential financial repercussions, offering a legal framework for addressing the aftermath of security breaches or other adverse events.

In tandem with liability considerations, contractual agreements in cloud security must address the issue of service level guarantees. These agreements typically include stipulations regarding the availability, performance, and reliability of the cloud services. Establishing clear metrics and remedies for service level deficiencies ensures that clients have legal recourse if the agreed-upon security standards are not met, thereby safeguarding their interests and investments in the cloud environment.

Vendor lock-in is a legal concern that organizations often grapple with in the context of cloud security. Contractual agreements should provide clients with the flexibility to migrate their data and applications seamlessly to alternative providers if necessary. This not only fosters healthy competition among CSPs but also safeguards clients against potential legal challenges that may arise if they decide to transition away from a particular service provider.

The issue of transparency is integral to cloud security, and contractual agreements should reflect a commitment to transparency on the part of the CSP. Clients have a legal right to understand the security measures implemented by the CSP, including encryption protocols, access controls, and auditing practices. Contractual provisions that ensure regular transparency reports and audits contribute to building trust and demonstrate a commitment to maintaining high-security standards.

Beyond contractual agreements, compliance with international standards and certifications adds another layer of legal assurance in the realm of cloud security. Certifications such as ISO 27001 for information security management and SOC 2 for service organizations attest to a CSP's commitment to robust security practices. Inclusion of these certifications in contractual agreements provides clients with a legal basis for trusting that the CSP adheres to globally recognized security standards.

In conclusion, the legal aspects related to cloud security, particularly within contractual agreements, are intricate and multifaceted. Crafting comprehensive and legally sound contracts is imperative to navigate the evolving landscape of data protection laws, industry-specific regulations, and the dynamic nature of cloud computing. Addressing issues such as data protection, jurisdiction, liability, and transparency in contractual agreements not only mitigates legal risks but also fosters a secure and trust-based relationship between cloud service providers and their clients in an era where data integrity and privacy are paramount.

Explore the development and implementation of governance policies in cloud security.

The development and implementation of governance policies in cloud security have become imperative in the contemporary digital landscape, where organizations increasingly rely on cloud computing to store, process, and manage their data. This evolution is marked by the need for comprehensive frameworks that address the unique challenges and risks associated with cloud environments. One key driver behind the formulation of governance policies is the inherent shift in responsibility from traditional on-premises infrastructure to third-party cloud service providers. As organizations migrate their operations to the cloud, the dynamic nature of this environment necessitates a proactive approach to security governance.

The first step in this process involves the establishment of a robust governance framework that outlines the overall strategy, objectives, and principles guiding cloud security. This framework typically integrates with the broader information security governance structure, aligning cloud-specific policies with the organization's overarching security goals. By articulating clear roles and responsibilities, such frameworks provide a foundation for effective decision-making and accountability in the cloud security context.

A critical aspect of governance policy development is risk assessment and management. Cloud environments introduce a diverse set of risks, ranging from data breaches and unauthorized access to service outages and compliance violations. Effective governance policies involve a comprehensive risk assessment that considers factors such as data sensitivity, regulatory requirements, and the shared responsibility model inherent in cloud services. These policies should articulate risk tolerance levels and delineate strategies for risk mitigation, transfer, or acceptance.

To address the multifaceted nature of cloud security, governance policies often encompass a variety of domains, including data protection, identity and access management, and compliance. Data protection policies outline encryption protocols, data classification, and incident response plans to safeguard sensitive information stored in the cloud. Identity and access management policies establish protocols for user authentication, authorization, and monitoring, crucial in an environment where access controls are often decentralized.

Furthermore, compliance considerations play a pivotal role in shaping governance policies for cloud security. Organizations must navigate a complex landscape of regional, industry-specific, and international regulations governing data protection and privacy. Effective governance policies not only ensure compliance with these regulations but also facilitate ongoing monitoring and adaptation to changes in the regulatory environment.

As organizations increasingly adopt multi-cloud or hybrid cloud architectures, governance policies must address the intricacies of managing security across diverse cloud platforms. Interoperability, data portability, and consistent security controls become paramount considerations in such scenarios. Governance policies should therefore provide clear guidelines on selecting and managing cloud service providers, including criteria for evaluating their security postures and contractual obligations.

The implementation phase of cloud security governance involves translating policies into practical measures and procedures. This may include deploying security technologies such as firewalls, intrusion detection systems, and security information and event management (SIEM) solutions. Additionally, organizations must invest in ongoing monitoring and auditing mechanisms to ensure that their cloud environments adhere to the established policies.

Employee training and awareness programs play a pivotal role in the successful implementation of governance policies. As human factors remain a significant source of security vulnerabilities, organizations must educate their workforce on cloud security best practices, phishing awareness, and the importance of adhering to established policies. Training initiatives should be tailored to the specific nuances of cloud security, emphasizing the shared responsibility model and the role each individual plays in maintaining a secure cloud environment.

Continuous improvement is an integral component of effective cloud security governance. Regular reviews and audits of governance policies and their implementation help organizations adapt to evolving threats, technology advancements, and changes in business requirements. This iterative process ensures that governance policies remain relevant, effective, and aligned with the organization's overall risk appetite and strategic objectives.

In conclusion, the development and implementation of governance policies in cloud security represent a dynamic and multifaceted endeavor. As organizations embrace the cloud to enhance flexibility, scalability, and efficiency, the need for robust governance becomes paramount. A comprehensive governance framework, encompassing risk management, data protection, compliance, and operational considerations, provides the foundation for securing cloud environments. The successful implementation of these policies requires a holistic approach that integrates technology, employee training, and continuous improvement mechanisms. By addressing the complexities of cloud security through effective governance, organizations can navigate the digital landscape with confidence and resilience.

Emphasize the role of training and awareness programs in maintaining compliance.

Training and awareness programs play a pivotal role in maintaining compliance within organizations operating in today's complex regulatory landscape. As industries grapple with an ever-evolving set of rules and standards governing data protection, privacy, and various other aspects of business operations, the need for a well-informed and vigilant workforce becomes increasingly crucial. Compliance is not a static state but a continuous process, and employees are both the front line and the last line of defense in ensuring that organizations adhere to the myriad of regulations that apply to them.

These training programs are designed to educate employees about the specific compliance requirements relevant to their roles and the broader organizational context. For instance, in the realm of data protection, employees must be well-versed in regulations such as the General Data Protection Regulation (GDPR) or the Health Insurance Portability and Accountability Act (HIPAA), depending on the industry and geographic location of the organization. Training helps employees understand the implications of these regulations on their day-to-day tasks, fostering a culture of compliance from the ground up.

One of the primary focuses of compliance training is on data protection and privacy. Employees need to grasp the significance of handling sensitive information responsibly, understanding the classification of data, and recognizing the potential risks associated with mishandling or unauthorized disclosure. Training programs often cover the importance of obtaining explicit consent for data processing, the secure storage of data, and the necessity of notifying appropriate parties in the event of a data breach. By instilling a deep understanding of data protection principles, organizations empower their workforce to make informed decisions that align with regulatory requirements.

Furthermore, compliance training extends beyond data protection to encompass broader topics such as ethical conduct, anti-corruption measures, and industry-specific regulations. Employees need to be aware of the ethical standards and legal obligations that govern their professional conduct, especially in industries where corruption risks are prevalent. Anti-corruption training programs emphasize the importance of fair business practices, discouraging bribery, and promoting transparency in financial transactions, all of which are crucial components of maintaining compliance.

The advent of technology and the increasing reliance on digital platforms in the workplace introduce additional dimensions to compliance training. Employees should be educated on the secure use of technology, recognizing phishing attempts, and adhering to cybersecurity best practices. With cyber threats becoming more sophisticated, organizations must ensure that their workforce is equipped to identify and mitigate potential risks to data integrity and confidentiality.

Importantly, compliance training is not a one-time event but a continuous process that evolves alongside regulatory changes and organizational developments. Regular updates and refresher courses are essential to keep employees informed about new regulations, revised policies, and emerging risks. These ongoing initiatives help reinforce a culture of compliance, ensuring that employees remain vigilant and responsive to the ever-changing regulatory landscape.

In addition to formal training programs, awareness campaigns contribute significantly to maintaining a compliance-centric culture within an organization. These campaigns utilize various communication channels, including internal newsletters, posters, and intranet platforms, to disseminate information about compliance requirements, policy updates, and success stories. By showcasing the positive impact of compliance efforts and highlighting the consequences of non-compliance, awareness campaigns create a sense of shared responsibility among employees.

Beyond regulatory compliance, training programs also address industry-specific standards and certifications that organizations may pursue to demonstrate their commitment to best practices. For example, in the realm of information security, employees may undergo training to prepare for certifications such as Certified Information Systems Security Professional (CISSP) or Certified Information Security Manager (CISM). These certifications not only enhance employees' knowledge and skills but also contribute to the organization's overall compliance with industry standards.

The effectiveness of training and awareness programs in maintaining compliance is closely tied to the commitment of leadership in fostering a culture of compliance. When organizational leaders prioritize and actively participate in compliance initiatives, it sends a powerful message throughout the workforce. Leaders should lead by example, demonstrating ethical behavior, adhering to compliance requirements, and actively engaging in training programs. This top-down approach reinforces the importance of compliance as a core organizational value.

In conclusion, training and awareness programs are indispensable components of an organization's strategy for maintaining compliance. These initiatives empower employees with the knowledge and skills needed to navigate the complex web of regulations governing their industry. By fostering a culture of compliance, organizations can mitigate risks, enhance their reputation, and build trust with stakeholders. Continuous training, coupled with awareness campaigns and leadership commitment, ensures that compliance remains a dynamic and integral aspect of the organizational fabric. As industries evolve and regulations change, the adaptability and awareness instilled through these programs position organizations to navigate the complexities of compliance with resilience and confidence.

Discuss the importance of metrics in measuring and reporting on cloud security compliance.

The importance of metrics in measuring and reporting on cloud security compliance cannot be overstated in the dynamic and complex landscape of cloud computing. As organizations increasingly leverage cloud services to store, process, and manage their data, the need for a robust system of metrics arises to assess and ensure compliance with the myriad of security standards and regulations. Metrics serve as quantifiable indicators that enable organizations to gauge the effectiveness of their security measures, identify potential vulnerabilities, and demonstrate adherence to established compliance frameworks.

One fundamental aspect of cloud security metrics involves assessing the implementation of controls outlined in governance policies. These controls, which may cover areas such as data encryption, access management, and incident response, are critical in safeguarding sensitive information in the cloud. By measuring the effectiveness of these controls through metrics, organizations can ascertain whether their security measures align with industry best practices and regulatory requirements. For instance, metrics may track the percentage of data encrypted, the frequency of access reviews, or the time taken to respond to security incidents.

Metrics play a pivotal role in evaluating the compliance of cloud environments with specific industry standards and regulations. Whether it be the General Data Protection Regulation (GDPR), the Health Insurance Portability and Accountability Act (HIPAA), or industry-specific standards like the Payment Card Industry Data Security Standard (PCI DSS), organizations must demonstrate adherence to these frameworks. Metrics provide a quantitative means to assess compliance, offering insights into key performance indicators (KPIs) such as data breach incidents, audit outcomes, and the status of security controls related to regulatory requirements.

Furthermore, metrics contribute to the continuous monitoring of security postures in the cloud. Given the dynamic nature of cloud environments, where resources can be provisioned and de-provisioned rapidly, ongoing monitoring is essential for detecting and responding to emerging threats. Metrics related to real-time monitoring of network traffic, system logs, and user activities enable organizations to proactively identify anomalous behavior, potential security incidents, and unauthorized access. This proactive approach is crucial for maintaining the integrity and confidentiality of data stored in the cloud.

In the realm of identity and access management, metrics provide insights into user authentication and authorization processes. By tracking metrics such as login success rates, failed login attempts, and the frequency of privileged access, organizations can evaluate the effectiveness of access controls. These metrics not only help in assessing compliance with security policies but also assist in identifying potential security breaches or insider threats. The ability to measure and report on these metrics is particularly important in cloud environments where user access may be decentralized across various services.

Moreover, metrics contribute to the assessment of the overall risk posture of cloud environments. Risk metrics, such as the likelihood and impact of security incidents, help organizations prioritize mitigation efforts and allocate resources effectively. By quantifying risk factors, organizations can make informed decisions on security investments, remediation strategies, and incident response planning. This risk-centric approach is essential in the context of cloud security, where the shared responsibility model necessitates a clear understanding of risk ownership and management between the cloud service provider and the organization.

Metrics also play a critical role in communicating the effectiveness of security measures to stakeholders, including executives, boards of directors, and regulatory bodies. Clear and concise metrics provide a tangible way to demonstrate the return on investment in security initiatives and the organization's commitment to maintaining a secure cloud environment. Additionally, regular reporting on security metrics fosters transparency, building trust with customers, partners, and regulatory authorities. In an era where data breaches and cyber threats are prevalent, organizations that can effectively communicate their security posture through metrics are better positioned to instill confidence in their stakeholders.

The establishment of a comprehensive set of cloud security metrics requires a thoughtful approach that aligns with the organization's risk tolerance, business objectives, and regulatory environment. Metrics should be tailored to the specific nuances of the cloud environment, accounting for factors such as multi-cloud or hybrid cloud architectures. The selection of relevant metrics should be a collaborative effort involving security professionals, compliance officers, and other key stakeholders, ensuring that the metrics chosen are meaningful and aligned with organizational goals.

In conclusion, the importance of metrics in measuring and reporting on cloud security compliance is multifaceted. Metrics provide a quantitative means to assess the effectiveness of security controls, monitor compliance with regulatory frameworks, and evaluate the overall risk posture of cloud environments. The ability to measure and report on these metrics is crucial for organizations seeking to demonstrate their commitment to security, communicate effectively with stakeholders, and navigate the complexities of the ever-changing cloud landscape. As cloud adoption continues to grow, the role of metrics in ensuring and reporting on cloud security compliance remains a cornerstone of a robust and resilient cybersecurity strategy.

Highlight the iterative nature of compliance efforts.

The iterative nature of compliance efforts underscores a fundamental reality in the dynamic and ever-evolving landscape of regulations, standards, and business environments. Achieving and maintaining compliance is not a one-time project but an ongoing and adaptive process that requires continuous attention, refinement, and adaptation. Organizations operate within a context where external factors, such as changes in legislation, industry standards, and technological advancements, necessitate a proactive and iterative approach to compliance.

The iterative nature of compliance efforts begins with the establishment of a robust foundation, often in the form of a comprehensive compliance program. This program serves as a framework that outlines the organization's commitment to adhering to relevant regulations, industry standards, and internal policies. However, this initial phase is just the starting point, and the real challenge lies in sustaining and enhancing compliance over time. This is where the iterative cycle comes into play, emphasizing the ongoing commitment to improvement and adaptation.

One critical aspect of this iterative process involves regular risk assessments. As the business environment evolves, so do the risks that organizations face. Regular risk assessments enable organizations to identify and evaluate new and emerging threats, vulnerabilities, and compliance challenges. By conducting periodic assessments, organizations can stay ahead of the curve, adjusting their compliance strategies to address the changing risk landscape. This iterative risk management approach is essential for maintaining a resilient and adaptive compliance posture.

Moreover, the iterative nature of compliance efforts is evident in the continuous cycle of policy development, implementation, and refinement. Organizations must establish and communicate clear policies that reflect current regulatory requirements and industry best practices. However, the effectiveness of these policies is contingent on their relevance to the evolving business landscape. Therefore, organizations must regularly review and update their policies, ensuring that they align with the latest legal and industry standards. This iterative policy management approach ensures that compliance efforts remain aligned with the organization's strategic objectives and external regulatory expectations.

In the context of technology and cybersecurity, the iterative nature of compliance efforts is particularly pronounced. As organizations adopt new technologies, cloud services, and digital platforms, they must continuously assess and enhance their security measures to address emerging threats. This involves an ongoing process of implementing security controls, monitoring their effectiveness, and adjusting strategies based on real-world feedback and incidents. The dynamic nature of cyber threats necessitates constant adaptation, and the iterative approach ensures that security measures evolve in tandem with the evolving threat landscape.

The iterative cycle also plays a crucial role in the realm of employee training and awareness programs. As regulations change, new compliance requirements emerge, and organizational priorities shift, employees need to stay informed and educated. Regular training sessions and awareness campaigns help reinforce compliance principles, update employees on policy changes, and instill a culture of compliance within the workforce. This iterative approach to employee education is essential for cultivating a vigilant and informed workforce that actively contributes to the organization's compliance efforts.

Furthermore, external audits and assessments contribute to the iterative nature of compliance efforts. Organizations often undergo regular audits conducted by internal teams, external auditors, or regulatory bodies. These audits serve as checkpoints in the compliance journey, providing insights into the effectiveness of existing controls and areas that may require improvement. The findings from audits feed into a continuous improvement loop, prompting organizations to refine their processes, update policies, and implement corrective actions. This iterative feedback loop ensures that compliance efforts remain aligned with regulatory expectations and industry standards.

The iterative nature of compliance efforts is closely intertwined with the concept of continuous improvement. Organizations committed to compliance understand that they operate in a dynamic environment where change is constant. The goal is not merely to achieve compliance at a specific point in time but to cultivate a culture of continuous improvement that permeates every aspect of the organization. This involves fostering a mindset of adaptability, responsiveness, and a commitment to learning from both successes and challenges in the compliance journey.

In conclusion, the iterative nature of compliance efforts reflects the dynamic and evolving nature of the regulatory landscape and business environments. Organizations must move beyond viewing compliance as a static achievement and embrace an ongoing, adaptive process that involves regular risk assessments, policy refinement, technology updates, employee education, and external audits. This iterative approach ensures that compliance efforts remain relevant, effective, and resilient in the face of changing circumstances. By embedding a culture of continuous improvement, organizations not only meet their current compliance obligations but also position themselves to navigate future challenges with agility and confidence.

Chapter 7: Incident Response and Recovery Strategies

Define incident response and its crucial role in mitigating security threats.

Incident response is a comprehensive and structured approach to addressing and managing the aftermath of a security incident or cyberattack. It encompasses a set of coordinated activities, processes, and procedures designed to identify, contain, eradicate, recover from, and learn from security incidents. The primary goal of incident response is to minimize the impact of security breaches and ensure the swift restoration of normal operations while preserving and analyzing digital evidence to understand the nature and scope of the incident. In essence, incident response is a strategic and proactive capability that organizations deploy to effectively deal with the inevitable reality that security incidents will occur.

The crucial role of incident response in mitigating security threats becomes evident when considering the evolving and sophisticated nature of cyber threats in today's digital landscape. Organizations face a wide array of potential security incidents, ranging from malware infections and data breaches to denial-of-service attacks and insider threats. The rapid detection and response to these incidents are imperative to prevent or limit damage, protect sensitive data, and maintain the trust of stakeholders. Incident response acts as a crucial line of defense, enabling organizations to react promptly, efficiently, and systematically when faced with a security incident.

A key element of incident response is the early detection of security incidents. Through continuous monitoring of network traffic, system logs, and user activities, organizations aim to identify unusual patterns or behaviors that may indicate a potential security breach. Early detection is essential because it allows for a swift response, reducing the time attackers have to carry out their objectives and minimizing the impact on the organization's systems and data. Incident response teams leverage a combination of security technologies, threat intelligence, and skilled analysts to enhance their ability to detect and respond to security incidents in a timely manner.

Once a security incident is detected, the containment phase of incident response comes into play. Containment involves taking immediate actions to prevent the further spread of the incident and limit its impact. This may involve isolating affected systems, blocking malicious network traffic, or disabling compromised user accounts. The goal is to prevent the incident from escalating and causing more extensive damage to the organization's infrastructure, data, and reputation. The effectiveness of the containment phase is crucial in mitigating the overall impact of a security incident.

Eradication is the phase where incident response teams focus on completely removing the threat from the organization's systems. This involves identifying the root cause of the incident, eliminating any remaining malicious artifacts, and patching vulnerabilities that may have been exploited. The eradication phase is essential to prevent a recurring incident and strengthen the organization's security posture. It often requires a combination of technical measures, such as deploying security patches and updates, and procedural changes to address underlying issues in the organization's security architecture.

Following eradication, the recovery phase of incident response focuses on restoring affected systems and services to normal operations. This involves validating the integrity of restored systems, monitoring for any signs of persistent threats, and ensuring that all necessary safeguards are in place to prevent a recurrence of the incident. The recovery phase is critical for minimizing downtime and disruptions to business operations. Organizations often develop and implement recovery plans in advance to streamline the process and facilitate a rapid return to normalcy.

Beyond the immediate response to a security incident, incident response includes a crucial element of post-incident analysis and learning. This phase involves a detailed examination of the incident to understand its root causes, tactics, techniques, and procedures (TTPs) employed by the attackers, and any vulnerabilities exploited. The knowledge gained from post-incident analysis informs future security measures, allowing organizations to enhance their defenses and better prepare for similar incidents in the future. Continuous improvement is a central tenet of incident response, as organizations strive to learn from each incident and adapt their security strategies accordingly.

Incident response is not solely a technical process but involves a multidisciplinary approach that includes technology, people, and processes. Effective incident response requires skilled professionals with expertise in cybersecurity, digital forensics, and crisis management. It also necessitates well-defined incident response plans and procedures that are regularly tested through simulations and drills. The collaboration between different departments within an organization, including IT, legal, communications, and executive leadership, is crucial for a coordinated and effective response to security incidents.

In conclusion, incident response plays a crucial role in mitigating security threats by providing organizations with a systematic and proactive approach to identifying, containing, eradicating, recovering from, and learning from security incidents. In the face of evolving and persistent cyber threats, incident response serves as a critical line of defense, enabling organizations to respond swiftly and effectively to mitigate the impact of security incidents. Through early detection, containment, eradication, recovery, and post-incident analysis, incident response contributes to the resilience and security posture of organizations in an increasingly complex and interconnected digital landscape.

Explore methods for promptly identifying and classifying security incidents.

Promptly identifying and classifying security incidents is a fundamental aspect of effective cybersecurity, enabling organizations to respond swiftly and decisively to potential threats. Various methods and technologies contribute to this crucial capability, aligning with the dynamic and sophisticated nature of today's cyber landscape.

One primary method for identifying security incidents is through continuous monitoring of network traffic. Network monitoring involves analyzing the flow of data across an organization's network to detect any unusual patterns or behaviors that may indicate a security breach. This method relies on intrusion detection systems (IDS) and intrusion prevention systems (IPS) that use signature-based detection, anomaly detection, or behavioral analysis to identify potential threats. By analyzing network traffic in real-time, organizations can quickly spot indicators of compromise, such as suspicious communication patterns or unauthorized access attempts, facilitating the prompt identification of security incidents.

In addition to network monitoring, endpoint detection and response (EDR) solutions play a crucial role in identifying security incidents at the device level. EDR solutions are deployed on individual endpoints, such as computers and servers, to monitor and analyze activities at the endpoint level. These solutions can detect malicious behavior, unauthorized access, or abnormal processes indicative of a security incident. By promptly identifying unusual activities on endpoints, organizations can isolate and investigate potential security incidents, preventing further compromise and mitigating the impact of a breach.

Security information and event management (SIEM) systems offer another method for promptly identifying and classifying security incidents. SIEM solutions aggregate and correlate data from various sources, including logs from network devices, servers, and applications. Through advanced analytics and correlation rules, SIEM systems can highlight events that may indicate a security incident. These events are then categorized and prioritized based on predefined criteria. SIEM solutions provide a centralized view of the organization's security posture, enabling security teams to quickly identify and respond to potential incidents based on the information provided by the system.

Furthermore, threat intelligence plays a critical role in promptly identifying security incidents by providing context and proactive insights. Threat intelligence involves the collection, analysis, and dissemination of information about potential cyber threats. Security teams can leverage threat intelligence feeds to stay informed about the latest attack vectors, known malicious actors, and emerging threats. By integrating threat intelligence into their security monitoring processes, organizations can enhance their ability to identify security incidents promptly and understand the context and potential impact of those incidents.

User and entity behavior analytics (UEBA) is another method focused on promptly identifying security incidents by monitoring the behavior of users and entities within the organization. UEBA solutions use machine learning algorithms to establish a baseline of normal behavior for users and entities. Deviations from this baseline can indicate suspicious or malicious activities, prompting the identification of potential security incidents. By analyzing patterns of behavior, UEBA solutions contribute to the early detection of insider threats, compromised accounts, or unauthorized access attempts.

Email security solutions and advanced threat protection mechanisms are crucial for promptly identifying security incidents related to phishing attacks and malicious email content. These solutions employ techniques such as email filtering, sandboxing, and analysis of email headers and content to identify and block malicious emails. Given the prevalence of email as a vector for cyberattacks, the ability to quickly recognize and classify phishing attempts or malicious attachments is essential for preventing further escalation of security incidents.

Anomaly detection techniques leverage statistical analysis and machine learning algorithms to identify deviations from normal patterns of behavior within the organization's IT environment. By establishing a baseline of normal behavior, anomaly detection systems can identify abnormal activities that may indicate a security incident. This method is particularly effective in detecting zero-day attacks or previously unknown threats that may not be identified through traditional signature-based detection methods.

Incident classification is a crucial aspect of the identification process, enabling organizations to prioritize and respond appropriately to different types of incidents. Classification criteria often include the severity of the incident, the potential impact on business operations, and the type of threat or attack involved. Automation plays a significant role in incident classification, as organizations can use predefined rules and criteria to automatically categorize incidents based on their characteristics. This automation enhances the speed and efficiency of incident response by ensuring that security teams can focus their attention on the most critical and high-impact incidents.

Collaboration and information sharing within the cybersecurity community also contribute to the prompt identification and classification of security incidents. Information sharing platforms, threat intelligence consortiums, and industry-specific forums allow organizations to stay informed about emerging threats and incidents observed by others in their sector. This collective knowledge helps security teams identify and classify incidents more rapidly, leveraging the insights and experiences of the broader cybersecurity community.

Employee training and awareness programs are instrumental in enhancing the human element of incident identification. Security awareness initiatives educate employees about common attack vectors, social engineering techniques, and the importance of reporting suspicious activities. By cultivating a culture of vigilance among employees, organizations empower their workforce to promptly identify and report security incidents, whether it be a phishing attempt, a suspicious email, or unusual behavior on the network.

Regular security assessments, including penetration testing and vulnerability scanning, contribute to the proactive identification of security incidents. Penetration tests simulate real-world attacks to identify vulnerabilities and weaknesses in the organization's defenses. Vulnerability scanning tools systematically scan the IT environment for known vulnerabilities. By conducting these assessments regularly, organizations can discover potential weaknesses before malicious actors exploit them, allowing for timely remediation and reducing the risk of security incidents.

In conclusion, promptly identifying and classifying security incidents is a multifaceted process that involves the integration of various methods and technologies. From continuous monitoring of network traffic and endpoint detection to the use of SIEM systems, threat intelligence, and advanced analytics, organizations deploy a comprehensive toolkit to detect and understand security incidents promptly. Automation, collaboration within the cybersecurity community, employee training, and regular security assessments further enhance the organization's ability to identify and classify incidents rapidly. In a landscape where cyber threats are persistent and diverse, the timely recognition of security incidents is paramount to effective incident response and the overall resilience of an organization's cybersecurity posture.

Discuss the development of a tailored incident response plan for cloud environments.

The development of a tailored incident response plan for cloud environments is a critical undertaking for organizations seeking to effectively navigate the unique challenges and complexities posed by cloud computing. As organizations increasingly rely on cloud services to store, process, and manage their data, the need for a comprehensive and adaptable incident response plan becomes paramount. A well-crafted incident response plan specific to cloud environments not only acknowledges the shared responsibility model inherent in cloud services but also addresses the dynamic nature of cloud infrastructure, the distributed nature of data, and the potential for novel attack vectors.

The initial phase of developing a tailored incident response plan involves a thorough understanding of the cloud environment's architecture, services, and deployment models. This foundational knowledge is essential for crafting an incident response strategy that aligns with the organization's specific use of cloud resources. Cloud environments often span multiple service models such as Infrastructure as a Service (IaaS), Platform as a Service (PaaS), and Software as a Service (SaaS). The incident response plan should consider the implications of incidents on each service model and delineate the responsibilities of both the cloud service provider and the organization.

A crucial component of the incident response plan for cloud environments is the delineation of roles and responsibilities within the organization and in collaboration with the cloud service provider. The shared responsibility model in cloud computing emphasizes that while the provider is responsible for the security of the cloud infrastructure, the organization retains responsibility for securing its data, applications, and access controls. The incident response plan must clearly define the roles of the internal incident response team, cloud service provider's incident response team, and any other third-party entities involved. This collaborative approach ensures a coordinated response that leverages the expertise of all relevant stakeholders.

In the context of a cloud incident response plan, organizations must incorporate the principles of the National Institute of Standards and Technology (NIST) framework for incident response. This framework provides a structured and adaptable approach to incident response, encompassing preparation, detection, containment, eradication, recovery, and lessons learned. Adapting these principles to the cloud environment requires considering the rapid scalability, elasticity, and automation inherent in cloud services. The incident response plan should articulate how these principles apply to cloud-specific scenarios, such as incidents involving cloud-based applications, storage, or identity and access management.

Preparation is a foundational stage in incident response planning, and in the context of cloud environments, it involves developing and testing incident response procedures tailored to the unique characteristics of the cloud. This includes defining incident categories specific to the cloud, such as unauthorized access to cloud resources, data breaches, or disruptions in cloud service availability. Organizations should conduct scenario-based exercises that simulate cloud-specific incidents to validate the effectiveness of the incident response plan and familiarize the response team with the intricacies of responding to incidents in a cloud environment.

Detecting security incidents in the cloud requires a combination of continuous monitoring, threat intelligence, and anomaly detection mechanisms. The incident response plan should detail how the organization will monitor activities across cloud services, analyze logs and events, and integrate threat intelligence to identify potential security incidents promptly. Cloud-specific tools and services, such as cloud security information and event management (Cloud SIEM), play a crucial role in enhancing the detection capabilities for cloud environments. Integrating these tools into the incident response plan ensures a comprehensive and context-aware approach to incident detection.

In the containment phase of incident response in cloud environments, organizations need to leverage the native capabilities provided by cloud service providers. This may involve isolating compromised instances, adjusting access controls, and utilizing cloud-native security groups or firewalls to contain the incident. The incident response plan should specify the procedures for isolating affected resources, coordinating with the cloud service provider to implement necessary controls, and preventing the lateral movement of attackers within the cloud environment. Additionally, communication and coordination mechanisms with relevant cloud provider support and incident response teams should be established in advance.

Eradication involves identifying and eliminating the root cause of the incident to prevent its recurrence. In a cloud environment, this may involve updating security configurations, patching vulnerabilities, or implementing new security controls. The incident response plan should outline how the organization will collaborate with the cloud service provider to address underlying issues in the cloud infrastructure. Automated processes for implementing security updates, leveraging Infrastructure as Code (IaC) practices, and ensuring consistent security configurations across cloud resources contribute to the effective eradication of security threats in the cloud.

Recovery in a cloud incident response plan extends beyond restoring affected systems to encompass the restoration of cloud services and data. Cloud environments allow for dynamic scaling and redundancy, facilitating a resilient recovery strategy. The incident response plan should detail how the organization will prioritize the recovery of critical cloud services, validate the integrity of restored data, and communicate with stakeholders about the restoration process. Cloud-based backup and recovery solutions, coupled with well-defined recovery time objectives (RTOs) and recovery point objectives (RPOs), contribute to the organization's ability to recover swiftly from security incidents in the cloud.

Post-incident analysis and lessons learned are integral components of the incident response lifecycle. In the context of cloud environments, organizations should conduct thorough post-incident reviews to understand the impact of the incident on cloud services, identify areas for improvement, and refine incident response procedures. This iterative process ensures that the incident response plan evolves alongside the organization's use of cloud services and the evolving threat landscape. Additionally, organizations should consider sharing lessons learned with the broader cloud security community to contribute to collective knowledge and improve the overall resilience of cloud environments.

Given the global nature of cloud services and the potential for cross-border data flows, the incident response plan should also address legal and regulatory considerations. Organizations must be aware of the data protection and privacy laws applicable to the regions where they operate and store data. The plan should include procedures for notifying regulatory authorities, customers, and other stakeholders in the event of a data breach, ensuring compliance with relevant regulations. Establishing relationships with legal counsel experienced in cloud compliance and data protection is crucial for navigating these complex aspects of incident response in cloud environments.

Continuous improvement is a core principle in the development of a tailored incident response plan for cloud environments. Regularly reviewing and updating the plan to incorporate lessons learned from incidents, changes in cloud services, and emerging threats is essential. Organizations should stay abreast of advancements in cloud security best practices, regulations, and technologies, adjusting their incident response strategies accordingly. By embracing a mindset of continuous improvement, organizations can enhance their resilience and readiness to respond effectively to security incidents in the dynamic and rapidly evolving landscape of cloud computing.

Highlight the importance of collaboration with cloud service providers during incident response.

The importance of collaboration with cloud service providers (CSPs) during incident response cannot be overstated in the complex and interconnected landscape of cloud computing. As organizations increasingly rely on cloud services for storing, processing, and managing their data, the nature of incidents has become more dynamic, necessitating a collaborative approach between organizations and their CSPs. The shared responsibility model inherent in cloud computing underscores the significance of clear communication, coordinated efforts, and mutual support during incident response activities.

In the event of a security incident, the initial collaboration with a CSP begins with timely and accurate communication. Transparency between the organization and the CSP is paramount, as both parties need to understand the nature and scope of the incident to formulate an effective response strategy. The organization should promptly notify the CSP about the incident, providing relevant details such as the affected resources, potential impact, and any actions taken to contain or mitigate the incident. This proactive communication sets the stage for a collaborative incident response effort.

A key aspect of collaboration with CSPs during incident response lies in understanding the delineation of responsibilities outlined in the shared responsibility model. While CSPs are responsible for the security of the cloud infrastructure, the organization retains responsibility for securing its data, applications, and access controls. Clarifying these roles ensures a coordinated response where each party focuses on their specific areas of expertise. The incident response plan should clearly articulate the division of responsibilities, minimizing confusion and facilitating a streamlined collaboration during the different phases of incident response.

CSPs often offer a range of tools and services that can enhance incident detection, investigation, and response within their cloud environments. Leveraging these native tools, such as cloud security information and event management (Cloud SIEM), identity and access management (IAM) logs, and threat intelligence feeds provided by the CSP, can significantly augment the organization's incident response capabilities. Collaboration with the CSP in configuring and optimizing these tools ensures that the organization benefits from the full spectrum of security features available in the cloud environment.

During the detection phase of incident response, organizations may rely on CSP-specific tools to monitor activities across cloud services. The CSP's insight into the infrastructure and the ability to analyze logs and events at scale contribute to the early identification of security incidents. Collaborative efforts in fine-tuning detection mechanisms, developing custom alerts, and integrating threat intelligence feeds allow the organization to harness the full potential of the CSP's tools for timely and effective incident detection.

In the containment phase, collaboration with the CSP is crucial for implementing controls that isolate affected resources, prevent further spread of the incident, and mitigate potential damage. Cloud-native security groups, firewalls, and access controls provided by the CSP offer granular control over network traffic and resource access. Coordinating with the CSP to adjust these controls based on the incident's characteristics and impact helps in containing the incident swiftly and efficiently. Additionally, understanding how the CSP manages incidents on their end ensures alignment in the containment efforts and minimizes any disruptions to the organization's operations.

The eradication phase involves addressing the root cause of the incident to prevent its recurrence. Collaboration with the CSP is essential in identifying and mitigating any vulnerabilities or misconfigurations in the cloud infrastructure that may have been exploited. This may involve adjusting security configurations, patching vulnerabilities, or implementing additional security controls. The organization and the CSP should work in tandem to eradicate the underlying issues, applying best practices for securing cloud resources and ensuring a resilient and secure cloud environment.

In the recovery phase, the organization collaborates with the CSP to restore affected cloud services and validate the integrity of recovered data. Cloud environments offer unique advantages in terms of rapid scalability and redundancy, facilitating a robust recovery strategy. Coordination with the CSP in prioritizing the recovery of critical services, performing validation checks, and communicating progress to stakeholders is instrumental in achieving a swift and effective recovery. This collaborative effort ensures that the organization leverages the inherent capabilities of the cloud environment for seamless restoration of operations.

Continuous communication and coordination with the CSP extend to the post-incident analysis and lessons learned phase. Collaborative efforts in conducting a thorough post-incident review, analyzing the incident's impact on cloud services, and identifying areas for improvement contribute to the iterative enhancement of incident response procedures. Sharing insights and lessons learned between the organization and the CSP fosters a culture of continuous improvement, where both parties benefit from the collective knowledge gained through each incident. This collaborative learning approach strengthens the overall resilience of the organization's cloud security posture.

Collaboration with CSPs becomes particularly vital in scenarios involving advanced threats or sophisticated cyberattacks. Threat actors are continually evolving their tactics, techniques, and procedures (TTPs), making it challenging for organizations to stay ahead. CSPs, with their extensive view of activities across multiple customer environments, are well-positioned to identify emerging threats and share threat intelligence with their customers. Collaborative efforts in threat intelligence sharing enhance the organization's ability to proactively defend against evolving threats and strengthen its overall cybersecurity posture.

In addition to technical collaboration, organizations benefit from engaging with their CSPs in tabletop exercises, simulations, and joint training initiatives. These collaborative activities help build familiarity with the CSP's incident response processes, improve coordination mechanisms, and ensure that both parties are well-prepared to respond effectively to security incidents. Joint training sessions also facilitate a better understanding of the specific tools, features, and capabilities provided by the CSP, enabling the organization to make optimal use of these resources during incident response.

Legal and regulatory considerations add another layer to the importance of collaboration with CSPs during incident response. Cloud environments often involve the processing and storage of data across different jurisdictions, each with its own data protection and privacy laws. Collaboration with the CSP in navigating legal and regulatory requirements ensures that incident response activities adhere to applicable laws. This includes considerations for data breach notification requirements, data sovereignty, and any other legal obligations that may impact incident response efforts.

In conclusion, collaboration with cloud service providers during incident response is indispensable for organizations operating in cloud environments. The shared responsibility model, clear delineation of roles, and effective communication lay the foundation for a collaborative incident response approach. Leveraging the tools and services provided by CSPs, aligning incident response procedures with cloud-specific considerations, and continuous coordination contribute to the effectiveness of incident response efforts. This collaborative partnership not only enhances the organization's ability to respond swiftly to security incidents but also fosters a shared commitment to the ongoing improvement of cloud security practices in the face of evolving cyber threats.

Outline a step-by-step approach to responding to data breaches in the cloud.

Responding to data breaches in the cloud requires a meticulous and well-orchestrated step-by-step approach to effectively mitigate the impact, preserve evidence, and ensure the organization's recovery. This process involves a combination of technical, organizational, and legal considerations, reflecting the complexities of today's cloud environments. The step-by-step approach begins with the initial detection of the data breach and progresses through containment, eradication, recovery, post-incident analysis, and communication with relevant stakeholders.

The first crucial step in responding to a data breach in the cloud is detection. Early detection is fundamental to minimizing the impact of the breach, and cloud environments offer various tools and mechanisms for continuous monitoring. Security information and event management (SIEM) solutions, cloud-native monitoring tools, and anomaly detection systems play a vital role in identifying suspicious activities, unauthorized access, or abnormal patterns in data flows. Timely detection relies on configuring these tools to generate alerts for potential incidents, and organizations should have robust procedures in place to promptly investigate and validate these alerts.

Upon detecting a data breach, the next step is to initiate containment measures. Cloud environments provide unique capabilities for isolating affected resources, adjusting access controls, and preventing the lateral movement of attackers. This phase involves coordinating with the cloud service provider (CSP) to implement controls such as adjusting security groups, isolating compromised instances, and restricting access to sensitive data. The objective is to prevent further dissemination of the breach, limit the potential damage, and create a controlled environment for subsequent investigation and response.

Eradication focuses on identifying and eliminating the root cause of the breach. This step involves a thorough examination of the affected cloud resources, analysis of logs, and collaboration with the CSP to address underlying vulnerabilities or misconfigurations. The organization should work towards ensuring that the vulnerabilities exploited by the attackers are patched, misconfigurations are corrected, and any lingering artifacts of the breach are removed. The eradication phase is essential to prevent a recurrence of the incident and fortify the overall security posture of the cloud environment.

Recovery involves restoring affected systems, services, and data to normal operations. Cloud environments facilitate resilient recovery strategies through features like data redundancy, backups, and dynamic scalability. Organizations should prioritize the recovery of critical services and data, taking into account the potential impact on business operations. Collaboration with the CSP is crucial during this phase to ensure a coordinated effort in restoring cloud services, validating the integrity of recovered data, and implementing any necessary security measures to prevent a similar incident in the future.

Post-incident analysis is a critical step in the response process, focusing on understanding the nature and impact of the data breach. This involves conducting a thorough investigation to determine how the breach occurred, what data was affected, and the extent of the compromise. Cloud-specific tools and logs provided by the CSP, as well as external forensic experts, may be engaged to aid in this analysis. The organization should also leverage threat intelligence to identify the tactics, techniques, and procedures (TTPs) employed by the attackers. This knowledge is invaluable for improving security defenses and preventing similar incidents.

Communication is a parallel and ongoing aspect of the response process. Organizations must communicate transparently with both internal and external stakeholders throughout the response effort. Internally, effective communication is essential among members of the incident response team, executive leadership, and relevant departments. Externally, organizations may need to communicate with customers, regulatory authorities, law enforcement, and other third parties affected by the breach. Timely and transparent communication helps build trust, manage reputational impact, and fulfill any legal or regulatory obligations related to data breach notifications.

Engaging legal counsel early in the response process is crucial to navigating the legal and regulatory aspects of a data breach. Legal considerations include compliance with data protection and privacy laws, contractual obligations with the CSP, and potential legal actions that may arise from the breach. Legal counsel can guide the organization in understanding and fulfilling notification requirements, preserving evidence for potential investigations, and managing any legal implications stemming from the breach. Collaboration with legal experts ensures that the response aligns with applicable laws and regulations.

Simultaneously, organizations should collaborate with their CSP throughout the entire response process. Early and continuous communication with the CSP is vital for understanding the shared responsibilities, coordinating technical efforts, and leveraging the CSP's expertise in securing cloud infrastructure. Collaboration with the CSP during incident detection helps in analyzing cloud-specific logs and telemetry data to identify the extent of the breach. In the containment phase, coordination is essential to adjust security controls, isolate compromised resources, and prevent further unauthorized access. The eradication and recovery phases benefit from joint efforts to address underlying vulnerabilities and restore affected cloud services securely.

The effectiveness of the response process is further enhanced by incorporating lessons learned into future incident response planning and security practices. Organizations should conduct a comprehensive post-incident review, analyzing the strengths and weaknesses of their response efforts. This analysis contributes to refining incident response procedures, updating security policies, and strengthening overall security posture. Continuous improvement is a guiding principle, and the organization should use the insights gained from each incident to enhance its resilience against evolving cyber threats in the cloud.

In conclusion, responding to data breaches in the cloud demands a methodical and well-coordinated approach that spans detection, containment, eradication, recovery, post-incident analysis, communication, legal considerations, and collaboration with the CSP. The dynamic nature of cloud environments requires organizations to adapt traditional incident response strategies to the unique challenges posed by cloud computing. By embracing a step-by-step response process and emphasizing collaboration with the CSP, organizations can effectively mitigate the impact of data breaches, learn from each incident, and continuously enhance their ability to safeguard sensitive information in the evolving landscape of cloud security.

Explore recovery strategies for cloud-based systems after a security incident.

Recovery strategies for cloud-based systems after a security incident constitute a critical phase in the overall incident response process. Cloud environments offer unique challenges and opportunities in the aftermath of a security breach, necessitating a comprehensive and adaptive approach to restore affected systems, services, and data while fortifying the organization's security posture. The recovery phase involves a series of strategic steps that span technical considerations, collaboration with cloud service providers (CSPs), legal aspects, and communication with stakeholders.

One fundamental aspect of recovery in cloud-based systems is the restoration of affected services and data to normal operations. Cloud environments inherently support resilient recovery strategies through features such as data redundancy, automated backups, and dynamic scalability. Organizations must prioritize the recovery of critical services based on their impact on business operations. Cloud service providers play a crucial role in this process, offering tools and services that facilitate the rapid restoration of cloud resources. Leveraging these native recovery capabilities enables organizations to minimize downtime and swiftly bring their systems back to a fully operational state.

Collaboration with the CSP is a key component of effective recovery strategies in cloud-based systems. During the recovery phase, organizations should engage with their CSP to ensure a coordinated effort in restoring cloud services. This collaboration involves transparent communication about the incident's impact, joint planning for recovery actions, and leveraging the expertise of the CSP in securing cloud infrastructure. The CSP's insights into cloud-specific tools, configurations, and best practices contribute to a more efficient and secure recovery process. Establishing clear communication channels and coordinating recovery efforts with the CSP is essential for a successful and synchronized recovery operation.

Validation of the integrity of recovered data is a critical step in the recovery phase for cloud-based systems. Organizations must ensure that the restored data is free from any alterations or compromises introduced during the security incident. Cloud environments often provide mechanisms for data validation, such as checksums, cryptographic hashing, and integrity checks. The organization, in collaboration with the CSP, should employ these mechanisms to verify the authenticity and accuracy of recovered data. This validation step is integral to maintaining data integrity, particularly when sensitive information is involved, and contributes to rebuilding trust in the reliability of cloud-based systems.

In the context of cloud-based systems, recovery planning should include a focus on the configuration and security settings of cloud resources. Cloud environments allow organizations to define and manage their infrastructure as code (IaC), facilitating the rapid and consistent deployment of resources. Incorporating security best practices into IaC templates ensures that recovered resources are configured with the necessary security controls in place. This proactive approach enhances the security posture of the recovered systems, reducing the risk of recurring vulnerabilities and potential exploitation by threat actors.

The recovery phase presents an opportunity for organizations to conduct a thorough review of their incident response procedures and identify areas for improvement. This reflective analysis is crucial for refining incident response plans, updating security policies, and strengthening overall cybersecurity resilience. Lessons learned from the incident, including the effectiveness of recovery measures and any challenges encountered, should inform the organization's ongoing efforts to enhance its incident response capabilities. Continuous improvement is a guiding principle in the recovery phase, ensuring that the organization evolves and adapts its security practices based on insights gained from the incident.

Legal and regulatory considerations are integral to the recovery strategies for cloud-based systems after a security incident. Organizations operating in different jurisdictions must navigate the complex landscape of data protection and privacy laws. The recovery process should align with legal obligations related to data breach notifications, incident reporting, and compliance with relevant regulations.

Engaging legal counsel during the recovery phase ensures that the organization adheres to legal requirements, manages potential liabilities, and fulfills any obligations to notify regulatory authorities, customers, or other affected parties about the security incident.

Communication is a parallel and ongoing aspect of the recovery phase, encompassing both internal and external stakeholders. Internally, effective communication is essential among members of the incident response team, executive leadership, IT departments, and any other relevant personnel. Clear and timely communication fosters collaboration and ensures that everyone involved is aware of the recovery progress. Externally, organizations may need to communicate with customers, partners, regulatory authorities, and the broader public. Transparent communication about the incident, the recovery process, and the steps taken to prevent future incidents is vital for maintaining trust, managing reputational impact, and complying with legal and regulatory requirements.

Engaging in post-incident analysis and lessons learned is an integral part of recovery strategies for cloud-based systems. This phase involves a detailed examination of the incident, the organization's response, and the effectiveness of the recovery measures. Cloud-specific logs, telemetry data, and forensic analysis contribute to understanding the nature and impact of the incident. Lessons learned from the recovery process inform updates to incident response procedures, security policies, and the organization's overall cybersecurity strategy. The iterative nature of post-incident analysis ensures that the organization continually improves its security posture based on the insights gained from each incident.

Technical considerations during the recovery phase extend beyond the restoration of services and data. Organizations must conduct a thorough assessment of the affected cloud environment to identify and remediate any residual vulnerabilities or misconfigurations. This involves collaborating with the CSP to address underlying issues that may have contributed to the security incident. Remediation actions may include applying security patches, updating configurations, and enhancing access controls. The organization should also consider implementing additional security measures to strengthen the overall resilience of the cloud-based systems against future security threats.

Recovery in cloud-based systems should not be viewed as a standalone process but rather as part of a broader strategy for building resilience. Organizations should take this opportunity to reassess their overall security posture, including proactive measures for threat detection, continuous monitoring, and preventive controls. Integrating the lessons learned from the recovery phase into the organization's broader cybersecurity framework ensures that future security incidents are met with a more robust and adaptive defense.

In conclusion, recovery strategies for cloud-based systems after a security incident demand a multifaceted approach that spans technical, organizational, legal, and communication considerations. Leveraging the capabilities of cloud environments, collaborating effectively with CSPs, ensuring data integrity, and adhering to legal and regulatory obligations are critical aspects of the recovery process. Continuous improvement, post-incident analysis, and lessons learned contribute to the organization's ability to adapt and evolve its cybersecurity practices in the dynamic landscape of cloud security.

Discuss the significance of post-incident analysis in improving future incident response.

The significance of post-incident analysis in improving future incident response cannot be overstated, as it serves as a cornerstone for organizational learning, refinement of security strategies, and the enhancement of overall cybersecurity resilience. Post-incident analysis, often referred to as a post-mortem or lessons learned exercise, represents a critical phase in the incident response lifecycle, offering valuable insights into the dynamics of security incidents, the effectiveness of response measures, and areas for improvement.

One of the primary objectives of post-incident analysis is to gain a comprehensive understanding of the incident's nature, scope, and impact. This involves conducting a thorough examination of the incident's timeline, from its initial detection to containment, eradication, and recovery. By reconstructing the sequence of events, security teams can identify the tactics, techniques, and procedures (TTPs) employed by threat actors, shedding light on their methods of intrusion and exploitation. Understanding the anatomy of the incident is foundational to developing targeted and effective response strategies for future incidents.

In addition to understanding the technical aspects of an incident, post-incident analysis delves into the organizational and procedural dimensions of incident response. This includes an evaluation of how well-defined incident response plans were executed, the effectiveness of communication and collaboration among response team members, and the efficiency of coordination with external entities, such as law enforcement or third-party incident response providers. Analyzing these aspects provides insights into the human and process-related factors that influence the overall success of incident response efforts.

Post-incident analysis plays a pivotal role in identifying the strengths and weaknesses of an organization's incident response capabilities. It highlights areas where the response was swift, effective, and aligned with established procedures, as well as areas where improvements are needed. This introspective examination enables organizations to refine their incident response plans, ensuring that they are agile, adaptable, and reflective of the evolving threat landscape. It also helps organizations identify gaps in their security posture, such as inadequate detection mechanisms, insufficient access controls, or outdated response procedures, which can be addressed to bolster overall cybersecurity defenses.

A key outcome of post-incident analysis is the formulation of actionable recommendations and best practices derived from the lessons learned during the incident response process. These recommendations cover a spectrum of domains, including technical measures, procedural enhancements, training and awareness initiatives, and investments in new technologies. By distilling insights from the incident, organizations can develop targeted and strategic recommendations that directly address the root causes and contributing factors identified during the analysis. Implementing these recommendations positions the organization to proactively mitigate similar risks in the future.

The iterative nature of post-incident analysis fosters a culture of continuous improvement within an organization. Each analysis contributes to an evolving body of knowledge that informs subsequent incident response efforts. This iterative process ensures that organizations do not merely react to incidents but actively learn from them, refining their cybersecurity posture over time. It fosters a proactive mindset, encouraging security teams to anticipate emerging threats, adapt response strategies accordingly, and continuously enhance the organization's resilience to evolving cyber risks.

Post-incident analysis is instrumental in fostering a culture of organizational learning and knowledge sharing. The insights gained from analyzing security incidents are valuable not only for the incident response team but for the broader cybersecurity workforce. Sharing lessons learned, best practices, and recommendations derived from post-incident analyses contributes to the collective knowledge of the organization. This shared knowledge empowers all stakeholders, from security professionals to IT staff and executives, to better understand the nuances of cyber threats and actively contribute to the organization's overall security posture.

Furthermore, post-incident analysis contributes to the development of threat intelligence within an organization. By dissecting the tactics used by threat actors during an incident, organizations can build a more nuanced understanding of the threat landscape. This intelligence informs proactive threat detection measures, allowing organizations to anticipate and counteract emerging threats before they manifest into security incidents. The integration of threat intelligence into incident response planning and overall cybersecurity strategy enhances an organization's ability to stay ahead of adversaries and respond effectively to new and evolving cyber threats.

Legal and regulatory compliance considerations are integral to post-incident analysis. Many jurisdictions require organizations to conduct post-incident analysis as part of their obligations to report and respond to data breaches. Post-incident analyses help organizations fulfill their legal and regulatory responsibilities by documenting the incident, detailing response actions taken, and providing evidence of due diligence in safeguarding sensitive information. Organizations that systematically conduct post-incident analyses are better positioned to demonstrate compliance with relevant data protection laws, industry regulations, and contractual obligations.

Post-incident analysis serves as a foundation for building resilience through scenario-based training and simulation exercises. Organizations can simulate realistic incident scenarios based on the lessons learned from previous incidents, allowing response teams to practice and refine their skills in a controlled environment. These exercises provide an opportunity to validate the effectiveness of incident response plans, enhance communication and collaboration among team members, and identify areas for further improvement. Scenario-based training transforms theoretical knowledge gained from post-incident analyses into practical skills that can be applied during real-world incidents.

Effective communication is another dimension of post-incident analysis, as organizations must convey their findings and recommendations to relevant stakeholders. This includes internal communication to executive leadership, IT departments, and incident response teams, as well as external communication to customers, regulatory authorities, law enforcement, and other third parties affected by the incident. Clear and transparent communication about the incident, the response efforts, and the lessons learned contributes to building trust, managing reputational impact, and fostering a culture of accountability and responsibility.

In conclusion, the significance of post-incident analysis in improving future incident response is multifaceted and far-reaching. It serves as a linchpin for organizational learning, providing insights into the technical, procedural, and human dimensions of security incidents. By systematically analyzing incidents, distilling lessons learned, and implementing targeted recommendations, organizations can iteratively enhance their incident response capabilities. The culture of continuous improvement fostered by post-incident analysis empowers organizations to adapt to evolving cyber threats, refine their security posture, and build resilience in the face of an ever-changing cybersecurity landscape.

Discuss legal and compliance aspects related to incident response activities.

Legal and compliance aspects related to incident response activities are integral components of an organization's efforts to navigate the complex landscape of cybersecurity and data protection. As organizations increasingly face the inevitability of security incidents, understanding and adhering to legal and compliance requirements during incident response becomes paramount. These aspects encompass a range of considerations, including data protection laws, industry regulations, contractual obligations, and engagement with law enforcement. Navigating these legal and compliance dimensions effectively ensures that incident response activities are conducted within the bounds of the law, safeguarding sensitive information and mitigating potential liabilities.

Data protection laws form a foundational framework for legal and compliance considerations in incident response. Organizations operating in different jurisdictions must be cognizant of the specific data protection regulations applicable to their operations. For instance, the European Union's General Data Protection Regulation (GDPR) imposes stringent requirements on organizations regarding the protection and processing of personal data. In the event of a security incident involving personal data, organizations must adhere to GDPR's notification requirements, promptly informing the relevant supervisory authority and affected individuals. Similar data breach notification requirements are present in various data protection laws worldwide, emphasizing the need for organizations to tailor their incident response plans to comply with these regulations.

Industry-specific regulations further contribute to the legal and compliance landscape of incident response. For example, healthcare organizations in the United States must adhere to the Health Insurance Portability and Accountability Act (HIPAA), which imposes strict standards for the protection of patients' health information. Financial institutions are subject to regulations such as the Gramm-Leach-Bliley Act (GLBA) and the Payment Card Industry Data Security Standard (PCI DSS), each with its own incident response requirements. Compliance with industry regulations necessitates a nuanced understanding of sector-specific legal obligations, shaping how organizations structure and execute their incident response activities to meet these standards.

Contractual obligations and agreements with third parties introduce another layer of legal considerations in incident response. Organizations often engage with vendors, cloud service providers, and other business partners, and these relationships are governed by con-

tracts that outline specific security and incident response requirements. Organizations must ensure that their incident response plans
align with contractual obligations, including reporting timelines, information sharing protocols, and cooperation mechanisms. Failure
to adhere to contractual commitments may not only result in legal
consequences but can also strain business relationships and impact
the organization's reputation.

Engaging with law enforcement is a nuanced legal aspect of incident response activities. In certain situations, organizations may
need to collaborate with law enforcement agencies to investigate and
mitigate the impact of a cyber incident. Cooperation with law enforcement is subject to legal considerations, including privacy laws
and the preservation of evidentiary integrity. Organizations must
strike a balance between assisting law enforcement in their investigations and safeguarding the rights of individuals affected by the incident. Legal counsel plays a crucial role in guiding organizations
through the complexities of interacting with law enforcement, ensuring that such collaborations are conducted in compliance with applicable laws.

The legal concept of attorney-client privilege becomes particularly relevant in incident response activities. Engaging legal counsel
early in the incident response process allows organizations to benefit
from attorney-client privilege, protecting certain communications
from disclosure during legal proceedings. This privilege extends to
the work product of legal counsel, fostering an environment where
organizations can candidly discuss and strategize incident response
without fear of subsequent legal repercussions. Leveraging attorney-
client privilege enhances the organization's ability to conduct a thorough and effective incident response while safeguarding sensitive information.

In some instances, incidents may lead to legal actions, either initiated by affected parties or regulatory authorities. Organizations

should be prepared for the possibility of litigation arising from a security incident. This preparation involves preserving evidence, maintaining detailed records of incident response actions, and engaging legal counsel to navigate potential legal proceedings. The organization's ability to demonstrate due diligence in its incident response efforts becomes a crucial factor in legal proceedings, emphasizing the importance of thorough documentation and adherence to legal and compliance standards throughout the incident response lifecycle.

Cross-border data considerations further complicate the legal landscape of incident response. Many organizations operate globally, leading to the processing and storage of data across different jurisdictions. The legal requirements for incident response may vary based on the location of affected individuals and the organization's operations. Navigating cross-border data flows necessitates a nuanced understanding of international data protection laws, such as the extraterritorial reach of the GDPR. Organizations must be mindful of the potential impact of these legal considerations on their incident response strategies, ensuring compliance with relevant laws in each jurisdiction where they operate.

Legal and compliance aspects extend to the communication strategies employed during and after incident response. Transparency and timely communication are essential components of effective incident response, but organizations must carefully navigate legal requirements and potential liabilities. Crafting public statements, notifying affected individuals, and communicating with regulatory authorities demand a delicate balance between providing necessary information and protecting the organization's legal position. Legal counsel plays a crucial role in advising on communication strategies, ensuring that organizations fulfill their legal obligations while minimizing the risk of adverse legal consequences.

Post-incident analysis, a critical phase in incident response, also has legal implications. Conducting a thorough analysis of the incident, identifying root causes, and implementing corrective measures contribute to the organization's ability to fulfill legal and compliance requirements. The insights gained from post-incident analysis inform not only technical and procedural improvements but also contribute to demonstrating due diligence in the event of legal scrutiny. Organizations that systematically conduct post-incident analyses are better positioned to showcase their commitment to cybersecurity and compliance, potentially mitigating legal liabilities.

In conclusion, legal and compliance aspects are integral dimensions of incident response activities, shaping how organizations prepare for, respond to, and recover from security incidents. The dynamic and evolving nature of cybersecurity laws and regulations underscores the importance of maintaining a proactive and adaptive approach to legal considerations in incident response. Engaging legal counsel, understanding jurisdiction-specific requirements, aligning incident response plans with contractual obligations, and preserving evidence for potential legal actions are essential components of a comprehensive and legally sound incident response strategy. By navigating these legal and compliance aspects effectively, organizations can enhance their resilience, protect sensitive information, and demonstrate a commitment to cybersecurity best practices within the bounds of the law.

Address the importance of clear and effective communication during security incidents.

The importance of clear and effective communication during security incidents cannot be overstated, as it plays a pivotal role in minimizing the impact of the incident, fostering collaboration among stakeholders, and preserving the organization's reputation. In the dynamic and high-stakes environment of cybersecurity, where threats can evolve rapidly, effective communication becomes a linchpin for successful incident response. Clear and timely communication serves as a guiding principle throughout the various stages of an incident, including detection, response, recovery, and post-incident analysis.

During the initial detection phase of a security incident, the speed at which information is communicated is critical. Security teams must be equipped with the means to promptly detect and validate potential incidents, and this necessitates clear communication channels and well-defined reporting procedures. Establishing a robust incident reporting mechanism ensures that individuals who detect suspicious activities or anomalies can convey this information swiftly to the incident response team. Timely communication at this stage sets the foundation for a rapid and effective response, enabling security teams to investigate and assess the severity of the incident promptly.

Once an incident is confirmed, the need for clear and effective communication intensifies during the response phase. Internally, within the organization's incident response team, transparency and collaboration are paramount. Team members must share information seamlessly, ensuring that everyone involved is well-informed about the nature of the incident, the assets affected, and the actions being taken to mitigate the threat. Clear communication within the response team facilitates a coordinated effort, aligning individual efforts toward the common goal of containing and eradicating the incident.

Externally, effective communication extends to stakeholders beyond the immediate incident response team. This includes executive leadership, IT departments, legal counsel, public relations teams, and any other relevant personnel. Executives need accurate and comprehensive information to make informed decisions about resource allocation, risk mitigation, and communication strategies. IT departments must be aware of potential disruptions and collaborate on technical measures to contain and remediate the incident. Legal counsel plays a crucial role in navigating the legal implications of the incident, while public relations teams focus on managing the organization's external messaging and reputation.

Transparency is a key component of effective communication during the response phase. Providing clear and honest updates to internal and external stakeholders about the incident's status, the steps being taken to address it, and any potential impact on operations instills confidence and trust. Transparency also enables stakeholders to make informed decisions about their own roles and responsibilities in the response effort. Open lines of communication contribute to a culture of shared responsibility, where all stakeholders are actively engaged in the organization's response to the incident.

Externally, communication with customers, partners, and regulatory authorities is essential during a security incident. Depending on the nature of the incident and relevant legal requirements, organizations may be obligated to notify affected individuals or entities about the breach. Clear and transparent communication in such instances is crucial for building trust and managing reputational impact. Crafting messages that convey the severity of the incident, the steps being taken to address it, and guidance for affected individuals demonstrates accountability and responsibility. Failure to communicate effectively with external stakeholders may exacerbate the reputational damage and erode trust in the organization.

Legal and compliance considerations further underscore the importance of clear communication during security incidents. Engaging legal counsel early in the response process helps organizations navigate the legal implications of the incident, including potential obligations for data breach notifications and compliance with relevant regulations. Clear communication with legal experts ensures that the organization adheres to legal requirements and mitigates potential liabilities. Moreover, the coordination between legal counsel and communication teams is essential to align messaging with legal strategies, maintaining a balance between transparency and legal prudence.

In the recovery phase of a security incident, communication remains a critical factor. Stakeholders, both internal and external, are eager for updates on the progress of recovery efforts and the restoration of normal operations. Effective communication during the recovery phase involves providing clear timelines, outlining the measures being taken to prevent a recurrence, and addressing any lingering concerns. Internal communication ensures that all relevant departments are aware of the recovery status, enabling a coordinated effort to resume normal business operations. Externally, continued transparency with customers, partners, and regulatory authorities contributes to rebuilding trust and confidence in the organization's ability to manage and recover from security incidents.

Post-incident analysis, an essential component of the incident response lifecycle, also benefits from clear and effective communication. Communicating the findings of the analysis internally helps the organization understand the root causes of the incident, identify areas for improvement, and refine incident response procedures. Clear communication of lessons learned contributes to the organization's overall cybersecurity resilience, shaping future incident response strategies based on insights gained from past incidents.

The role of communication becomes even more pronounced in the context of advanced and sophisticated cyber threats. In scenarios involving advanced persistent threats (APTs) or complex attack vectors, organizations may face challenges in rapidly understanding and responding to the incident. Clear and effective communication becomes a strategic asset in such situations, allowing security teams to disseminate threat intelligence, share insights about evolving tactics, and coordinate responses across the cybersecurity community. Collaboration with external entities, such as industry information sharing groups and government agencies, relies on clear communication to ensure a collective and coordinated defense against advanced threats.

Building a culture of security awareness within the organization is closely tied to effective communication during security incidents. Employees and end-users are integral components of the overall security posture, and clear communication about security incidents helps raise awareness about potential threats, phishing attacks, or social engineering attempts. Regular communication regarding best practices for security hygiene, incident reporting procedures, and ongoing training initiatives empowers individuals throughout the organization to play an active role in maintaining a vigilant and secure environment.

In conclusion, the importance of clear and effective communication during security incidents permeates every phase of the incident response lifecycle. From the initial detection of an incident through response, recovery, and post-incident analysis, communication serves as a linchpin for successful outcomes. Transparency, collaboration, and timely dissemination of information among internal and external stakeholders contribute to a resilient incident response strategy. Recognizing the critical role of communication in the dynamic landscape of cybersecurity positions organizations to not only navigate incidents successfully but also build trust, demonstrate accountability, and continually improve their cybersecurity posture.

Emphasize the iterative nature of incident response improvement.

The iterative nature of incident response improvement is a fundamental principle that underscores the dynamic and evolving landscape of cybersecurity. Unlike a linear or one-time approach, the iterative process recognizes that incident response is an ongoing and adaptive practice. It encompasses a continuous cycle of assessment, learning, enhancement, and implementation, ensuring that organizations evolve their incident response capabilities in tandem with emerging cyber threats. This iterative approach is crucial for staying ahead of adversaries, refining response strategies, and building resilience in the face of an ever-changing threat landscape.

The first stage of the iterative process involves a comprehensive assessment of past incidents. Organizations analyze the details of each incident, dissecting the events, tactics, and vulnerabilities that contributed to the security breach. This retrospective analysis forms the foundation for understanding the unique challenges posed by different incidents, allowing organizations to distill valuable lessons learned. By delving into the specifics of each incident, security teams gain insights into the tactics, techniques, and procedures (TTPs) employed by threat actors. This knowledge becomes a strategic asset, informing subsequent improvements to incident response strategies.

The learning phase within the iterative cycle is paramount for organizations seeking to adapt and enhance their incident response capabilities. Lessons learned from past incidents contribute to a collective knowledge base that extends beyond the immediate incident response team. Security professionals gain insights into the evolving tactics of cyber adversaries, emerging vulnerabilities, and the efficacy of different response measures. This shared knowledge becomes a critical resource for organizations aiming to fortify their defenses against recurrent threats and anticipate new attack vectors. The learning phase is not confined to technical aspects but also encompasses organizational and procedural insights, fostering a holistic understanding of incident dynamics.

Enhancement represents the proactive application of lessons learned to bolster incident response capabilities. This phase involves refining and optimizing incident response plans, procedures, and technical controls based on the insights gained from past incidents. Enhancements may span various dimensions, including the integration of new technologies, adjustments to communication protocols, and the optimization of detection and response processes. By actively implementing improvements, organizations position themselves to address known weaknesses and better respond to future incidents. This forward-looking approach aligns with the iterative nature of incident response, as enhancements are continually refined based on evolving threat landscapes and organizational requirements.

Implementation is the practical execution of enhanced incident response measures. This phase involves putting the refined incident response plans and procedures into action. Implementation extends beyond the technical realm to include organizational and human factors, such as training programs, awareness initiatives, and the cultivation of a security-conscious culture. Clear communication of the revised incident response processes to relevant stakeholders ensures a cohesive and coordinated response effort. The effectiveness of implementation is gauged through the organization's ability to respond promptly and effectively to security incidents, integrating the lessons learned and enhancements made during the iterative cycle.

The continuous nature of the iterative process in incident response is exemplified by the post-incident analysis of implemented improvements. After responding to an incident and implementing enhanced measures, organizations conduct a thorough review of their performance. This post-incident analysis includes an evaluation of how well the enhanced incident response measures aligned with the organization's objectives. It provides an opportunity to assess the effectiveness of the improvements, identify any unanticipated challenges, and gather additional insights for further refinement. This ongoing analysis contributes to the iterative cycle by closing the feedback loop, enabling organizations to adapt their incident response strategies based on real-world outcomes.

The iterative nature of incident response improvement aligns with the principle of continuous improvement, a core tenet of effective cybersecurity practices. Organizations that recognize the need for constant adaptation and refinement position themselves to navigate an ever-evolving threat landscape. Iterative improvement is not a one-size-fits-all process; it is tailored to the organization's specific needs, risk profile, and the lessons gleaned from its unique experiences. This adaptability is particularly crucial in the context of diverse industries, where the nature of threats and regulatory landscapes may vary significantly.

In a rapidly changing cybersecurity landscape, the iterative approach allows organizations to be agile and responsive. Cyber threats evolve, and threat actors continually refine their tactics. An iterative incident response strategy acknowledges this dynamic reality, ensuring that organizations are not only reactive but also proactive in their approach. The ability to iterate empowers organizations to quickly adjust their response measures, fortify defenses, and stay ahead of emerging threats. This agility is a strategic advantage in a landscape where the only constant is change.

The iterative nature of incident response improvement dovetails with the concept of threat intelligence integration. Organizations actively collecting and analyzing threat intelligence benefit from a continuous influx of information about emerging threats, vulnerabilities, and adversary tactics. This threat intelligence informs the iterative cycle, providing valuable context for understanding the relevance of past incidents and guiding the prioritization of enhancements. By integrating threat intelligence into the iterative process, organizations enrich their incident response strategies with real-time insights, enabling a more proactive and informed defense.

Organizations committed to the iterative improvement of incident response also embrace a culture of resilience. Recognizing that security incidents are not a matter of if but when, organizations cultivate a mindset that values adaptability and continuous learning. A resilient culture acknowledges that incidents are opportunities for growth and refinement, rather than setbacks. It encourages a proactive stance toward incident response, where each iteration builds on the strengths of the previous one, creating a more robust and adaptive security posture.

Collaboration and information sharing within the cybersecurity community are amplified by the iterative nature of incident response improvement. Organizations contributing to and benefiting from collective knowledge enhance their ability to respond effectively to shared threats. The iterative cycle encourages collaboration among industry peers, allowing for the exchange of insights, best practices, and lessons learned. This collaborative approach extends beyond organizational boundaries, fostering a community-wide resilience against common threats.

In conclusion, the iterative nature of incident response improvement is a cornerstone of effective cybersecurity practices. It embodies a continuous cycle of assessment, learning, enhancement, and implementation, ensuring that organizations evolve their incident response capabilities in response to evolving cyber threats. By embracing this iterative approach, organizations position themselves to navigate a dynamic threat landscape, fortify their defenses, and cultivate a culture of resilience. The iterative cycle, grounded in lessons learned and driven by continuous improvement, represents a strategic and adaptive response to the ever-changing challenges of cybersecurity.

Chapter 8: Future Trends in Cloud Security

Discuss the rapid evolution of technology and its impact on cloud security.

The rapid evolution of technology has ushered in an era of unprecedented advancements, profoundly impacting various facets of the digital landscape, and perhaps nowhere is this transformation more pronounced than in the realm of cloud security. As technology continues its relentless progression, cloud computing has emerged as a linchpin for the deployment and delivery of a myriad of services, ranging from data storage and processing to application development and deployment. The multifaceted impact of technological evolution on cloud security is deeply intertwined with the dynamic interplay of innovation, challenges, and the imperative for adaptive cybersecurity measures.

The proliferation of cloud services and the pervasive adoption of cloud computing represent a transformative force driven by technological evolution. Organizations across diverse industries leverage the cloud to scale their operations, enhance agility, and streamline resource management. This shift from traditional on-premises infrastructure to cloud-based models has redefined the cybersecurity landscape. The rapid evolution of cloud technology, epitomized by the emergence of Infrastructure as a Service (IaaS), Platform as a Service (PaaS), and Software as a Service (SaaS), has afforded businesses unparalleled flexibility and scalability. However, this evolution has also introduced a complex set of security considerations, necessitating innovative approaches to safeguarding digital assets in an increasingly interconnected and dynamic environment.

One of the central implications of the rapid evolution of technology on cloud security is the dynamic nature of the threat landscape. The sophisticated capabilities of cyber adversaries evolve in tandem with technological advancements, posing formidable challenges to cloud security. As organizations embrace cutting-edge technologies such as artificial intelligence (AI), machine learning (ML), and the Internet of Things (IoT), the attack surface expands, providing threat actors with new vectors for exploitation. The fluidity of the threat landscape demands continuous vigilance, adaptability, and the integration of advanced security measures to detect and thwart emerging threats.

The transformative impact of technology on cloud security is accentuated by the imperative for automation and orchestration in cybersecurity measures. The sheer scale and complexity of cloud environments necessitate the automation of security processes, from threat detection to incident response. Technologies like Security Orchestration, Automation, and Response (SOAR) systems have become indispensable in orchestrating the diverse components of cloud security, streamlining workflows, and enabling rapid, data-driven decision-making. The evolution of automation in cloud security not only enhances operational efficiency but also empowers organizations to respond proactively to security incidents in real time.

The advent of containerization and microservices architectures represents a paradigm shift in application development and deployment, profoundly influencing cloud security strategies. Container orchestration platforms like Kubernetes have gained prominence, enabling organizations to build, scale, and manage containerized applications efficiently. While these technologies contribute to enhanced agility and scalability, they also introduce unique security considerations. The rapid evolution of container security solutions underscores the need for adaptive measures to address vulnerabilities associated with containerized environments. Security tools, policies, and best practices must evolve in tandem with containerization trends to ensure robust protection without compromising the advantages offered by these innovative technologies.

The convergence of cloud computing with edge computing further exemplifies the rapid evolution of technology and its impact on cloud security. Edge computing, characterized by the processing of data closer to the point of generation, introduces new paradigms for computing and storage. As organizations decentralize their computing infrastructure to meet the demands of latency-sensitive applications, the security implications extend beyond traditional cloud boundaries. The integration of edge computing into the broader cloud security landscape requires a holistic approach that considers the unique challenges posed by distributed computing environments, emphasizing the need for decentralized security controls and real-time threat intelligence.

The evolution of technology is also reflected in the growing prominence of Zero Trust security frameworks in cloud environments. Traditional network perimeters are no longer sufficient in an era characterized by remote work, cloud services, and mobile devices. Zero Trust models assume that threats can originate from within and outside the network, requiring continuous verification of identities and strict access controls. This paradigm shift aligns with the dynamic nature of modern technology ecosystems, emphasizing a proactive and adaptive approach to cloud security. Continuous authentication, encryption, and least privilege access become paramount as organizations strive to mitigate the risks associated with the evolving threat landscape.

Amidst the rapid evolution of technology, the increased reliance on DevOps practices has reshaped the landscape of software development and deployment, influencing cloud security strategies. DevOps, characterized by the integration of development and operations teams, emphasizes speed, collaboration, and automation. This cultural shift has given rise to DevSecOps, where security is integrated into the entire DevOps lifecycle. The evolution of DevSecOps underscores the importance of embedding security into the fabric of cloud-native applications, fostering a proactive security posture that aligns with the pace of technological change.

The evolution of cloud security is inextricably linked with advancements in cryptographic protocols and encryption technologies. As organizations migrate sensitive data to the cloud, the protection of data in transit and at rest becomes paramount. Quantum computing, a nascent but rapidly advancing technology, introduces both opportunities and challenges to cryptographic systems. The development of quantum-resistant encryption algorithms represents a proactive response to the potential threat posed by quantum computers, highlighting the necessity for continual evolution in cryptographic strategies to ensure the confidentiality and integrity of data in cloud environments.

The regulatory landscape further underscores the impact of technology evolution on cloud security. As governments and regulatory bodies grapple with the complexities of a digitized world, privacy and data protection regulations evolve in response to technological advancements. Compliance with regulations such as the General Data Protection Regulation (GDPR) and the California Consumer Privacy Act (CCPA) necessitates a dynamic approach to cloud security, as organizations navigate the intricacies of data governance, consent management, and the secure processing of personal information in cloud environments.

The rapid evolution of technology in cloud security is inseparable from the imperative for continuous innovation in threat detection and prevention. Advanced threat detection mechanisms leverage AI and ML algorithms to analyze vast datasets, identify patterns indicative of malicious activity, and enhance the accuracy of security alerts. The integration of behavioral analytics and anomaly detection further exemplifies the symbiotic relationship between technology evolution and adaptive security measures. As threat actors employ increasingly sophisticated tactics, the evolution of security technologies becomes indispensable for maintaining effective defenses in cloud environments.

Cloud-native security solutions have emerged as a direct consequence of the rapid evolution of technology. These solutions, purpose-built for cloud environments, leverage native cloud services and APIs to provide seamless integration with cloud platforms. Cloud-native security tools address the unique challenges posed by the dynamic nature of cloud infrastructure, ensuring that security measures align with the ephemeral, scalable, and decentralized characteristics of cloud environments. The evolution of cloud-native security exemplifies the industry's commitment to staying ahead of emerging threats and adapting to the changing landscape of technology.

In conclusion, the rapid evolution of technology exerts a profound and multifaceted impact on cloud security. The transformative influence of cloud computing, containerization, edge computing, automation, and cryptographic advancements reshapes the cybersecurity landscape. The dynamic interplay between technological innovation and security challenges necessitates an adaptive and proactive approach to cloud security. Organizations navigating this evolving landscape must continually reassess their security postures, embrace emerging technologies, and cultivate a culture of resilience to effectively address the complexities of the modern threat landscape. The symbiotic relationship between technology evolution and cloud security underscores the imperative for continuous innovation, collaboration, and vigilance in safeguarding digital assets in an era of unprecedented technological advancement.

Explore the principles of a zero-trust security model.

The principles of a Zero Trust security model represent a paradigm shift in cybersecurity, challenging traditional assumptions about network trust and emphasizing a proactive, continuous verification approach. In a Zero Trust model, the fundamental concept is to treat all users, devices, and applications as potentially untrusted, regardless of their location within or outside the network perimeter. This departure from the traditional castle-and-moat approach acknowledges the dynamic and evolving nature of cyber threats, urging organizations to adopt a more robust and adaptive security posture. The principles of a Zero Trust model encompass a holistic and comprehensive strategy that involves continuous verification, least privilege access, micro-segmentation, comprehensive visibility, and dynamic risk assessment.

Continuous verification is a cornerstone of the Zero Trust security model, emphasizing the need to continually validate the identities and security posture of users, devices, and applications. Unlike the traditional model that relies on static, perimeter-based trust, Zero Trust demands ongoing authentication and authorization at every access attempt. Users and devices are not granted implicit trust based solely on their location within the network but must undergo continuous scrutiny and validation throughout their interactions with resources. This dynamic verification process minimizes the risk of unauthorized access, as trust is never assumed and is continuously reaffirmed based on real-time conditions and contextual factors.

Least privilege access is a guiding principle of the Zero Trust model, advocating for the restriction of access permissions to the minimum necessary for users and systems to perform their designated functions. Unlike the traditional model where users often enjoy broad access privileges once inside the network, a Zero Trust approach follows the principle of granting the least amount of access required for specific tasks. This minimizes the attack surface, limiting the potential impact of a security breach. By adhering to the principle of least privilege, organizations can significantly reduce the risk of lateral movement by threat actors within the network, enhancing overall security posture.

Micro-segmentation is a key architectural component of the Zero Trust security model, focusing on dividing the network into smaller, isolated segments to contain and control lateral movement. Rather than relying on a one-size-fits-all security approach for the entire network, micro-segmentation allows organizations to enforce specific security policies at the granular level of individual workloads or applications. This segmentation strategy impedes the lateral spread of threats, confining potential breaches to limited segments and preventing unauthorized access to critical assets. Micro-segmentation aligns with the Zero Trust philosophy by assuming that threats may exist anywhere within the network and proactively isolating and securing segments accordingly.

Comprehensive visibility is an imperative principle of Zero Trust, emphasizing the need for organizations to gain real-time insights into user activities, device behaviors, and network traffic. Visibility extends beyond traditional network perimeters to encompass all endpoints, both on-premises and in the cloud. By maintaining a comprehensive view of the network, organizations can effectively monitor and analyze user behavior, detect anomalous activities, and respond swiftly to potential security incidents. Comprehensive visibility ensures that security teams have the necessary context to make informed decisions and continuously assess the security posture of the environment.

Dynamic risk assessment is a fundamental tenet of the Zero Trust security model, acknowledging that the risk landscape is not static and must be continuously evaluated. Traditional security models often rely on static, periodic risk assessments that may become outdated quickly in the face of evolving threats. In contrast, a Zero Trust model incorporates real-time risk assessments that consider factors such as user behavior, device posture, and threat intelligence. Dynamic risk assessment enables organizations to adapt their security measures based on the evolving threat landscape, ensuring that security controls are responsive to changing conditions and emerging risks.

Zero Trust principles also emphasize the importance of encrypting data both in transit and at rest. Encrypting communications between users, devices, and applications helps safeguard sensitive information from interception and unauthorized access. In a Zero Trust model, encryption serves as an additional layer of protection, especially in scenarios where network traffic traverses untrusted environments, such as public networks or the internet. By applying encryption consistently across the network, organizations enhance the confidentiality and integrity of their data, aligning with the principle of assuming that threats may exist both outside and inside the traditional network perimeter.

User and device authentication play a crucial role in Zero Trust, and organizations are encouraged to implement multi-factor authentication (MFA) as a standard practice. Multi-factor authentication requires users to provide multiple forms of identification before gaining access to resources, significantly enhancing the security of authentication processes. By incorporating factors such as passwords, biometrics, or smart cards, MFA reduces the risk of unauthorized access resulting from compromised credentials. In a Zero Trust model, user and device authentication are essential components of the continuous verification process, reinforcing the principle of never assuming trust based solely on the user's location or initial authentication.

Behavioral analytics is an integral part of the Zero Trust security model, leveraging machine learning algorithms to analyze user and entity behaviors. By establishing baseline behavior profiles for users and devices, organizations can detect anomalies and potentially malicious activities. Behavioral analytics contribute to the continuous verification process, allowing security teams to identify deviations from normal behavior and respond promptly to potential security incidents. This proactive approach aligns with the Zero Trust philosophy, emphasizing the importance of actively monitoring and assessing the dynamic nature of user interactions within the network.

Automation and orchestration are essential components of the Zero Trust security model, empowering organizations to streamline security processes, respond rapidly to incidents, and enforce policies consistently. Automation allows for the execution of routine tasks, such as updating access controls or applying security patches, without manual intervention. Orchestration ensures the coordination and integration of different security tools and processes, creating a cohesive and responsive security ecosystem. In a Zero Trust model, automation and orchestration support the continuous verification of user and device identities, enabling organizations to adapt quickly to changing conditions and maintain a proactive security posture.

Integration with threat intelligence is a key principle of the Zero Trust model, emphasizing the importance of leveraging external insights to enhance security measures. Threat intelligence provides organizations with information about the latest cyber threats, vulnerabilities, and attack techniques. By integrating threat intelligence feeds into security processes, organizations can contextualize their risk assessments, identify potential threats more effectively, and implement proactive measures to mitigate emerging risks. The integration with threat intelligence aligns with the dynamic risk assessment principle of Zero Trust, allowing organizations to stay informed about the evolving threat landscape.

In conclusion, the principles of a Zero Trust security model represent a comprehensive and adaptive approach to cybersecurity, acknowledging the dynamic and evolving nature of modern threats. Continuous verification, least privilege access, micro-segmentation, comprehensive visibility, dynamic risk assessment, encryption, multi-factor authentication, behavioral analytics, automation, orchestration, and integration with threat intelligence collectively form a holistic framework that challenges traditional notions of network trust. By embracing the principles of Zero Trust, organizations can enhance their security posture, mitigate risks, and proactively respond to the complexities of the contemporary cybersecurity landscape. The Zero Trust model advocates for a mindset shift, urging organizations to question assumptions about trust and adopt a proactive, continuous, and comprehensive approach to securing their digital assets.

Discuss the increasing role of AI and machine learning in cybersecurity.

The increasing role of Artificial Intelligence (AI) and Machine Learning (ML) in cybersecurity represents a transformative paradigm shift, fundamentally altering how organizations defend against an evolving landscape of cyber threats. AI and ML technologies have emerged as powerful tools, augmenting human capabilities, automating complex tasks, and providing a dynamic and adaptive defense against sophisticated adversaries. As the volume, velocity, and complexity of cyber threats continue to escalate, the integration of AI and ML into cybersecurity practices has become indispensable for enhancing threat detection, response efficiency, and overall resilience.

In the realm of threat detection, AI and ML play a pivotal role by enabling organizations to move beyond traditional signature-based approaches. These technologies excel in analyzing vast datasets to discern patterns, anomalies, and deviations from normal behavior. Through unsupervised learning, ML algorithms can autonomously identify patterns indicative of potential threats, even in the absence of predefined signatures. This capability is particularly valuable in the detection of novel and previously unseen threats, providing a proactive defense against rapidly evolving cyber risks.

One of the key applications of AI and ML in cybersecurity is in the field of anomaly detection. ML algorithms can establish a baseline of normal behavior within a network, user, or system, and subsequently identify deviations from this baseline. Anomalous patterns, which may indicate potential security incidents, can be detected in real-time, allowing organizations to respond swiftly to emerging threats. The ability to autonomously adapt to changing environments and evolving threat landscapes makes anomaly detection a crucial component in fortifying cybersecurity defenses.

Behavioral analytics, an extension of anomaly detection, leverages AI and ML to analyze user and entity behavior over time. By creating behavioral profiles and identifying deviations from established norms, organizations can detect suspicious activities that may be indicative of malicious intent. Behavioral analytics not only enhances the accuracy of threat detection but also reduces false positives, enabling security teams to focus on high-priority alerts. The integration of behavioral analytics aligns with the evolving nature of cyber threats, where understanding and adapting to dynamic behaviors is critical for effective defense.

Intrusion detection and prevention systems powered by AI and ML technologies significantly enhance an organization's ability to identify and thwart malicious activities. These systems can analyze network traffic, identify unusual patterns, and correlate multiple indicators of compromise to pinpoint potential intrusions. The proactive nature of AI-driven intrusion detection allows organizations to respond rapidly to security incidents, preventing or minimizing the impact of cyber attacks. ML algorithms continually learn from new data, adapting to evolving tactics used by threat actors and enhancing the accuracy of intrusion detection over time.

AI and ML are increasingly utilized in the domain of threat intelligence, assisting organizations in processing and analyzing vast amounts of data to derive actionable insights. By automating the analysis of threat feeds, dark web forums, and other sources, AI-driven threat intelligence platforms can identify emerging threats, vulnerabilities, and tactics employed by cybercriminals. The integration of threat intelligence enhances situational awareness, allowing organizations to make informed decisions, prioritize vulnerabilities, and proactively fortify their defenses against imminent threats.

The deployment of AI and ML in security information and event management (SIEM) systems has revolutionized the way organizations handle log data and security events. These technologies excel in correlating disparate data sources, detecting patterns, and identifying potential security incidents. AI-driven SIEM solutions provide a more efficient and accurate means of triaging alerts, enabling security teams to focus on high-priority threats. Moreover, the automation of routine tasks, such as log analysis and event correlation, allows security professionals to allocate their time and expertise to more strategic aspects of cybersecurity.

AI and ML technologies also play a critical role in the realm of endpoint security. Endpoint detection and response (EDR) solutions leverage these technologies to detect and respond to malicious activities on individual devices. ML algorithms analyze endpoint data in real-time, identifying unusual behavior, malicious processes, and indicators of compromise. The ability to detect and respond to threats at the endpoint level is essential in a landscape where cyber adversaries often target individual devices as entry points into larger networks. AI-driven EDR solutions contribute to a more proactive and adaptive defense strategy, enhancing the overall resilience of organizations against advanced threats.

Phishing and social engineering attacks, which often rely on exploiting human vulnerabilities, have witnessed a surge in sophistication. AI and ML are employed in email security solutions to enhance the detection of phishing attempts and malicious email content. These technologies analyze email patterns, content, and user behavior to identify suspicious emails, phishing links, and malicious attachments. The ability to learn from evolving email threats enables AI-driven email security systems to provide real-time protection against novel and highly targeted phishing attacks, safeguarding organizations from one of the most prevalent and deceptive forms of cyber threats.

AI and ML technologies have demonstrated their efficacy in the realm of malware detection and analysis. Traditional signature-based antivirus solutions are often inadequate in detecting polymorphic and zero-day malware variants. ML algorithms, however, can learn from features and behaviors associated with malware, enabling them to identify previously unseen threats. By analyzing large datasets of known malware and continuously adapting to new samples, AI-driven malware detection systems enhance the accuracy of threat identification and mitigate the risk of malware infections.

Security orchestration, automation, and response (SOAR) platforms harness the power of AI and ML to streamline and automate incident response processes. These platforms enable organizations to create orchestrated workflows that automate repetitive tasks, facilitate collaboration among security teams, and integrate with various security tools. AI-driven automation enhances the speed and efficiency of incident response, allowing organizations to respond rapidly to security incidents, contain threats, and reduce the overall impact of cyber attacks. The adaptive nature of AI and ML in SOAR platforms ensures that incident response processes evolve based on the evolving threat landscape.

The integration of AI and ML in vulnerability management transforms how organizations identify, prioritize, and remediate security vulnerabilities. These technologies can analyze vast datasets of vulnerabilities, assess the potential impact, and prioritize remediation efforts based on risk. ML algorithms can predict the likelihood of exploitation for specific vulnerabilities, allowing organizations to focus resources on addressing high-risk issues first. The automation of vulnerability scanning and analysis through AI-driven tools accelerates the identification of security weaknesses, providing organizations with a proactive approach to securing their digital infrastructure.

The evolving nature of AI and ML in cybersecurity extends to the domain of deception technologies. These technologies leverage AI-driven decoys and traps to detect and divert attackers away from critical assets. By creating deceptive environments that mimic real systems and data, organizations can actively engage and deceive adversaries, providing security teams with valuable insights into their tactics and techniques. The adaptive nature of deception technologies, guided by AI, ensures that deceptive elements evolve to match the changing strategies employed by threat actors.

While AI and ML technologies offer significant advancements in cybersecurity, their adoption also introduces challenges and considerations. Adversarial machine learning, where threat actors attempt to manipulate or evade ML models, is an emerging concern. Organizations must continually refine and adapt their ML models to counter adversarial techniques, ensuring the robustness of their defense mechanisms. Additionally, ethical considerations, transparency, and the interpretability of AI-driven decisions in cybersecurity are crucial aspects that demand careful attention to maintain trust and accountability.

In conclusion, the increasing role of AI and ML in cybersecurity represents a transformative force, empowering organizations to bolster their defenses against the escalating complexity of cyber threats. From threat detection and response to vulnerability management and orchestration, these technologies provide a dynamic and adaptive approach to cybersecurity. The integration of AI and ML augments human capabilities, automates routine tasks, and enhances the accuracy of security measures. As the cyber threat landscape continues to evolve, organizations that embrace and leverage AI and ML technologies are better positioned to navigate the complexities of modern cybersecurity, proactively responding to emerging threats and fortifying their digital resilience. The symbiotic relationship between human expertise and artificial intelligence is paramount in establishing a robust cybersecurity posture for the digital age.

Explore the security challenges associated with edge computing.

Edge computing, heralded for its promise to bring computation closer to data sources and end-users, introduces a unique set of security challenges that demand nuanced and adaptive solutions. The decentralized nature of edge computing, where computing resources are distributed across a multitude of devices and locations, poses distinct risks that require careful consideration. One of the primary security challenges associated with edge computing is the expanded attack surface. Unlike centralized cloud infrastructures, edge environments encompass a diverse array of devices, including Internet of Things (IoT) devices, sensors, and edge servers. Each of these devices presents a potential entry point for cyber adversaries, magnifying the complexity of securing the overall ecosystem.

The heterogeneity of devices within edge computing environments contributes to another significant security challenge—device diversity. Various devices may run different operating systems, have varying levels of computational capacity, and possess disparate security postures. Managing the security of a diverse fleet of devices becomes a complex endeavor, as standardized security measures may not uniformly apply across the entire spectrum of edge devices. This diversity necessitates a tailored and context-aware security approach that accommodates the unique characteristics and limitations of each device while ensuring a cohesive defense strategy.

The proximity of edge computing to end-users and data sources brings forth concerns related to physical security. Edge devices are often deployed in distributed and sometimes uncontrolled environments, such as manufacturing floors, retail spaces, or remote industrial locations. The physical accessibility of these devices to unauthorized individuals raises the risk of tampering, theft, or manipulation. Ensuring the physical security of edge devices becomes crucial, demanding measures such as secure enclosures, tamper-resistant hardware, and location-based access controls to mitigate the potential impact of physical security breaches.

Another security challenge associated with edge computing stems from the reliance on network connectivity. Edge devices are interconnected through networks that may include both wired and wireless connections. The dynamic and diverse nature of these networks introduces vulnerabilities, making edge computing environments susceptible to network-based attacks. Threats such as man-in-the-middle attacks, eavesdropping, and network spoofing pose risks to the integrity and confidentiality of data transmitted between edge devices. Implementing robust network security measures, including encryption, authentication, and intrusion detection, becomes imperative to mitigate these risks.

The distributed nature of edge computing introduces challenges related to data privacy and compliance. Edge devices often process and generate sensitive data in close proximity to the data source. This raises concerns about the collection, storage, and processing of personal or regulated data, especially considering that data privacy regulations vary across regions. Ensuring compliance with privacy regulations, such as the General Data Protection Regulation (GDPR) or the Health Insurance Portability and Accountability Act (HIPAA), becomes a complex undertaking. Organizations operating in edge computing environments must implement privacy-preserving mechanisms, robust data encryption, and clear data governance policies to navigate these regulatory challenges.

Edge computing's reliance on decentralized processing introduces latency as a critical consideration, especially in applications requiring real-time or low-latency responses. While the aim is to minimize latency by processing data closer to the source, this decentralized approach introduces potential security implications. Decentralized processing may involve executing critical security functions, such as authentication and authorization, on edge devices with limited computational capabilities. Striking a balance between optimizing latency and maintaining the integrity of security processes becomes a delicate challenge, requiring careful design and optimization of security mechanisms tailored to the specific demands of edge computing applications.

The dynamic and ephemeral nature of edge environments contributes to the challenge of maintaining visibility and control. Traditional security tools designed for centralized architectures may struggle to provide comprehensive visibility into the diverse and distributed edge infrastructure. This lack of visibility poses challenges for monitoring, threat detection, and incident response. Organizations need to invest in specialized tools capable of monitoring edge devices, detecting anomalous activities, and orchestrating responses in real-time. Additionally, the integration of edge security solutions with centralized security operation centers (SOCs) becomes crucial for holistic threat management and response.

Security updates and patch management represent another formidable challenge in edge computing. The sheer volume and diversity of edge devices, coupled with their distributed deployment, make it challenging to enforce timely and consistent security updates. Unlike traditional data centers where patching can be centralized, edge devices may be scattered across geographically dispersed locations, making manual updates impractical. Implementing efficient and automated mechanisms for patching and updating edge devices is essential to address vulnerabilities promptly and prevent exploitation by malicious actors.

The interdependence of edge devices within an ecosystem introduces the challenge of securing the entire supply chain. Edge computing environments often involve a multitude of vendors providing diverse components, from sensors to edge servers. The compromise of a single component within the supply chain could have cascading effects on the security of the entire system. Organizations engaging in edge computing must adopt rigorous supply chain security practices, including vendor risk assessments, secure software development practices, and continuous monitoring of the supply chain for potential vulnerabilities or compromises.

The inherent lack of a standardized security framework for edge computing exacerbates the security challenges associated with this paradigm. Unlike cloud computing, which has established security best practices and frameworks, edge computing is still in the process of developing standardized security guidelines. This lack of standardization complicates security efforts, as organizations may need to tailor their security approaches based on proprietary or vendor-specific implementations. Collaborative industry efforts to establish standardized security frameworks for edge computing are crucial to providing organizations with clear guidelines and best practices to enhance the security of their edge environments.

The convergence of operational technology (OT) and information technology (IT) within edge computing environments introduces a convergence of security challenges. Edge deployments often involve the integration of traditional IT systems with industrial control systems and OT devices. Bridging the gap between IT and OT security poses challenges related to differing priorities, protocols, and risk tolerances. The convergence of IT and OT security requires a holistic approach that considers the unique requirements of both domains, ensuring that security measures address the complexities introduced by the integration of these traditionally separate environments.

The transition from centralized control to distributed autonomy in edge computing introduces challenges related to trust and assurance. With the delegation of decision-making to edge devices, organizations must ensure that these devices make trustworthy and secure decisions. Trust in the integrity and authenticity of data processed at the edge is critical, as decisions based on compromised or manipulated data can have severe consequences. Establishing mechanisms for trusted execution, secure data provenance, and attestation becomes imperative to instill confidence in the security of edge computing deployments.

The evolving threat landscape and the potential for novel attack vectors demand proactive security measures within edge computing environments. Threat actors may leverage the distributed nature of edge computing to exploit vulnerabilities, launch coordinated attacks, or target specific edge devices. Security professionals must adopt threat intelligence-driven strategies, conduct regular risk assessments, and stay abreast of emerging threats to proactively defend against evolving attack vectors. Collaborative efforts within the cybersecurity community are essential to share threat intelligence and best practices for securing edge environments.

In conclusion, the security challenges associated with edge computing are multifaceted and require a comprehensive and adaptive approach. The decentralized, diverse, and dynamic nature of edge environments introduces complexities that demand careful consideration of physical security, device diversity, network vulnerabilities, data privacy, compliance, latency optimization, visibility, patch management, supply chain security, standardization, IT-OT convergence, trust, and proactive threat defense. As organizations increasingly embrace edge computing for its benefits in latency reduction, bandwidth optimization, and real-time processing, addressing these security challenges becomes imperative to ensure the resilience and integrity of edge computing deployments. Collaborative industry efforts, innovative security solutions, and a proactive mindset are essential to navigate the evolving landscape of edge computing security successfully.

Discuss the potential impact of quantum computing on traditional cryptography.

The potential impact of quantum computing on traditional cryptography represents a profound and paradigm-shifting challenge that has garnered significant attention in the field of cybersecurity. Quantum computing, a revolutionary approach to computation based on the principles of quantum mechanics, holds the promise of solving complex problems exponentially faster than classical computers. While this capability opens the door to transformative advances in various fields, it simultaneously poses a substantial threat to the foundations of traditional cryptographic algorithms that underpin the security of digital communication, data storage, and authentication mechanisms.

Classical cryptographic systems, including widely used algorithms like RSA and ECC (Elliptic Curve Cryptography), rely on the difficulty of certain mathematical problems, such as factoring large numbers or solving discrete logarithm equations. These problems form the basis of asymmetric encryption, digital signatures, and key exchange protocols. Quantum computers, leveraging principles like superposition and entanglement, have the potential to efficiently solve these mathematical problems that are considered computationally hard for classical computers. The most notable quantum algorithm in this context is Shor's algorithm, which, when executed on a sufficiently powerful quantum computer, can factor large integers and break widely deployed public-key cryptography.

The most immediate and significant impact of quantum computing on traditional cryptography is the vulnerability of widely used public-key cryptosystems. RSA, for example, relies on the difficulty of factoring the product of two large prime numbers, a task that Shor's algorithm can perform exponentially faster than the best-known classical algorithms. Similarly, ECC relies on the computational infeasibility of solving certain elliptic curve discrete logarithm problems, which can also be efficiently solved by quantum computers. As a result, the security assurances provided by these cryptographic algorithms are fundamentally undermined in the era of quantum computing, necessitating a paradigm shift in cryptographic approaches.

To address the impending threat posed by quantum computing, the field of post-quantum cryptography has emerged. Post-quantum cryptography aims to develop cryptographic algorithms that resist the computational power of quantum computers. These algorithms explore alternative mathematical problems, such as lattice-based cryptography, hash-based cryptography, code-based cryptography, and multivariate polynomial cryptography, which are believed to be hard for quantum algorithms to solve efficiently. The transition to post-quantum cryptography is essential for ensuring the long-term security of digital communication and data protection in the face of advancing quantum technologies.

The migration to post-quantum cryptographic algorithms is, however, not a seamless process. It involves challenges and considerations that extend beyond algorithmic replacements. The transition must be carefully managed to avoid security gaps during the coexistence of classical and quantum-safe cryptographic systems. Cryptographic agility, or the ability of systems to adapt to new cryptographic algorithms seamlessly, becomes a critical requirement. Organizations need to develop strategies for the systematic integration of post-quantum algorithms into existing systems, taking into account interoperability, backward compatibility, and the potential need for hybrid cryptographic solutions during the transition period.

Apart from the impact on public-key cryptography, quantum computing also poses challenges to symmetric-key cryptography. Grover's algorithm, another quantum algorithm, demonstrates the ability to perform an exhaustive search of an unsorted database or find the pre-image of a hash function in roughly the square root of the classical time complexity. While this poses a threat to symmetric-key algorithms by halving their effective key lengths, it is important to note that the impact is more manageable compared to the complete breaking of public-key cryptosystems by Shor's algorithm. Consequently, symmetric-key algorithms need to employ larger key sizes to maintain their security in a post-quantum era.

Hash-based cryptographic primitives, commonly used for data integrity and digital signatures, also face potential vulnerabilities due to quantum attacks. Lamport signatures and Merkle tree-based constructions are examples of hash-based cryptographic solutions that are considered quantum-resistant. These hash-based approaches rely on the computational hardness of reversing cryptographic hash functions, a task for which no efficient quantum algorithms are known. Research and standardization efforts in post-quantum cryptography include the exploration and development of hash-based cryptographic primitives to ensure the resilience of digital signatures and hash functions against quantum threats.

The impact of quantum computing on cryptographic protocols extends beyond encryption and signatures to key exchange mechanisms. Quantum Key Distribution (QKD) is an emerging technology that leverages the principles of quantum mechanics to enable the secure exchange of cryptographic keys between parties. QKD utilizes the principles of quantum superposition and the no-cloning theorem to establish a quantum-secure key exchange. While QKD represents a quantum-resistant alternative to classical key exchange protocols, its practical deployment faces challenges related to cost, distance limitations, and the need for specialized infrastructure. Additionally, the broader integration of QKD into existing communication systems requires careful consideration of its compatibility with conventional networking technologies.

The financial and logistical implications of transitioning to quantum-resistant cryptographic solutions are significant. Industry sectors, government agencies, and organizations with long-term security requirements must proactively prepare for the post-quantum era. This preparation includes research and development efforts to identify and standardize quantum-resistant cryptographic algorithms, the implementation of cryptographic agility in systems, and the development of migration strategies that mitigate the risks associated with quantum vulnerabilities.

The timeline for the widespread adoption of quantum computers remains uncertain, and it is contingent on advancements in quantum hardware, error correction, and the resolution of various technical challenges. However, the potential impact of quantum computing on cryptography necessitates proactive measures to ensure the resilience and longevity of cryptographic systems. International collaborations, industry standards, and ongoing research initiatives play a crucial role in shaping the trajectory of post-quantum cryptography. Organizations should invest in research and development efforts, engage in security assessments of their cryptographic infrastructures, and formulate strategies for the seamless integration of quantum-resistant algorithms to safeguard sensitive information in the face of evolving technological landscapes.

In conclusion, the potential impact of quantum computing on traditional cryptography is a complex and multifaceted challenge that demands strategic and timely responses from the cybersecurity community. The vulnerabilities introduced by quantum algorithms like Shor's and Grover's pose a threat to widely deployed cryptographic systems, necessitating the development and adoption of post-quantum cryptographic algorithms. The transition to quantum-resistant cryptography involves considerations of cryptographic agility, algorithm standardization, symmetric-key resilience, hash-based primitives, and the exploration of quantum-safe key exchange mechanisms. As quantum technologies continue to advance, the proactive adoption of quantum-resistant cryptographic solutions becomes imperative for ensuring the long-term security and confidentiality of digital communication, data storage, and authentication mechanisms in an era where the computational landscape is fundamentally reshaped by the power of quantum computing.

Explore the concept of continuous authentication for enhanced identity security.

Continuous authentication stands at the forefront of identity security, presenting a paradigm shift from traditional, static methods towards a dynamic and adaptive approach that aligns with the evolving threat landscape. In the digital era, where the boundaries of cyberspace blur, and identity breaches pose severe consequences, the need for a robust and resilient authentication mechanism becomes paramount. Traditional authentication methods, often relying on static credentials such as passwords or biometrics, face inherent vulnerabilities. Continuous authentication addresses these shortcomings by introducing a continuous and real-time verification process that continuously assesses the user's identity throughout their interaction with a system or application.

The essence of continuous authentication lies in its ability to monitor and analyze user behavior, contextual information, and various factors in real-time to ascertain the ongoing legitimacy of a user's identity. Unlike traditional authentication, which verifies the user only during the initial login phase, continuous authentication maintains a persistent vigilance, adapting to the dynamic nature of user activities. Behavioral biometrics, a key component of continuous authentication, capitalizes on the unique patterns of a user's behavior – such as keystroke dynamics, mouse movements, or even typing cadence – to create a continuously updated profile that serves as a distinctive digital fingerprint. This nuanced approach enables a more accurate and context-aware verification process, reducing the reliance on static credentials susceptible to theft, sharing, or compromise.

Machine learning and artificial intelligence play a pivotal role in the implementation of continuous authentication. These technologies enable systems to learn and recognize the patterns of normal user behavior, establishing a baseline against which anomalies can be detected. Through continuous analysis, the system adapts to changes in user behavior over time, accommodating legitimate changes while raising alerts for potentially suspicious activities. The dynamic nature of machine learning algorithms allows continuous authentication to evolve alongside user habits, addressing the challenges posed by a dynamic and diverse user base.

The integration of contextual information enriches the continuous authentication process by considering the environmental factors surrounding a user's interaction. Contextual elements, such as the user's location, device characteristics, network environment, and time of access, contribute to a comprehensive understanding of the user's digital context. Deviations from established patterns within this context trigger alerts or additional verification measures, adding layers of security beyond traditional static authentication. For example, a user attempting to access an account from an unusual location or at an unexpected time may prompt the system to request further verification through multifactor authentication.

Multifactor authentication (MFA) plays a complementary role in enhancing the security of continuous authentication. While continuous authentication focuses on real-time behavioral analysis, MFA introduces additional layers of verification through multiple independent factors, such as possession of a physical token, biometric verification, or one-time passcodes. The combination of continuous authentication and MFA creates a robust and layered defense, where each factor reinforces the security posture, and the continuous assessment ensures that access remains authenticated even after the initial login.

Continuous authentication finds application across diverse domains, ranging from traditional login scenarios to critical infrastructure protection and financial transactions. In the realm of online banking, for instance, continuous authentication can monitor user behavior throughout a session, providing an additional layer of security beyond the initial login credentials. In healthcare, where sensitive patient data is handled, continuous authentication ensures that only authorized personnel with continuously verified identities can access critical information, safeguarding patient privacy and compliance with regulations.

The healthcare sector also exemplifies the need for a balance between security and user experience in continuous authentication. While the goal is to enhance identity security, the user experience must not be unduly compromised. Continuous authentication aims to seamlessly integrate into the user's workflow, ensuring that the verification process remains unobtrusive and minimally disruptive. Striking this balance is crucial for the widespread adoption and acceptance of continuous authentication solutions across various industries.

The concept of continuous authentication becomes particularly pertinent in the context of the remote and mobile-centric work environments prevalent in today's digital landscape. As organizations increasingly embrace flexible work arrangements and remote access, the traditional perimeter-based security model becomes less effective. Continuous authentication, with its focus on user behavior and context, provides a more adaptive approach that aligns with the fluid nature of modern work environments. Whether an employee is accessing corporate resources from the office, home, or a public space, continuous authentication continuously evaluates the legitimacy of their identity, mitigating the risks associated with unauthorized access.

The advent of the Internet of Things (IoT) further amplifies the relevance of continuous authentication. In an interconnected ecosystem of devices, ranging from smart appliances to industrial sensors, ensuring the integrity of user identities becomes a complex challenge. Continuous authentication, when extended to IoT devices, establishes a dynamic and adaptive security framework where each device continuously verifies its user's identity based on behavioral patterns, ensuring that only authorized users can interact with and control these devices. This approach is crucial in preventing unauthorized access to critical infrastructure or personal devices, especially in environments where the impact of security breaches extends beyond data compromise to physical consequences.

Despite its numerous advantages, continuous authentication is not without challenges. Balancing accuracy and false positives is a delicate consideration. Striking the right threshold for recognizing anomalies while avoiding unnecessary disruptions requires fine-tuning and ongoing refinement. Additionally, privacy concerns must be addressed to ensure that continuous authentication methods respect user privacy and comply with regulatory requirements. Transparent communication with users about the nature of continuous authentication, the types of data being analyzed, and the security measures in place is essential for fostering trust in these systems.

The regulatory landscape also plays a role in shaping the adoption of continuous authentication. As privacy and data protection regulations evolve, organizations implementing continuous authentication must navigate compliance requirements to ensure that user data is handled responsibly and transparently. Compliance frameworks such as the General Data Protection Regulation (GDPR) in Europe underscore the importance of user consent, data minimization, and clear communication regarding data processing activities, principles that are especially relevant in the context of continuous authentication.

Continuous authentication represents a transformative step towards a more adaptive and resilient identity security framework. The evolution from static authentication methods to dynamic, context-aware verification aligns with the demands of a digital landscape characterized by mobility, remote work, and interconnected devices. As organizations grapple with the imperative of fortifying their defenses against evolving cyber threats, continuous authentication emerges as a potent strategy to enhance identity security, reduce the risk of unauthorized access, and provide a seamless and unobtrusive user experience. The journey towards continuous authentication is marked by ongoing research, technological innovation, and a commitment to striking the delicate balance between security, user experience, and privacy in the pursuit of a more secure and adaptive digital future.

Discuss advancements in security automation and orchestration.

Advancements in security automation and orchestration represent a transformative leap forward in the field of cybersecurity, introducing efficiency, scalability, and adaptability to counter the ever-evolving landscape of cyber threats. Automation, in the context of cybersecurity, refers to the use of technology to perform tasks with minimal human intervention. Orchestrating these automated processes involves the integration and coordination of diverse security tools and technologies to create a cohesive and responsive security ecosystem. The driving force behind these advancements lies in the recognition that manual intervention alone is inadequate to defend against the scale and sophistication of modern cyber threats.

One of the key areas where automation has demonstrated its impact is in the realm of threat detection and response. Automated threat detection systems leverage machine learning algorithms and behavioral analytics to sift through vast datasets, identify patterns indicative of potential threats, and generate alerts in real-time. These systems excel in rapidly processing and analyzing large volumes of data, enabling security teams to focus their attention on high-priority threats. Automation extends to the response phase, where predefined playbooks or workflows guide the automated mitigation of identified threats. This proactive approach enhances the speed and efficiency of threat response, minimizing the dwell time of adversaries within a network.

The orchestration of security processes amplifies the effectiveness of automation by connecting disparate security tools and technologies into a unified and coordinated defense mechanism. Security orchestration platforms act as the central nervous system, facilitating communication and collaboration between various security tools. For example, when a threat is detected by an intrusion detection system, an orchestrated response may involve isolating the affected system, updating firewall rules, and notifying relevant stakeholders—all executed seamlessly through automated workflows. This level of coordination ensures a synchronized and swift response to security incidents, reducing the manual effort required to manage and mitigate threats.

Incident response, a critical component of cybersecurity, has witnessed significant advancements through automation and orchestration. Automated incident response platforms enable organizations to create and execute response plans tailored to specific types of incidents. These plans encompass a series of automated actions, from isolating compromised systems to gathering forensic data and notifying incident response teams. Orchestrating these response plans ensures a standardized and consistent approach to incidents, mitigating the risk of human error and ensuring that critical steps are not over-looked during the heat of an incident. The result is a more stream-lined and efficient incident response process.

The integration of threat intelligence into automated security processes further enhances the ability to proactively defend against emerging threats. Threat intelligence feeds, which provide informa-tion about the latest cyber threats, vulnerabilities, and attack tech-niques, can be automatically ingested into security platforms. Auto-mated correlation of this threat intelligence with existing security da-ta allows organizations to contextualize their risk assessments, iden-tify potential threats more effectively, and implement proactive mea-sures to mitigate emerging risks. The continuous integration of up-dated threat intelligence ensures that security processes remain in-formed and adaptive to the evolving threat landscape.

Security automation and orchestration also play a crucial role in vulnerability management. Automated vulnerability scanning tools can systematically assess an organization's infrastructure for known vulnerabilities, streamlining the identification process. Once vulner-abilities are detected, orchestrated workflows guide the remediation process, automating tasks such as applying patches, reconfiguring systems, or isolating vulnerable assets. This automated approach to vulnerability management is instrumental in reducing the window of exposure to potential threats, minimizing the risk of exploitation and data breaches.

The realm of security information and event management (SIEM) has evolved significantly with the integration of automation and orchestration. SIEM platforms collect and analyze logs and events from various sources to identify potential security incidents. Automation enhances the analysis process by automatically correlat-ing disparate data points, recognizing patterns, and generating ac-tionable insights. Orchestrating responses based on SIEM alerts en-sures a coordinated and timely reaction to potential threats. For example, if a SIEM alert indicates a series of failed login attempts from a specific IP address, an orchestrated response may involve blocking the IP address, notifying the user, and escalating the incident to the appropriate response team.

Automation is also reshaping the landscape of security awareness and training programs. Automated phishing simulation tools, for instance, can simulate phishing attacks to test an organization's resilience to social engineering threats. These tools automatically generate realistic phishing scenarios, track user responses, and provide metrics for assessing the effectiveness of security awareness training. Orchestrating these simulations ensures a systematic and ongoing approach to testing and improving the security awareness of an organization's workforce, reducing the risk of falling victim to real-world phishing attacks.

The role of automation and orchestration extends beyond the confines of individual organizations to collaborative efforts within the cybersecurity community. Threat information sharing platforms leverage automation to enable the rapid dissemination of threat intelligence among organizations and industries. Automated feeds of indicators of compromise (IOCs), malware signatures, and attack patterns allow organizations to enhance their collective defenses by learning from the experiences of others. Orchestrating the sharing and analysis of threat intelligence ensures a coordinated response to widespread threats, creating a collective defense ecosystem that is more resilient against large-scale cyber campaigns.

Security automation and orchestration are pivotal in addressing the complexities introduced by cloud environments. As organizations migrate to cloud-based infrastructures, the dynamic and distributed nature of cloud environments necessitates a more adaptive and automated approach to security. Automated cloud security solutions can continuously monitor and assess configurations, detect misconfigurations or vulnerabilities, and automatically apply security policies to ensure compliance. Orchestrating security processes across hybrid and multi-cloud environments ensures a unified defense strategy that seamlessly spans on-premises and cloud-based resources.

Advancements in security automation and orchestration are closely tied to the principles of DevSecOps, where security is integrated into the entire software development and deployment lifecycle. Automation tools are leveraged to embed security checks and controls at every stage, from code development to deployment and operations. Orchestrating security processes within DevSecOps pipelines ensures that security is not a bottleneck but an integral and continuous part of the development lifecycle. Automated security testing, code analysis, and compliance checks contribute to the creation of more secure and resilient applications.

Despite the transformative impact of security automation and orchestration, certain challenges persist. Integration complexities arise from the diverse and often proprietary nature of security tools. Orchestrating workflows that span different technologies, vendors, and protocols requires standardized interfaces and protocols to ensure seamless interoperability. Additionally, the dynamic nature of cyber threats demands continuous refinement of automated processes to keep pace with evolving tactics, techniques, and procedures employed by adversaries.

Privacy concerns also come into play, particularly when automated processes involve the collection and analysis of sensitive data. Striking a balance between effective security measures and privacy considerations is essential to ensure compliance with regulations and build trust among users. Transparent communication about the types of data being processed, how it is used, and the security measures in place becomes crucial in gaining user acceptance and meeting regulatory requirements.

In conclusion, advancements in security automation and orchestration mark a pivotal shift in cybersecurity strategies, providing organizations with the tools to defend against the complexities of modern cyber threats. The marriage of automation and orchestration streamlines threat detection and response, incident management, vulnerability remediation, and collaborative threat intelligence sharing. As the cyber landscape continues to evolve, the adaptive and scalable nature of security automation and orchestration will be instrumental in building resilient defenses, fostering collaboration within the cybersecurity community, and ensuring that security remains a dynamic and integral component of the digital ecosystem.

Discuss the evolution of biometric authentication technologies.

The evolution of biometric authentication technologies represents a fascinating journey through advancements in science, engineering, and information security. Biometrics, the measurement and statistical analysis of people's unique physical and behavioral characteristics, has emerged as a powerful authentication method, offering a more secure and convenient alternative to traditional methods such as passwords or PINs. The earliest forms of biometric identification date back to ancient civilizations, where individuals were recognized based on unique physical traits, such as facial features or handprints. However, it is in the modern era that biometrics has undergone a profound evolution, driven by technological innovations and the increasing need for robust identity verification.

Fingerprint recognition stands as one of the earliest and most widely adopted forms of biometric authentication. The uniqueness and persistence of fingerprint patterns have made them a natural choice for personal identification. Early fingerprinting techniques, dating back to the late 19th century, involved ink and paper. However, the advent of digital imaging and pattern recognition technologies in the late 20th century paved the way for automated fingerprint identification systems (AFIS). AFIS revolutionized law enforcement and security by enabling rapid and accurate matching of fingerprints against large databases. As technology progressed, mobile devices incorporated fingerprint sensors, bringing biometric authentication to the fingertips of millions and popularizing its use in daily life.

The evolution of facial recognition technology represents another landmark in biometric authentication. Early facial recognition systems relied on simple geometric measurements of facial features. However, the advent of computer vision and artificial intelligence (AI) has transformed facial recognition into a sophisticated and widely deployed biometric modality. Deep learning algorithms, capable of analyzing complex facial patterns, have enabled highly accurate and real-time facial recognition. This evolution has found applications in various domains, from secure access control systems to user authentication on smartphones and social media platforms. Nevertheless, the widespread adoption of facial recognition has raised concerns about privacy, bias, and the ethical use of such technologies.

Iris recognition, leveraging the unique patterns in the colored part of the eye, has emerged as a highly accurate and secure biometric modality. The intricate and stable nature of iris patterns, combined with advancements in camera technology and image processing, has made iris recognition a viable choice for applications demanding a high level of security. Airport security, border control, and government authentication programs have increasingly embraced iris recognition for its accuracy and resistance to fraud. As the technology continues to evolve, efforts are being made to integrate iris recognition into consumer devices, broadening its use beyond specialized applications.

Voice recognition, or speaker recognition, represents a biometric modality rooted in the distinct characteristics of an individual's voice. Early voice recognition systems relied on simple acoustic features, but the evolution of signal processing and machine learning has propelled voice biometrics to new heights. The use of dynamic features, such as pitch, intonation, and speech patterns, has enhanced the accuracy and reliability of voice recognition systems. Voice biometrics find applications in call centers, financial institutions, and voice-controlled devices. The advent of natural language processing and voice assistants has further fueled the integration of voice recognition into everyday technology, offering a hands-free and convenient authentication method.

The advent of behavioral biometrics has ushered in a new era in identity verification by analyzing unique patterns in human behavior. Keystroke dynamics, for example, assess the rhythm and timing of a person's typing, creating a distinct behavioral profile. This form of biometrics finds applications in securing access to computers and networks. Similarly, gait analysis leverages the distinct walking patterns of individuals for identification. Behavioral biometrics offer continuous and passive authentication, adapting to changes in behavior over time. As the Internet of Things (IoT) continues to proliferate, behavioral biometrics hold promise for securing a wide range of connected devices.

The integration of biometric authentication into mobile devices has played a pivotal role in its widespread adoption. The introduction of fingerprint sensors on smartphones marked a turning point, offering users a convenient and secure method to unlock their devices and authorize transactions. As technology progressed, facial recognition and iris scanning became common features in flagship smartphones, further enhancing the user experience. Biometric authentication not only replaced traditional methods but also facilitated the transition towards passwordless authentication, reducing the reliance on easily forgotten or compromised credentials.

Continuous advancements in sensor technology have fueled the evolution of biometric modalities. Wearable devices equipped with biometric sensors, such as smartwatches or fitness trackers, enable continuous monitoring of physiological signals like heart rate or electrodermal activity. These physiological characteristics can serve as unique biometric identifiers, adding an additional layer of security. The fusion of multiple biometric modalities, known as multimodal biometrics, enhances the robustness of authentication systems by combining the strengths of different biometric characteristics. Multimodal biometrics can include combinations like fingerprint and facial recognition or iris and voice recognition, creating a more comprehensive and resilient authentication framework.

The shift towards contactless biometric authentication has gained momentum, particularly in response to the global COVID-19 pandemic. Contactless modalities, such as facial recognition and iris scanning, align with hygiene concerns associated with physical contact surfaces. Additionally, contactless authentication methods support the seamless integration of biometrics into various public spaces, including airports, public transportation, and retail environments. The convenience and speed of contactless biometric authentication contribute to its growing acceptance and deployment in diverse applications.

The advent of decentralized identity solutions, leveraging blockchain and distributed ledger technologies, has introduced new possibilities for secure and user-centric biometric authentication. Decentralized identity platforms empower individuals to control and share their biometric data selectively, enhancing privacy and reducing the risk of centralized data breaches. Blockchain's immutability ensures the integrity of biometric records, instilling trust in identity verification processes. As decentralized identity ecosystems continue to evolve, biometric authentication may play a central role in providing individuals with secure and portable digital identities.

Challenges in biometric authentication persist, ranging from concerns about privacy and data security to the potential for bias in certain biometric systems. Privacy-preserving technologies, such as homomorphic encryption or federated learning, aim to address privacy concerns by allowing computations on encrypted data without exposing sensitive information. Standardization efforts and ethical guidelines are crucial in ensuring that biometric technologies are deployed responsibly and uphold principles of fairness and inclusivity. Ongoing research and innovation are essential to addressing these challenges and advancing the capabilities of biometric authentication.

In conclusion, the evolution of biometric authentication technologies is a testament to the relentless pursuit of more secure, convenient, and user-friendly methods of identity verification. From the early days of fingerprinting to the current era of multimodal and contactless biometrics, technological advancements have propelled biometrics into diverse applications, ranging from personal devices to critical infrastructure. The fusion of biometrics with artificial intelligence, machine learning, and decentralized identity solutions is poised to shape the future of identity verification, offering a dynamic and adaptive approach to securing digital interactions in an interconnected world. As biometric technologies continue to mature, their role in enhancing security, user experience, and privacy will become increasingly integral to the digital ecosystems we navigate daily.

Discuss anticipated regulatory developments in cloud security.

The anticipated regulatory developments in cloud security reflect the ongoing efforts to address the complex and evolving challenges posed by the migration of data and services to cloud environments. As organizations increasingly leverage cloud computing to enhance agility, scalability, and efficiency, regulators around the world are scrutinizing the need for robust frameworks to ensure the security, privacy, and compliance of cloud-based systems. One of the prominent regulatory trends is the pursuit of comprehensive and harmonized cloud security standards. Governments and regulatory bodies are recognizing the need for internationally accepted standards that provide a common baseline for assessing and managing security risks in cloud environments. The development of such standards aims to facilitate interoperability, foster global trust, and streamline compliance efforts for organizations operating across borders.

Privacy considerations loom large in the regulatory landscape, prompting the evolution of data protection regulations tailored to the cloud. The General Data Protection Regulation (GDPR) in the European Union has set a precedent by introducing stringent requirements for the processing and storage of personal data, including provisions related to cloud service providers (CSPs). As cloud adoption continues to grow, regulators globally are examining and enhancing their data protection laws to align with the principles of GDPR. Anticipated regulatory developments may include the refinement of data protection requirements specific to cloud services, addressing issues such as data residency, cross-border data transfers, and the obligations of both data controllers and processors in cloud environments.

In the context of cloud security, transparency and accountability have become focal points for regulators seeking to empower organizations and individuals with clearer insights into the security postures of cloud service providers. Governments and regulatory bodies are expected to promote transparency by encouraging CSPs to provide comprehensive documentation on their security practices, incident response capabilities, and data handling procedures. Additionally, there is an anticipation of increased scrutiny on third-party security assessments and certifications, with regulators emphasizing the importance of independent validations to instill confidence in the security measures adopted by CSPs.

The emergence of sector-specific regulations tailored to industries with unique security and compliance requirements is another notable trend in anticipated regulatory developments. Sectors such as finance, healthcare, and critical infrastructure are likely to witness regulations that specifically address cloud security within the context of their industry-specific challenges. Regulators are expected to collaborate with industry stakeholders to craft regulations that strike a balance between fostering innovation and ensuring the resilience of critical systems in the face of cyber threats. Such sector-specific regulations may introduce additional security controls, incident reporting requirements, and compliance measures tailored to the nuances of each industry's cloud adoption landscape.

A heightened focus on supply chain security is anticipated in regulatory developments pertaining to cloud security. Recognizing the interconnected nature of cloud ecosystems and the potential risks introduced by third-party vendors, regulators are expected to emphasize the importance of robust supply chain risk management practices. This includes encouraging organizations to conduct thorough assessments of the security practices of their cloud service providers, scrutinizing the security controls implemented by upstream suppliers, and ensuring the integrity of software and hardware components within the cloud supply chain. Anticipated regulations may mandate increased transparency and disclosure regarding the security postures of all entities within the cloud supply chain.

Incident response and notification requirements in the cloud are likely to be a key area of regulatory focus. As cyber threats continue to evolve, regulators are expected to mandate stringent incident response measures for organizations leveraging cloud services. This may include requirements for organizations to develop and test incident response plans specific to their cloud environments, establish clear communication channels with cloud service providers, and adhere to predefined notification timelines in the event of a security incident. Regulators may also encourage collaboration between organizations and government agencies to facilitate swift and coordinated responses to cloud security incidents with broader implications.

In the realm of cloud security compliance, regulators are anticipated to place an increased emphasis on the automation of compliance processes. Recognizing the dynamic and rapidly evolving nature of cloud environments, regulators may encourage the integration of automated tools and technologies for continuous monitoring, assessment, and reporting of compliance with security standards and regulations. This shift towards automation aims to enhance the agility and responsiveness of organizations in maintaining and demonstrating compliance in the face of evolving regulatory requirements.

Cross-border data governance is poised to become a key consideration in anticipated regulatory developments in cloud security. With organizations increasingly relying on cloud services to store and process data across borders, regulators are expected to address the complexities associated with jurisdictional differences in data protection and security laws. Efforts to establish international frameworks for cross-border data flows, such as the APEC Cross-Border Privacy Rules (CBPR) system, may influence the direction of future regulations. Regulators may work towards harmonizing cross-border data governance to provide a consistent and clear regulatory landscape for organizations engaging in global cloud operations.

Regulatory developments are likely to encompass measures aimed at enhancing the resilience of cloud services against emerging threats, such as those posed by quantum computing. As the field of quantum computing advances, regulators may anticipate the need for encryption algorithms and security measures that are resistant to quantum attacks. Regulatory frameworks may evolve to encourage organizations to adopt quantum-safe cryptographic practices and to define standards for the security of quantum technologies within cloud environments.

Cybersecurity risk management is expected to be a central theme in future regulatory developments, with an emphasis on a risk-based approach tailored to the unique characteristics of cloud environments. Regulators may encourage organizations to conduct comprehensive risk assessments specific to their cloud deployments, considering factors such as data sensitivity, industry regulations, and the shared responsibility model inherent in cloud computing. The integration of risk management into overall corporate governance practices may be a focal point for regulators seeking to instill a culture of proactive risk mitigation within organizations leveraging cloud services.

In conclusion, the anticipated regulatory developments in cloud security reflect a nuanced and multifaceted approach to addressing the challenges and opportunities presented by the widespread adoption of cloud computing. From privacy considerations and supply chain security to incident response requirements and cross-border data governance, regulators are expected to craft comprehensive frameworks that balance the need for innovation with the imperative of ensuring the security, privacy, and compliance of cloud-based systems. As organizations navigate this evolving regulatory landscape, collaboration between regulators, industry stakeholders, and cybersecurity experts will play a crucial role in shaping effective and pragmatic regulations that foster a secure and resilient cloud computing ecosystem.

Address the ongoing importance of human factors in cybersecurity.

The ongoing importance of human factors in cybersecurity underscores the dynamic interplay between individuals, their behaviors, and the intricate technological landscape they inhabit. As the digital realm continues to permeate every aspect of our lives, the role of humans in shaping the cybersecurity landscape remains pivotal. Despite advancements in technology and the deployment of sophisticated security measures, humans remain both the primary users and potential vulnerabilities in the cybersecurity equation. Understanding, addressing, and harnessing the intricacies of human behavior is essential in fortifying the defense against cyber threats and ensuring the overall resilience of digital ecosystems.

Human factors manifest in various dimensions within the cybersecurity domain, starting with the fundamental aspect of user awareness and education. The awareness of cyber threats, phishing attacks, and social engineering tactics is a cornerstone of effective cybersecurity. Individuals, whether employees within organizations or the general populace, need to be equipped with the knowledge and skills to recognize and respond to potential threats. The ongoing challenge lies in the need for continuous education and awareness programs that evolve alongside the dynamic landscape of cyber threats. Organizations must cultivate a cybersecurity culture where individuals understand their roles and responsibilities in maintaining a secure digital environment.

The psychology of cybersecurity is deeply intertwined with human behavior, shaping how individuals perceive and respond to security measures. Behavioral economics, cognitive biases, and the psychology of decision-making all play critical roles in influencing the effectiveness of cybersecurity strategies. For instance, the concept of security fatigue highlights how individuals may become overwhelmed or disengaged with security measures, leading to lapses in judgment and compliance. Addressing security fatigue requires a nuanced understanding of human psychology, prompting the design of user-friendly and intuitive security interfaces that minimize cognitive load and foster a positive security experience.

In the realm of password security, human factors are evident in the challenges associated with creating and managing strong, unique passwords. Despite the proliferation of password managers and guidelines for secure password practices, individuals often exhibit predictable behaviors, such as using easily guessable passwords or reusing them across multiple accounts. Human-centric approaches to password security involve not only technological solutions but also the promotion of behavioral changes through effective communication, training, and the implementation of user-friendly authentication methods that reduce the burden on individuals.

The phenomenon of insider threats further underscores the role of human factors in cybersecurity. Insiders, whether unwittingly or maliciously, pose a significant risk to organizations. Understanding the motivations, pressures, and behaviors that may lead individuals to compromise security is essential in developing effective strategies for detection, prevention, and mitigation. Behavioral analytics, which leverages machine learning to analyze patterns of user behavior, offers a human-centric approach to identifying anomalous activities and potential insider threats. Balancing the need for security with respect for individual privacy is crucial in implementing monitoring and analytics solutions that effectively address insider threats.

Social engineering attacks, where cybercriminals exploit human psychology to manipulate individuals into divulging sensitive information or taking malicious actions, highlight the ongoing importance of human factors in cybersecurity. Phishing, pretexting, and other social engineering tactics rely on the inherent trust and social norms that govern human interactions. Recognizing and mitigating these threats require not only technological defenses such as email filters and secure communication channels but also continuous education and awareness programs that empower individuals to recognize and resist social engineering attempts.

The convergence of the physical and digital worlds in the era of the Internet of Things (IoT) introduces new dimensions to the human factors in cybersecurity. As individuals interact with an increasing number of connected devices, from smart home appliances to wearable technologies, the security implications extend beyond traditional computing environments. Human-centric considerations must encompass the privacy implications of ubiquitous data collection, the potential risks associated with insecure IoT devices, and the need for individuals to understand and control the security settings of their connected devices. Designing IoT interfaces that prioritize user understanding and control is essential in ensuring that individuals can make informed decisions about the security of their interconnected digital ecosystem.

The human factor extends to the workforce, where employees play a critical role in shaping the security posture of organizations. Cybersecurity awareness training programs are essential, not only for imparting technical knowledge but also for fostering a cybersecurity mindset among employees. A security-aware workforce becomes a human firewall, capable of recognizing and responding to security incidents, reporting potential threats, and adhering to security best practices. The ongoing challenge lies in making cybersecurity training engaging, relevant, and tailored to the diverse roles and responsibilities within an organization.

Human factors are particularly pronounced in the context of incident response and recovery. The effectiveness of incident response efforts hinges on the coordinated actions of individuals within an organization. The ability to communicate, collaborate, and make informed decisions under pressure is critical in mitigating the impact of a security incident. Simulated incident response exercises, often referred to as "cybersecurity drills," are valuable in not only testing technical capabilities but also in assessing the human factors involved in incident response. These drills enable organizations to evaluate the effectiveness of communication channels, decision-making processes, and overall preparedness for responding to cyber threats.

The ongoing importance of human factors in cybersecurity is evident in the concept of the "weakest link." No matter how advanced and resilient the technological defenses may be, the security of a system is often compromised by the actions or oversights of individuals. Recognizing this, organizations are investing in technologies that augment human decision-making rather than replace it. Human-centric security technologies, such as user behavior analytics, adaptive authentication, and explainable AI, aim to enhance the collaboration between humans and machines in the pursuit of cybersecurity goals.

Ethical considerations also play a vital role in shaping the ongoing importance of human factors in cybersecurity. As organizations deploy technologies such as artificial intelligence and machine learning for security purposes, ethical guidelines must govern their development and implementation. Bias in algorithms, discrimination in security practices, and the potential for misuse of advanced technologies underscore the need for a human-centric approach to cybersecurity ethics. Ensuring that technology serves human values, respects individual rights, and aligns with ethical standards is crucial in building a cybersecurity framework that reflects societal norms and expectations.

The intersection of human factors and cybersecurity extends to the regulatory landscape, where policymakers are grappling with the complexities of privacy, data protection, and the ethical use of technology. Regulations such as the General Data Protection Regulation (GDPR) acknowledge the importance of human-centric principles by emphasizing individual rights, transparency, and accountability in the processing of personal data. Anticipated regulatory developments are likely to further emphasize the role of individuals in shaping cybersecurity outcomes, with a focus on empowering users, promoting transparency, and holding organizations accountable for the ethical use of technology.

In conclusion, the ongoing importance of human factors in cybersecurity emphasizes the need for a holistic and human-centric approach to securing digital ecosystems. From user awareness and education to the psychology of decision-making, insider threats, social engineering, workforce training, incident response, and ethical considerations, the role of humans permeates every facet of cybersecurity. Recognizing and addressing human factors is not a static endeavor but an ongoing and dynamic process that requires collaboration between technology developers, security professionals, policymakers, and individuals. As the digital landscape continues to evolve, the success of cybersecurity strategies will be intricately tied to our ability to understand, adapt to, and leverage the nuances of human behavior in the pursuit of a secure and resilient digital future.

| Page